TABLE OF CONTENTS

S0-BCV-751

P. N. Tung

Harry Lewellyn's

Anza-Borrego Desert State Park

GLOVEBOX GUIDE™

3-20-1998

TO UNPAVED SOUTHERN CALIFORNIA

Second Edition
1993

Author
Harry Lewellyn

Editor
Linda Moffett

Page and map composition
Colin Lewellyn

Cover
Rainer Hanxleden

GLOVEBOX PUBLICATIONS
Anaheim, California 92817-8615

Unpaved road travel is potentially dangerous. Nothing in this Guide implies passibility and/or safe travel by everyone and/or everything, every time and/or everywhere. **Use discretion!**

Unpaved road directions are confusing. Nothing in this Guide implies accuracy or existence of field designations and/or everyone's safe return. **Use discretion!**

Unpaved road travel is frustrating. Nothing in this Guide implies and/or grants permission to use any trail. **Use discretion** by checking with the authorities and/or private property owners!

Unpaved road travel is fun. This Guide implies fun. **Have fun by using discretion!**

Published by
Glovebox Publications
Post Office Box 18615
Anaheim, California 92817-8615

Printed in the United States of America

Second Edition, January 1993

ISBN 0-944781-01-2

SECOND EDITION PREFACE

A lot has taken place since the first edition of the Glovebox Guide™ hit the streets. More people are using dirt roads. I've done the *California OHV Guidebook* for the State of California, Department of Parks and Recreation, Off-Highway Motor Vehicle Recreation Division. The college classes, seminars and tours have expanded, and you thirst for more.

The growing popularity of dual sport motorcycles and mountain bikes, and more 4WDs means more people using the backcountry. More people in the backcountry means we must become more sensitive to our precious environment. Ben Koski, Bureau of Land Management, California Desert District, El Centro Resource Area Manager, helped me become painfully aware of how unaware I am. I'm embarrassed to say the first edition used words like, worthless, lifeless and God forsaken, to describe some trail areas. Without making an excuse for editorial style, you will see a greater degree of respect and admiration for Mother Nature throughout this edition.

His comments also prompted me to strengthen several chapters. I could have added a resources chapter, but I wanted to maintain some consistency with the first edition. Those managing public lands have been kind enough to tell us first hand what their areas have to offer and how best we can retain our use privilege. I also present my perspective on those patrolling the areas - the rangers. And I've enhanced the Tips chapter by offering suggestions about safety, trespass, cameras in the backcountry and more. However, I still leave for another Glovebox Guide™ how to drive a 4WD.

Throughout this edition, I use material from past issues of the *4-Wheeling* newsletter which I publish. The Navigation chapter benefited from articles on speedometers, odometers, estimating distance and compasses. I feel the Survival chapter was improved with lists. The first aid kit list came from *4-Wheeling* too. The equipment "take" lists are from Rick Russell, the creator and editor of the Sidekick maps. The citizens band radio section was beefed up and I've added a section on leadership and leading trips.

Producing the *California OHV Guidebook* yielded side benefits. Most of the safety and resource conservation material comes directly from this book. The first edition maps had a degree of funky charm, but desktop publishing dictates I forego charm for quality. Besides, I hated cutting and pasting road names and symbols on hand drawn maps.

The college classes and my general tours have given me deeper insight into your guidebook needs. My Death Valley and Baja tours showed me these are prime adventure areas. Most everyone dreams of, or has gone to, these most delightful places. You have only to talk to someone from outside the USA to appreciate how much mystery and intrigue both present to foreigners. Travel in Baja is to Europeans as an African safari is to Americans.

Further, I trust the Products and Services chapter will answer your many questions about backcountry "things." It breaks new ground in that it is advertising, or more accurately, advertorials, in a conventional book. It informs of who does what, and will help you procure the best services and products. It also gives the companies a chance to tell you who they are, what they do and why you should consider them the next time you buy maps and equipment, stay in Death Valley or whatever. Many present a personal message from the owners and founders. There's a little history of sorts about how they got started. You'll also find a word about a very important public service, non-profit corporation, **TREAD LIGHTLY!**

I continue to break traditional book layout rules by not using those ridiculous lowercase, Roman numerals for pages preceding the first chapter. I write in a style where yeah and huh are OK. My index contains everything so you don't have to finger through glossaries, appendices and so on, to find what you want. I've designed the Guide to be functional and not follow archaic, impractical principles meant to impress the halls of Oxford and leave the reader frustrated and fumbling.

The functional features of the first edition have been retained. The spiral binding allows you to keep the Guide open to your trip of the day without damaging the spine. The new place-keeper flap/front spine gives the Guide identity on the bookshelf. The back cover map legend provides ready-reference for all maps. The *QUICK-LOOK* locator inside the front cover gives an overview of all the trails in the Guide exclusive of Death Valley and Baja.

About now, you usually get a barrage of acknowledgments and excuses why all of the contributors cannot be named. I've cured that. The contributors are acknowledged at their point of contribution throughout the text. Look for their names at the bottom of the trail text pages too. These helpful mappers pre-ran the trails. On the title page, along with back cover photographer John Torrey of Montrose, California, are those who made the Guide happen. Without all of their help and experience, the second edition would not be what it is. This Guide is not mine, it's yours. Only with your help, contributions and ideas has it become the standard of Southern California backcountry travel. And thanks for purchasing the Guide. I'm sure you will join me in saying thank you to all who have worked so hard to make the second edition of the *GLOVEBOX GUIDE TO UNPAVED SOUTHERN CALIFORNIA* the backcountry traveler's most useful companion.

Have as much fun using your Guide as we did creating it!

CHAPTER 1 INTRODUCTION

GETTING STARTED

ADVENTURE ABOUNDS

Southern California is rich in natural beauty and historic intrigue. Secluded mountain meadows draw the casual picnicker. A hanging tree and quaking aspens entice the photographer. Isolated Indian sites, gold mines or desert oases lure the adventuresome, or maybe we just want fresh air and exercise! Regardless, we all have an element of explorer within us and like to get away. With the advent of the four-wheel-drive (4WD) sport utility vehicle, the dual sport motorcycle and the mountain bike, exploration is well within the means of most. But where are these places? Is it legal to drive there? What is there to see along the way? The *GLOVEBOX GUIDE TO UNPAVED SOUTHERN CALIFORNIA* answers these questions. It offers backroad trips and tips. It tells how to plan, map, navigate and carry out back road trips.

SHARE THE TRAILS

Although originally conceived as a trail guide for 4WD sport utility vehicle owners, most of the trails are equally passable for the careful, two-wheel-drive adventurer. The dual sport motorcycles can safely cover far more ground than the 4Xs, and the mountain bikes will find the routes surprisingly void of other travelers.

ACTION ORIENTED

This Guide supports the trend to minimize reading and maximize action. Words are kept to a minimum, however, sufficient detail is provided to calibrate your odometer, learn compass fundamentals and other backcountry skills. It has two parts. Chapters 1 through 9 tell how to carry out unpaved adventures. Chapter 10 is the meat of the Guide and describes the trails. Most are within Southern California, but Death Valley and Baja have been added for the adventuresome.

LOST?

You may have purchased this Guide some time ago and have been waiting for just the right time to use the text chapters rather than just the trails. And the right time is now because you're lost! Check out Chapter 5 for getting unlost. I hope you're not also in need of Chapter 7! It offers advice on survival.

NEW TURF

If you're experienced, I imagine you're reading Chapter 10, Trails, right now. However, with the help of Chapters 2 through 9, you will be able to discover new trails. Some near your favorite turf; others I trust, in unexplored areas.

THE CHAPTERS

Read the chapters in any order. They provide useful information to plot and pursue enjoyable adventures. There's worthwhile information for all.

CHAPTER 2

Chapter 2, *USING THIS GUIDE*, introduces my form and format. It will help you understand and use the balance of the book. The Guide's cover, binding, page numbers, chapter subtitles, keywords and illustrations are designed for easy use.

CHAPTER 3

Preparation is the key to successful treks. Chapter 3, *PLANNING*, is on trip planning. It provides instructions and a simple trip planning form. It prescribes an even simpler safety practice - tell someone where you're going and when you return.

CHAPTER 4

Chapter 4, *MAPS*, addresses the love-hate relationship some people have with maps, teaches simplified map reading, and suggests where to buy them. The maps in this Guide only provide general outlines and trail references. Every trail in the Guide references other, more detailed maps for detailed navigational purposes.

CHAPTER 5

In Chapter 5, I sneak in the much avoided topic of *NAVIGATION*. My practical, common sense approach to navigation is useful to all. It describes a Trip Log for accumulating trip data and discusses getting unlost. Compass fundamentals, altimeter fundamentals, speedometer and odometer calibration, and estimating distance are also treated.

CHAPTER 6

I feel a sincere obligation to you, our environment and our means of travel to include *TIPS*, Chapter 6. It covers safety, protecting our environment (resource conservation), fire hazards, trespass, the responsibilities of being trip leader, backcountry practices and my perspective on rangers. Chapter 6 sometimes repeats material in other chapters. I trust this will help emphasize its importance.

CHAPTER 7

Chapter 7, *SURVIVAL*, is obviously not a complete survival guide. It stresses the importance of water for personal survival. You learn to maintain a positive attitude, carry lots of water and stick by your transportation. When you practice these simple guidelines, everything else seems to fall in place. This chapter is where you go for lists: first-aid, tools, radio and camera spares.

CHAPTER 8

PICKING PLACES, Chapter 8, helps you pick trails near home or on the way to grandma's. It helps you connect trails together into longer excursions. Also included are personal messages from the managers of various public lands. It's their chance to inform of where to go and welcome responsible appreciation of the backcountry.

CHAPTER 9

Chapter 9, *PRODUCTS AND SERVICES*, is new to this edition. My intent is to provide information to help you make informed decisions. I trust you will learn where to buy maps, what tires to use, where to stay and so on.

CHAPTER 10

Chapter 10 describes the *TRAILS*. Some are but a few miles and others require a weekend or more. Combine them to form your own personalized journeys. They vary in difficulty from not to very!

WORDS OF WISDOM

NOT ABOUT DRIVING

How to drive your 4X, dual sport or mountain bike are subjects for other Glovebox Guides™. What's more, learning to use them safely and properly requires that precious commodity time. Give yourself a chance to learn. Like other physical skills, practice makes perfect. Travel with others who have that skill and experience. The companionship is nice. Having the peace of mind knowing someone is along who knows what to do is even nicer. It takes the pressure off learning.

TOO ROUGH?

If you seek thrill rides and weekend war stories, this Guide is not for you. However, described herein are formidable trails with only subtle words of caution. For example, The Los Coyotes Indian Reservation is a beautiful place for trail exploration. It's also the occasional setting for the High Desert Roundup. The roughest of the tough break bone and Bronco alike at this yearly event. In contrast, the Guide lists Mulholland Drive which provides a grand panorama of Southern California and is usually tame enough for the family sedan.

COMMON SENSE

The Glovebox Guide's™ variety of trails will entertain both the novice and the gnarly. My emphasis is on routes that are passable to stock, sport utility vehicles (the family 4X). However, in the *Silver Coyote's book of rules*, it's fair to go slow, stop, check it out, and even go back. I frequently wonder how much good common sense was used when I hear, "It's too late to turn around!" Where and what you ride over is your choice. Exercise discretion.

FRIENDLY USERS

HELP OTHERS

I like to think backcountry travelers are a fraternal lot. In years past, I sometimes felt I was prying out the ol' fishin' hole secrets when inquiring about trails or asking for help. Those days are past. I find current travelers willing to help with tools, tows and topography. I've been watched from cliff side for an hour and received immediate response to my CB radio plea for winch support. Another time a passerby disassembled his rig to give me a part to fix my breakdown. That's paying your dues. I expect there are still a few old shotgun toting gruffs that say no, but they'll come around, just help them when they need it. And by the way, stop and say hello to ol' California *4WD XPRT* when you see me on the trail someday.

ENJOY

With that, I wish you many happy miles of safe, responsible and ecologically compatible backcountry adventures.

CHAPTER 2 USING THE GUIDE

EASY TO USE

USING THIS GUIDE

In designing the Glovebox Guide™, I wanted to provide an ever-present, easy-to-use trail guide. The Guide's small format lends itself to easy glovebox or fanny pack storage. Fold the pages back to back. The binding is designed for this. No more fumbling through a closed book to get back to your current trail. Toss it on the dash or in the seat beside you. This is not abuse, but intended use. Let's take the Guide from the top.

QUICK TRAIL REFERENCE

THE QUICK-LOOK REFERENCE

Inside the front cover is the *QUICK-LOOK* reference map. By number, it shows the general location of each trail in Southern California. Inside the back cover is a cross-reference from the trail reference-number to that trail's map page number. This maze of numbers can look complex at first, but just remember, the first number is the reference number, the number in parentheses is the mileage and the last number is simply the trail map page. Use the *QUICK-LOOK* to promptly find trails in specific locations. I'll skip the title page, table of contents and preface. Their content is traditional.

PAGE NUMBERS

THE PAGES

At the top of each page is the chapter title with the page number. For example, Chapter 5 on navigation has the word "NAVIGATION" on each of its pages. Open the Guide to any page and you instantly know what chapter (subject) you're in. The exceptions are the first page of each chapter that only has the chapter number and title in large type at the top, and the trail maps and text of chapter 10. The large trail titles clearly announce it's the Trails chapter.

CHAPTER SUBTITLES

The bold print, chapter subtitles in the text area group common subjects. Home right in on your area of interest.

KEYWORDS

Keywords, the stand-alone words in the margins, tell what's in the adjacent paragraph. Use them to skim a subject or skip known material. Note them when reading through the Guide for the first time. Want specific information while on the fly, in the field? Scan the keywords.

ILLUSTRATIONS

All illustrations and corresponding text are on the same or adjacent pages. No more page flipping. This is particularly useful in Chapter 10, Trails. Each map is on the left and the corresponding description is on the right. Chapter 10 treats using the maps and descriptions.

INDEX

The index is actually an appendix, a glossary, and more. The references are abundant. It's more than just a word index. Within are AREA trail summaries. All abbreviations are listed too. In the world of computer programs, the index is user friendly. Depend on it and use it freely.

BACK COVER

MAP LEGEND

The back cover has several features. The fold out flap can be tucked behind the front cover and serve as a spine for shelving the Guide. It also can be used as a place-keeper. The traditional inside of the back cover was discussed above. The inside of the fold-out flap is the legend for all of the trail maps. Although the symbols are few and easy to learn, the inside back cover provides a ready reference when in doubt.

FUNCTIONAL DESIGN

ENJOY

The functional design and printed aids make using the Guide easy. The small format makes it easy to store and carry. Your *GLOVEBOX GUIDE TO UNPAVED SOUTHERN CALIFORNIA* will serve you through many enjoyable miles.

CHAPTER 3 PLANNING

SUCCESSFUL TRIPS

CONTACT THE AUTHORITY

WHAT IS PLANNING?

ENJOY PLANNING

GETTING STARTED

PLANNING IS PARAMOUNT

The key to successful trips is planning. Know the details of your trip. Write them down or at least have them keenly in mind. A careful evening of planning can well offset a careless day of being lost.

The Glovebox Guide™ simplifies the task, but is not a replacement for complete planning. The **MAPS** paragraph in the trail text lists maps that provide far more detail than the Guide. **AUTHORITY** specifies who manages the area and how to get in touch with them. Take the time to call local Ranger Districts or Resource Areas to get the latest information. This is also a good time to order their maps and inquire about current conditions or permits.

Trip planning answers all the questions. Where do we start? Where do we finish? How far between gasoline stops? How difficult is the road? What is there to see? Where are we going to stay? Where will we eat? Who's going with us? Who has authority for the land we'll travel? Do we need fire or other permits? How long will we be gone? What will the weather be like? Do we need any special equipment? Do we need a tourist visa, foreign insurance or money? What do we do if something goes wrong? Answer these questions and you're well on your way to a terrific trip.

I used to anxiously chomp at the bit until we were 100 miles or more out of town, then I'd relax. Now my pleasures begin with planning. Gather together your fellow travelers and make an evening of it. It bonds the explorers and builds better excursions.

Adventures may be spurred by conversations with others, this Guide, classes, or any number of other resources. I was told by one Guide user, on Friday night, he and his friends would toss the Guide in the air and whatever trail it fell open to was their weekend trip! Sounds like fun to me. Regardless of your cue, establish the worthwhile habit of complete planning.

PLANNING TOOLS

THE TOOLS OF PLANNING

The tools of planning are:
  Others
    Word of mouth advertises trails best.
  Books
    They tell of places to go and things to see.
  Maps
    They provide the roads, trails and features.
  Classes
    They whet your appetite for special knowledge.
  The Local Authority
    Where you get the straight info.
  The Weather Man
    He fills many gaps.
  Trip Info Sheet
    It informs others of your plans.

OTHERS

My best trips start with other people. They spark my interest in a specific area or natural feature. Get all their information. Take notes. Have a map. Use the Trip Info Sheet to remind you of important questions. Ask how you may contact them in the future. People are usually willing to tell you what they know. Sometimes a friendly smile or extra thank you will yield special secrets.

BOOKS

Your trip source book may be about rocks (rockhounding), flowers (when and where they bloom) or photography (shooting hot springs). This Guide provides information on Southern California dirt roads, but it's just a start. Don't discount the old books. They lend a guiding hand to forgotten treasures.

MAPS

Having and using maps is important. I devote a whole chapter to maps and their use. In addition to roads and trails, use them for landmarks and points of interest. Maps are an expendable tool. Freely mark up your travel copy. Fill in features and distances from other sources. Save the travel copy and your trip log for future reference. Too old a map may get you in trouble. Too new may have dropped interesting sites. Compare several for omissions, mistakes and accuracy.

CLASSES

Classes in photography, bird watching, prospecting, biology, geology and many other subjects provide information about remote areas. They tell you where to go and what to see. They enrich your appreciation of what's there. On my 4-Wheeling classes and tours I frequently run into other classes. Exchange your skills and knowledge for theirs.

LOCAL AUTHORITY

Throughout this Guide, I recommend you contact the governing authority. Call them to get the latest information. You may be disappointed to learn what you didn't want to hear, "The trail is closed due to a fire." But better from home than at the locked gate! Pay particular attention to seasonal closures or locked gate symbols. They can spoil an otherwise perfect trip. This is also a good time to ask about permits. Do you need a fire permit for this time of year? Also learn office hours and plan to stop by before you hit the dirt. Public offices are filled with information that typically goes wanting for readers. Besides, the ranger's first-hand information could prove invaluable, particularly if it's your first time into an area.

WEATHER MAN

Weather information serves several purposes. Safety - is it flash flood or snow season? Are any storms expected for your travel period? Is it going to be extra hot and should you save this particular trek for cooler weather? Accessibility - will the road be snowed in? Did the rains wet the dry lake and make it impassable? Gear - how should we dress or will we need chains? Should we take our down sleeping bags or are the light ones OK? Know what the weather is and will be for the duration of your trip. This is essential!

CALIBRATE YOUR SOURCE

Learn to calibrate your source of information. A mountain biker's long way is shorter than a motorcyclist's. A new truck owner's tight bushes might mean near. To the old truck owner, tight might mean using low-low to push through them. Some exaggerate the difficulty to keep you out. Others exclaim it's easy to sucker you in. An old-timer's tough road can be very easy or real tough. Know and calibrate all your sources, spoken or written, text or map, me and the weather man included!

THE PLANNING PROCESS

SELECT THE ROUTE

Find where you want to go on a map or two. Spread them out on a big table with friends around. The additional eyes and points of view enhance planning.

Make sure you can trace a route from paved road to paved road. With topographic maps, you can also determine elevation gain and loss, and rate of climb and descent. This is important information, especially if you're concerned with peddle-power and endurance.

SELECT MAPS

Choose one map or set of maps to be your primary travel aids. Mark them up with information from other sources. On extended trips, it's practical to tack-up six or seven topos on the wall to trace your entire trip and get the big picture. I usually number the maps so I can readily move from one to the other when in the field. Highlighting the trail helps too. Other times I take the map that covers the most area and grid it off with the applicable topos. This way, I can use a single map for most of the trip, and easily refer to the more detailed maps when necessary.

CHECK THE ROUTE

Check the road designations on the maps and trail guides. Do you want to go over what's shown? Too rough? Too tame? Too long? Knowing what will be encountered is like being a Scout. You are prepared. If you insist on a challenge, the maps will show it. And the easier way will also be shown.

DETERMINE THE DISTANCE

Next, add up the miles. Figure the paved road miles from the gasoline station just before you start the dirt road to the one nearest where you come back to pavement. If you're bicycling, think about your drop-off and pick-up points, and how you handle getting back to the car.

DETERMINE GASOLINE NEEDS

Calculate your gasoline requirements as follows. I conservatively assume I get 5 miles per gallon (MPG) on dirt roads. Do you have enough gas? For example, assume 40 miles of pavement from the top-off station, plus 50 miles of dirt, then 60 miles of pavement to the next gas station. That's 100 miles of paved road at 20 MPG or 5 gallons. Then there is another 50 miles of dirt at 5 MPG or 10 gallons. I need 15 gallons total. My tank holds 20, so I'm OK. I actually get more than 5 MPG on dirt roads, but I like the added peace of mind using 5 MPG. It gives me a safety factor for fuel to explore the unknown or when temporarily disoriented.

GET THE BIG PICTURE

In Chapter 5, Navigation, I suggest you continually maintain orientation. Always know where you are and what surrounds you. Study a map that covers a large area and look for significant features. Mountain peaks like San Jacinto or large bodies of water like the Salton Sea, are all visible from a great distance. Your big picture reference points could be the landing pattern at March Air Force Base or man made structures. Have major reference points for all trips. Keep them in sight or know their direction throughout your trip. This skill improves with time and practice. Work on it. It is most useful when disoriented.

STUDY THE DETAILS

Study topo maps for finer details like springs, mines or buildings. These otherwise insignificant features can lead to great surprises. Springs mean animals and birds. Mines mean tailings, dumps and historical items like stamp mills. Old buildings can reveal intriguing history. Spend time with your maps.

MAP THE PAVED ROUTE TOO

Map out the paved route too. Allow plenty of travel time. Let the drive to the trail head be unwind time. Arrive fresh and relaxed versus wired and up tight. Calm, relaxed explorers are safe explorers. Think in terms of the whole trip, not just using the trails. A flat tire on the pavement is just as annoying as on the dirt. Check all trip-related items. Add maintenance tasks to your check-lists and perform them before each trip. Tune-up the whole trip!

THE TRIP INFORMATION SHEET

INFORM OTHERS

Always compile and use a Trip Information Sheet. Its purpose is to provide written travel plans and it doesn't have to be fancy. Just enough to let everyone involved know what's going on is sufficient. Each of your fellow travelers and a *home body* should have a copy. A *home body* is described below. List their name and telephone number on the sheet too.

A sample Trip Information Sheet is shown on page 14. Use the blanks as described.

TRIP INFORMATION SHEET

NAME: Give your trip a name. The area, the route, a feature, the destination or use your imagination. Naming your trip makes it easier to talk about.

DISCUSSION: This is a catch all: where you're going, how long you'll be gone, what you're doing, where you're staying, meal plans, special insurance or money considerations as in Baja, weather considerations and how to dress can all be covered in this section. Alternatives if rained out (contingency plans), others joining you along the way and so on can be covered in this section too.

DEPARTURE day, time and place: Tell from where and when you will leave. The phone number of the departure point is useful too.

ROUTE: In a few words describe where you start, what roads you'll use and eventually the route home. Indicate start, finish and trails for the unpaved adventure too. If some of your travelers weren't at the planning session, this, along with the **Discussion,** answers many of their questions.

ITINERARY: Give hour by hour, or day by day information for the trip. This typically summarizes the **Discussion**.

MAPS: Tell what maps are useful for the trip. Name the best map for the trip.

AUTHORITY: An emergency contact point in the field is primary for emergencies. The local governing agency is best. This may be determined along the way and phoned back to the home body.

EQUIPMENT: This is usually for the vehicle (extra gasoline, or water if you're peddling, chains for the snow, air pump for the sand) and sometimes for recreation (dive gear, snow shoes, high speed film for the caves).

CB: Tell what citizens band (CB) radio channel you will use. CBs are discussed in more detail later. Carry and use them. Appoint a tail or a person who will be at the end of your caravan. Stay in touch with them frequently.

TRAVELERS: Here's where you list your companions (CB handles are fun too). For pre-trip coordination, you may find home telephone numbers useful and cellular numbers may be an indispensable link for emergencies.

HOME BODY: This is the person near home that can be contacted for the duration of the trip. List their name and telephone number. The home body is used as a message exchange center in case the group gets separated. Explain how to use the home body to all travelers. The rules are upon separation, both the main group and those separated must call the home body when you reach a telephone. This exchange can forego an unnecessary, apparent emergency, or validate a real rescue. The better prepared you are to show you've done your homework, the quicker rescue personnel are likely to respond. You help them sift through requests for their limited, and valuable time and services.

INCLUDE BIG PICTURE MAP

Not shown on the sample form, and usually on the back, is a big picture map. This shows the entire trip. It highlights the paved routes, trail head, dirt road start and finish, and the way home. Highlighting the ranger stations along the way also helps.

INFORM OF SAFE RETURN

You conclude your planning responsibilities by telling the home body of your safe return.

CHAPTER 4 MAPS

LOVE/HATE

WHAT ARE MAPS FOR?

GETTING READY

MAPS PROVIDE DETAIL

THEY'RE LIKE ABSTRACT ART

THE UNPAVED LIFE JACKET

Some folks love them, some hate them and others can't use them. However you feel about maps, when you venture off the interstates, maps are a necessity! My approach to map reading is simple. Consider maps like life preservers and parachutes. They are indispensable.

Maps help you keep track of your location, where you're going and what there is to see. Maps represent a large physical area in relatively small printed form. Maps are the most important part of planning and navigating.

Read this chapter at the dining room table with the Guide in one hand and "the map" in the other hand. "The map" I'm referring to is the Automobile Club of Southern California's (ACSC) *Los Angeles and Vicinity* map. However, any other map of local Southern California will do fine. Open the map and have the non-text side up. You will also need a north seeking (magnetic) compass and a ruler. Any compass and straight-edge will do.

I can understand why maps both intimidate and please various people. This yin-yang phenomenon stems from the same basis. Maps must represent a very large chunk of geography on a relatively small piece of paper. Maps present a fair amount of detail with no apparent organization. We understand books and text because of the symmetrical printed layout. Text reads from left to right and top to bottom. There is a start, a finish, and all in-between follows a logical flow.

Maps have no beginning, no end and there is no logical flow. They are more like abstract art than text. They represent what is actually out there. In order to be accurate, they must tell it like it is - no creativity, imagination or apparent organization. Also, due to the size of the large geographic area represented, they must use unfamiliar symbols, lines and colors to represent the real world. All this means is text-reading techniques do not apply to maps. We must learn map-reading methods.

I find complicated things easier to understand when I break them into elements, learn the pieces, then reassemble the parts. So don't run off just yet. I'll explain the parts, then bring them back together.

MAP PARTS

FOUR BASIC PARTS

Maps have four basic parts: the **Legend**, **Main Body**, **Compass Rose** and **Coordinates**. The **Legend** is the part that tells what the symbols, lines and colors mean. In the ACSC map, the legend is in the lower left corner. Note a heavy red line is a freeway, a pair of dashed, black lines is a poor road, green means a park and so on. The **Main Body** shows geographic and man made features such as Santa Catalina Island and Avalon (to the right of the legend). The **Compass Rose,** which is just above the legend, indicates geographic north. It follows the universal convention that the top of the map is north. The **Coordinates** are the numbers and letters along all four borders. We will learn to use coordinates to locate points within the main body.

LEGEND

The **Legend** interprets what is in the main body. When you see something on a map you don't understand, go to the legend. It will tell you what that symbol means. The legend also contains the *scale*. The scale relates inches of map to miles of actual distance.

Some maps, such as the topographic maps (topos) produced by the Department of Interior, United States Geological Survey (USGS), use their precious paper to only show fine detail and do not have a legend printed on each map. These maps have companion booklets which explain the symbols and how to use their maps. More on this below.

MAIN BODY

The **Main Body** is where the meat is. It is also where confusion arises. Don't be intimidated by its size and apparent complexity. You don't have to understand the whole thing all at once, just a piece at a time. And speaking of time, this is where you spend most of it, in the **Main Body**.

COMPASS ROSE

To use maps for navigation in the field you must know which way *is north* and which way *north is* on the map. The **Compass Rose** shows the map's north. Your north seeking compass indicates earth's magnetic north. The objective is to align the map with magnetic north. "And what about magnetic variation," the experts clamor. They also make a fuss over variation versus declination versus deviation. Variation is the difference between magnetic north and true geographic north. See the Navigation chapter for more on this. My basic approach to backcountry travel assumes you stay on the roads and cover ground relatively quickly, so I usually neglect magnetic variation. Cross-country foot travel is another matter.

COORDINATES

Remember the left-to-right, top-to-bottom logic of text and books? **Coordinates** help bring order back to an otherwise randomly arranged map. I use coordinates to locate roads and points of interest in my trail descriptions. Coordinates are located in the margins around the main body and are usually numbers in one direction and letters in the other. The ACSC map's coordinates are numbers along the top and bottom, and letters along the left and right. Coordinates locate specific points within the main body.

USING A MAP

ALIGNING THE MAP

Spread the map out and place your north-seeking compass directly on the center of the compass rose. Rotate the map (don't touch the compass) until the "N" (north) on the map is under the head (north seeking part) of the compass needle. The map "S" should also be under the tail of the needle. By orienting the map to north, the mountain or lake to your left on the map is also to your left in the real world. This exercise brings the two into synchronization. Virtually every time you use a map in the field, you should orient the map. When doing this for real, use the compass at least 20 feet away from all large metal objects, particularly your 4Xs, motorcycles and even bicycles. Be aware power lines can affect magnetic readings too. Right now, it doesn't matter how the body of the compass is oriented. I'll cover that in Chapter 5, Navigation. The map is now oriented toward north.

Spend a few minutes reviewing the symbols in the legend. The scale (technically a *bar scale*) is particularly

STUDY THE LEGEND

important. It relates distance on the map to actual distance on the ground, and vice-versa. An inch on the ACSC map represents about 4½ miles. An inch on a 7.5' topographic map is only about 0.4 mile. The important thing to realize is map bar scales vary. Knowing this scale and surrounding terrain help estimate travel time and gasoline requirements.

SCALE DETAILS

If you're doing fine with maps so far, it might be wise to skip this paragraph. It's not really necessary to understand and use maps, just to talk about, and order them. It has to do with the *ratio scale*, not the *bar scale*, which I addressed above. The *fraction*, *ratio scale*, *fraction scale,* or *representative fraction* as the USGS puts it, is specified in terms of one to (:) some other number. For example, a 7.5' topo is a 1:24,000 scale map. This is a large scale map; it shows lots of detail. A small scale map covers more ground and show less detail. It still confuses me! It's one of those opposite things: large scale maps (small ratio number) show small areas; small scale maps (large ratio number) show large areas. Like I said, skip it if it doesn't make sense!

COORDINATE DETAILS

Coordinates divide the map into a logical grid. They make it easy to describe the location of, and find any thing on a map. Let's designate and locate the town of Thousand Oaks at coordinates "F-2" on the map. First find "F" in the left margin. (Yeah, I know you've already found Thousand Oaks, but follow along anyway!) The "F" part of F-2 means Thousand Oaks is somewhere within the left-to-right, "F" band. Think of it like a row or line of text. Next find the top-to-bottom, "2" band. Think of this like a column of numbers. Within the intersection of the "F" row and "2" column is Thousand Oaks. There are coordinates for any point on a map. Find Rimrock at F-20. You're doing great!

COMPLICATED COORDINATES

Some maps use more complicated coordinate terms. They can use legal plot descriptions, or latitude/longitude markers, but the overall intent is the same. One part of the coordinate shows the horizontal row and the other shows the vertical column. At the intersection of the two is what's specified.

PUTTING IT TOGETHER

In practice, you put it all together by first orienting the map to magnetic north. Next use the coordinates to find your start and finish. Lastly, trace your adventure via the legend's designations.

AN EXAMPLE

Find Rimrock at F-20 again. Find Baldwin Lake at E-18, and no it isn't cheating to look for the blue hash-marks of drying Baldwin Lake. Anything that simplifies map usage is OK in my book. Trace the graded dirt road (see the legend) from Rimrock, up and to the left to Baldwin Lake. The road measures 3 inches, call it 4 counting wiggles. The scale indicates 4½ miles per inch, so that's about 18 miles total (4" X 4½ miles per inch = 18 miles). With a little practice you can locate and plot any trail or feature on any map. Now you're an expert! By the way, you've just plotted my Pioneer Town trail.

OBTAINING MAPS

YELLOW PAGES

Like me, after you develop an affinity for maps, you'll also develop favorite sources. A good place to start is *Maps* in the yellow pages of the telephone book. Use the *Products and Services* Chapter of this Guide too. Other places to try are sporting goods centers, backpacking stores, off road marts and rockhound shops. With competent help, it's fun to mail-order maps. The mail-order experts at the Map Link in Santa Barbara were invaluable regarding *scales* above.

AUTO CLUB

The Automobile Club of Southern California (ACSC) has excellent maps. If you're a member, you've got it made. And non-members can now buy them. I just learned the ACSC is test marketing retail map sales to non-members through Barnes & Noble Book Stores.

DeLORME

Another excellent, comprehensive atlas is published by the DeLorme Mapping company. Their *Southern California Atlas & Gazetteer* (ISBN 0-89933-205-6) is a wealth of information.

LOCAL AUTHORITIES

Since I recommend you <u>always</u> check with local authorities before going out, why not pick up their maps and brochures. State and Federal agency maps are a bargain. They usually have the exact road designations as found in the field. Most other maps do not include

FOREST SERVICE

DESERT ACCESS GUIDES

TOPOGRAPHIC MAPS

FREE TOPO AIDS

Bureau of Land Management (BLM) or Forest Service designations. In addition, while you are there, you can update your map, by hand, from the desk copy.

The Forest Service has forest maps and specialty maps tailored to specific users.

The BLM has a series of maps designed to assist backroad users. They are called the Desert Access Guides of which there are 22. Most of the public land in Southern California is covered by these maps. They are my initial source for desert travel. They are excellent. Road designations, open and closed roads, points of interest, campsites and history are but a few of the subjects covered. I reference the Desert Access Guides and other official maps in the **MAPS** paragraph of the Chapter 10 trail descriptions. A focal point for the entire California Desert District is:

BLM, California Desert District
6221 Box Springs Boulevard
Riverside, California 92507-0714
(909) 697-5215

If you're map comfort level is still low, here's another section to skip. The Department of Interior, United States Geological Survey (USGS) makes available to the public maps of the finest detail - topographic maps (topos). Detail means topographic contour lines and more. They are cryptic and intimidating if you are new to maps. They are indispensable if you're looking for remote areas and seldom seen sites. I use them to locate springs, mines, roads, railroads and old buildings that have long since been removed from newer maps. The chapter on navigation makes use of them for orienteering.

There are three things you should have, at no cost, if you plan to use topos: 1) the *California Index to Topographic and other Map Coverage*; 2) the *Catalog of Topographic and other Published Maps*; and 3) *Topographic Maps*. The first two divide California to show the names of the topos and availability, and the third includes symbols. Each of my trails, under **MAPS**, provides the reference page number for item one above. With this book and mine, you can determine what topos apply to specific trails. Obtain these items from the sources mentioned above, your local USGS office or:

US Geological Survey
Box 25286, Federal Center, Bldg. 41
Denver, CO 80225

THE GUIDE'S TRAIL MAPS

GLOVEBOX MAPS LACK DETAIL

My maps lack detail. That makes them easy to use. My maps lack detail. That makes it a mistake to use them for navigation. They have no scale. They are occasionally condensed to bring start and finish points, and important paved intersections, within the map. Ranger stations and campsites may be shown on the wrong side of the road just to fit in. Their intent is to make it easy to use more detailed navigational maps. They are not intended for navigation. They are intended to help identify the trail and assist with planning. Use other maps for navigation.

MAPS AND WIND

Nowadays, the hardest part of using maps in the field for me is keeping them still in the wind and folding them back up! Inside the car or on the hood is not good magnetically. Rocks on the corners on the ground is the best bet to combat the wind.

FOLDING

I watch people unfold maps and then meticulously fold them completely back up with every usage. No wonder they hate maps! Learn to leave the map partially unfolded to about twice its fully-folded size. Leave it open to the area of use. As you become adept at this twice-size folding technique, you will be able to track on a couple sides of the map. The key to folding the map back to its original configuration starts with observing how you unfolded it in the first place. Also, most maps fold like an accordion and not like sheets and towels.

ENJOY

Have fun with maps. They are important to your survival!

CHAPTER 5 NAVIGATION

NAVIGATIONAL PHILOSOPHY

SIMPLE APPROACH

Avoided more than maps is navigation, and I understand why! It's like most things we do in life. We are told it has to be hard to be good. You know, "no pain, no gain." Well, I don't believe it! I hope my simple approach will make it more palatable. The fatal sound of *lost* should be motivation enough for you to give this chapter a chance.

TEMPORARILY DISORIENTED

I've never been lost. Lost sounds so permanent, so final, so fatal. I've occasionally been *temporarily disoriented*. In fact, I was once temporarily disoriented in Baja for two days. Just changing your mind set from lost to temporarily disoriented takes some of the pressure off getting unlost. And with proper planning and preparation, we manage to find our way back to the hustle, bustle of workday life. Throughout this book, *lost* is used in the context of only being *temporarily disoriented*.

PURPOSE OF NAVIGATION

Use navigation to determine where you are, where you're going and locate points of interest. Navigation takes you back and forth between the printed world of maps and books, and the real world of the trails and places.

ESTABLISH ORIENTATION EARLY

One of the most important principles is to maintain your orientation from the moment you leave home. Trying to get unlost, when lost, makes about as much sense as checking the brakes after you've gone off the cliff. Will you pass Mount Baldy along the way? Keep track of it from the interstate. Get a feel for its perspective from different angles. Your map shows a gypsum mine as you enter Fish Creek. Can you see dust on the way in? The dust plume may be visible for miles. Check it out as you approach. Simple stuff, but most useful when really needed.

Establish and maintain *big picture* reference points early in your journey. These are features that will be visible

BIG PICTURE REFERENCE

throughout most of your trip. Once into the wilderness, the details become obscure. Start your orientation on the paved road. This is where your planning pays off. Mountain peaks, lakes (both wet and dry), and other natural features along your route are easy to spot on maps and may be just what you need for big picture reference points. Mines, industrial sites, military bases and other man made features are worthwhile reference points too. For example, I once used the military aircraft landing pattern at March Air Force Base for orientation. Use whatever works. I sometimes think because we are in the backcountry, we feel we must use only *natural* reference points. This is part of that, "it's got to be hard" thinking. Shake it to become a resourceful and effective navigator.

DEVELOP A BACKCOUNTRY SENSE

Learn to second guess the direction you'll be going and what's up ahead. Are you headed out across 10 miles of wide open valley, up a canyon and onto a mesa? Got a hunch about which of the three mesas is yours? Estimate the distance to a future location. Make a guess as to which canyon you'll go up. Which way does the canyon turn when it looks like it dead ends? These mental gymnastics are like your muscles. They improve with exercise. Don't be disappointed with initial results. I'm frequently wrong and delight at being right. The skills of distance, direction and features do not emerge overnight.

THE TOOLS OF NAVIGATION

USEFUL TOOLS

ALTIMETER - To determine elevation.
BINOCULARS - To spot far off features.
BOOKS - For routes and attractions.
CB RADIO - For inter-group and emergency communication.
COMPASS - North seeking type to determine north.
COMPASS - To draw (not drive) in circles.
OTHERS - At home or along the way for trail information.
MAPS - Chapter 4 covered using them.
ODOMETER - For distance measurement.
OPSIOMETER - An expert's map distance measuring device.

PENCIL AND NOTE PAD - Part of the Trip Log.
PROTRACTOR - For the expert navigator.
RULER - To measure scale distance and triangulation.
TRIP LOG - To keep track of trip details.
And most important of all, *PLANNING, PREPARATION AND STUDY!*

NAVIGATIONAL SKILLS COME WITH TIME

I use the crawl before you walk before you run teaching technique. In light of making it easy, look at the above as a complete overkill. Don't feel you have to own all these items and be an Annapolis graduate for successful backcountry travel. As with maps in the preceding chapter, the following paragraphs briefly describe each item and how it applies to navigation. Then you'll learn to bring them together later in the chapter. Read through this portion of the Guide to get the gist of what is said and not become immediately proficient. Mastering navigation comes with time and experience.

ALTIMETERS

Altimeters indicate elevation, but a word of caution. Altimeters really only measure barometric pressure which varies with the weather. Take any given night on TV and look at the weather reports and satellite pictures. These pictures show two things. The weather fronts move and they vary over a given area. This leads me to a rule of thumb when using altimeters. If you move more than five miles, or more than one-half hour has passed, be suspect of your precise altimeter accuracy. You may have moved through a weather front or given time, the weather front may have moved by you. Once while sitting atop Mount Whitney, I watched the elevation change 150 feet in a matter of less than an hour. Mount Whitney did not change elevation, a weather front was moving through.

CALIBRATE FREQUENTLY

Opportunities for calibration occur when you reach a peak, cross a stream, climb abruptly out of, or down into a canyon, and pass known features such as camp sites. Use elevation markers along the road. Most maps give the elevation of peaks. Many times, campgrounds and points of interest give elevation along with other data. Another technique is to find where your trail crosses a stream or turns up or down on the topos. Read the elevation directly from the topographic contour lines. To effectively use altimeters for navigation, you must frequently calibrate them.

BINOCULARS

Binoculars are great navigational aids. Use them to pick out your destination. "The mountain peak with the lookout is the one we want." They can also change a faint reflection into that most welcome sign of cars on the interstates. Fast moving dust on the horizon may convert into a poleline road upon closer examination. Navigation takes time. Take time to look around.

BOOKS

Books vary from entertaining to specific navigation detail. They can exaggerate or lull you into an area. As mentioned before, calibrate the information regarding accuracy and adjectives. Otherwise, books are a good source of directional information.

CB RADIO

Using a CB radio for navigation is a long shot. You'll learn of more practical uses later on. For navigation, listen for other travelers local to you and ask for instructions. Call for help as explained in Chapter 7. In the Tips chapter, I recommend you always stop and chat with other explorers. Ask if they have CBs, and what channel they are using. This is worthwhile information when you need help.

COMPASS

The compass and maps need no further explanation at this time. More on compasses later.

CIRCLE DRAWING COMPASS

The circle drawing compass use will become evident when I explain "shrinking the map."

OTHERS

As with CB radio above, discussions with others are another good reason to be friendly along the way. Those you encounter may have just traveled what's up ahead for you, or they may have traveled the area before. It makes good sense to stop and chat with virtually everyone.

ODOMETER

Your odometer is your link to distance on the ground. I'm disappointed with the ones that do not include tenths of a mile. If you own that type, skip on. If not, here's a side trip on exactly how to determine the accuracy of your odometer. This method works equally well for 4X, motorcycle or mountain bike; however, lengthy bike checks require more personal energy. I'll address myself to 4WDs.

CALIBRATE

Calibrate your odometer. Dirt roads and directions are hard enough to follow without complicating things with inaccurate equipment. I've been within 50 feet of a road and not seen it! That's a one percent error in just one mile! Odometer inaccuracy is typically three to six percent. Professional speedometer calibration should also include odometer calibration.

CALIBRATE SAFELY

Knowing the accuracy of your speedometer has financial rewards. Being cited for excessive speed is no fun, particularly when your speedometer showed legal. More on speedometers at the end of this chapter. Knowing the accuracy of your odometer can make the difference between finding that *lost* oasis or being *lost*! With very little effort and time, it is possible to safely determine odometer accuracy. I throw in safely to remind you to keep your eyes on the road. This exercise, and the speedometer check later on, require driving and recording data while moving and at roadside stops. They are best carried out with the driver doing her job, the navigator doing his, and both paying attention to safety!

THE CENTER DIAL

Before we get started, I'll spin you through the mechanics of the center dial, then discuss calibration. For analog type speedometers (clock type), the numbers around the outside of the center dial indicate speed. In the USA, it's miles per hour (MPH). The smaller, colored numbers indicate kilometers per hour (km/h). And don't ask me why MPH is all caps and km/h is lower case. I suspect it has to do with the more scientific inclination of metric units.

TRIP ODOMETER

The rectangular array of yet smaller numbers within the speedometer is the odometer. It indicates distance, or in our case, miles. You may have two (or more) odometers. The six place readout shows total miles on the vehicle and the four place trip odometer can be reset. The trip odometer that shows tenths of a mile is best. The tenths dial (digit) contrasts with the balance of the numbers. It is usually printed in the reverse of the other digits.

MILE POST MARKERS

Along California's interstates and highways are mile post markers. The figure on page 30 shows the information they present. The markers are put up every mile, with interim markers at rivers, railroad crossings and other highway features. For this exercise, use the distance portion of the marker.

Highway Number **79**
County **SD**
Mileage **41**
00

California Mile Post

First you need to determine which way the tenths dial moves: does it increase rolling up or down? It's sometimes hard to tell what number is coming and which one is going without knowing your rolling direction. Is the number almost fully in view or is it just starting to roll away? My Ford Explorer rolls in the up direction. Note also that the tenths dial continually turns, whereas the units, tens and hundreds digits click from whole number to whole number.

Odometer checks are most safely performed along backcountry roads and not on interstate highways. On-the-fly, short, interstate odometer checks are not as accurate and safe as stop-and-go backroad checks. In contrast to speedometer checks, distance checks are not concerned with twists and turns, ups and downs, and rate of travel.

SHORT DISTANCE CALIBRATION IS DIFFICULT

Typical stock odometer error is less than six percent. This small error makes short distance checks more difficult than long distance. For short distance odometer checks you must interpolate, or guess at hundredths of a mile. This is where the direction of rotation comes into play. For example, if you choose to check distance over a mile or two, you will most likely find the tenths dial is just about to, or has just rolled past your starting tenths number.

GUESSING IN-BETWEEN

Interpolation is the art of guessing what portion of a rotation the tenths digit has made (see the figure on page 31). If the tenths dial is half way between 0 and 1 on a one-mile check, then you guess (interpolate) the reading is 1.05 miles, or 5% error. A third of a roll means about 1.03 (3% error); two-thirds roll means about 1.07 (7% error) and so on. As you'll see below, with a ten mile check, you can forget interpolation. With an exact ten mile check, the trip odometer directly indicates your correction factor. If arithmetic and this paragraph confuses you, a ten mile check is for you.

TEN MILE CHECK

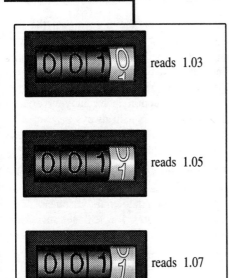

reads 1.03

reads 1.05

reads 1.07

SAFELY START

TRAVEL TEN MILES

CORRECTION FACTOR

In California, drive either north or east on any marked highway. In these directions, mileage increases and makes the math easier. California mile-post highway distance indications start at the highway's southern or western origin. In other words, distance increases traveling north or east.

Safely pull off the pavement near a mile-post marker and note the mileage. Pick one with no tenths to further simplify the arithmetic. Align the very front of the car, motorcycle or mountain bike with the mile-post. Do not pull along side a marker that leaves you on the pavement. Your vehicle may unsafely obstruct the highway. Also, stopping on blind curves and in blind dips is dangerous. Record this mileage. Reset your trip odometer to zero. Pay particular attention to the tenths dial. Has it gone completely and exactly to zero? This sometimes requires the complete depression and very slow, gentle release of the reset button. Add (subtract if you drive south or west) ten miles to this mileage.

Safely pull back onto the highway without spinning the tires and drive to the mile-post ten miles farther down the road. Again, safely pull off the highway with the mile-post properly aligned at the front of the vehicle. Carefully note the trip odometer reading. For a ten mile check, the tenths dial determines your correction factor (your percentage error).

For example, if the odometer reads 10.3 miles, your correction factor is 1.03. This means your odometer reads 3% high. If the distance is under 10 miles, say 9.6, your correction factor is 0.96 and your odometer reads 4% low. It doesn't take a genius to see the correction factor (multiplier) is the 10-mile-test digits with a simple one-place-to-the-left-shift of the decimal point. If you choose a 100 mile check-distance, shift the decimal point to the left two places.

ADJUST MAP READINGS

Use the odometer correction factor to *adjust* the distances given in maps and books. Multiply the map (book) reading by your correction factor. For example, the high reading odometer requires multiplying the map distance by 1.03. The low reading odo uses 0.96 as the multiplier. Write the correction factor in your owners manual or some location that will always be available. But remember, this error will change with tire wear, size changes, and axle ratio changes.

OPSIOMETER

I'm easily fascinated with adult toys, but an opsiometer borders on useless. It is a device that you roll along the map roads to accumulate trail distance. Two opsiometers and 10 years later, I'm still not successful at driving one. I overshoot the curves and skid on hairpins. I look at opsiometers like a trip to a bad movie: you have to go to figure out you shouldn't have! For six or seven bucks, they are an evening's entertainment.

PENCIL AND PAPER

You need something to keep a record of your adventure. Pencil and note pad are regular items in my 4X.

PROTRACTOR

Protractors are included in my list to satisfy the navigational techies. I very seldom use one and will not explain them.

RULER

Rulers are not a must, but they serve two purposes. Use them to measure (estimate) scale-mile distance. They are also useful for drawing triangulation lines.

THE TRIP LOG

DETAILS IMPORTANT

Just as planning is the key to successful trips, so are details to navigation. Besides, a written record will get you back to the same spot next time, or help a friend navigate the unknown. Prepare and use a Trip Log.

KEEP A LOG

A Trip Log is simply a written record of your adventure. Logging a trip is not complicated. There are three columns to a Trip Log. *Time* - When did you make a stop or pass a specific landmark? Use this to estimate your return via the same route. Three hours in means three hours out. Do you have enough daylight? *Miles* - What was the mileage reading at your stop? How many miles have you gone? Do you have enough gas for the balance of the trip? *Remarks* - What occurred at this stop (the current time and mileage)? Did you stop for lunch or pictures? This is useful information. Lunch time is not needed for the drive out. Same is true for pictures. Is there a reference landmark worth noting? Is it a "Y" in the road? Is there nothing significant on the map or your surroundings? Create your own reference. Put a mark on the map and note the feature. Put a trail duck (a small pile of three or more rocks) along side the road.

DON'T ABUSE FOR TRAIL MARKING

On trail markers: technically, it is against the law to leave trail markers in place. The pie plate that shows your buddies where you are camped is illegal if not removed. Ribbons or other markers tied to bushes and trees are wrong too. I'm particularly annoyed by off road racers who mark their way with day-glow paint on rocks and plants! They have no room to complain of losing race courses if they don't eliminate this unsightly practice and clean up their mess!

REMOVE TRAIL MARKERS

I've also learned so many people construct trail ducks, they are useless for long term reference. It seems like every person that has gone up a trail, right or wrong, leaves a trail duck, and doesn't remove it upon discovering it is incorrect! Trail ducks are very temporary things for me. Remove all forms of trail markers.

RECORD DETAILS

Your first entry in the trip log can be when you leave home, but must be when you start dirt road. From then on, every time you stop, make a turn, catch a breath, investigate a highlight, pass another road, or are in doubt about where you are, make an entry in the log. Side trips and doubling back are particularly confusing to me. I compute the *double back* mileage right as it occurs. I then enter and circle it in the **Remarks** section. This makes deducting it for the miles out easier. Same goes for picture breaks and other non travel time. Calculate and enter it under **Remarks** as it happens.

LOG OTHER DETAILS TOO

Use the log to keep track of other information too. How is the road according to the group coming out? What CB channel are they on? Did you note the REACT (Radio Emergency Associated Communications Teams, explained below) channels on the roadside sign? Did the geology class tell of caves up that side wash? Something to explore next time.

EASY WAY

You say you don't want to keep a trip log? Make it easy on yourself. Keep the trip log on your map. Make your notes on the map, exactly where it happens. Read the balance of this chapter on getting unlost, particularly shrinking the map, and then decide if a trip log is a useful navigation tool.

EXAMPLE

Here's a summary example. We turned off the pavement at mileage 39678 at 8 AM. Our day goes as shown in the example. Come mileage 39729 at 2:30 PM, it's time to go home. Total mileage was 51 less 7, as noted in *Remarks*. Time was 5 hours less 2 for breaks. We have 44 miles and need 3 hours to get back to paved road. The gas gauge shows half full and it doesn't get dark until 7 PM. We're in great shape!

Many of the items above elude to planning. Planning, preparation and study are the backbone of navigation.

NAME	GOLD CLIFF	DATE 9-9-87

TIME	MILES	REMARKS
8 A	39678.4	START DIRT
8:30	681.7	SIDE TRIP TO WILLOW SP
9	683.2	@ SPRINGS (T-:20)
9:20	"	LV " (M-3)
9:50	684.7	BACK TO MAIN TRAIL
10:30	693.1	PICTURES AT CAVE/CLIFF
10:40	"	LV " " (T-:10)
11:30	39707.0	HWY 66 - LUNCH
12:30	"	LV " (T-1:00)
1:00P	713.0	LOST??
1:10	"	LV ↑ (T-:10)
1:12	713.5	STREAM - YEA!
1:20	715.0	RT AT Y - DEAD END
1:40	719.0	BACK AT Y (T-:20) (M-4)
2:00	729.4	GOLD CLIFF - GOOD STUFF!
2:30	"	LV " " (T-:30)
6:00	39773.4	PAVED ROAD, GO FOR HOME

GETTING UNLOST

USE IMAGINATION

Understand this section as much with your feelings as your logic. I say to "shrink the map." Be confident you're really not hopelessly lost on the whole map, just a portion. When I say extend your arm in the direction of such and such mountain, see the mountain and your extended arm. Let your mind's eye see what I'm talking about. Can you hear the stream? Trust you are learning more than your logic lets you think. Go back over the technical parts after you get a feeling for the concepts.

ARE YOU REALLY LOST

Traveling an hour or two in the woods can be unnerving. Particularly if you haven't seen anyone or anything for 50 miles. We are restless under these situations. Check your trip plan to see where you should be. Check with your traveling companions. Are they lost too or are you just anxious? Sometimes just relaxing for a moment will bring it all into perspective. Nine times out of ten, I'm not lost, just impatient!

LEADING HAS PRESSURES

Impatience is particularly true for the leader. Both the teasing and real concerns will surface when temporarily disoriented. In the *Silver Coyote's book of rules*, it's OK to be lost. It is part of the adventure. I sometimes get harassed for not getting lost. Stop for a minute and pull out the maps. Explain to others, "I'm confused. I'm looking for a road to the north, but haven't found it. It should be right after we cross a stream. Does anyone have any ideas?" Then someone pops up, "We haven't crossed a stream yet, but I hear one!" Also, give others a chance and the responsibility to lead. One turn at leading brings into perspective its pressures and responsibilities.

LISTEN TO OTHERS

Listen to those with more or current local experience. Is there an old timer in the caravan who knows but "ain't say'n." I cannot drive and navigate. Trade off driving and catch up on navigating. Men, get your egos out of the way and listen to the ladies. Typically you've been driving and they've been reading the books and studying the maps. There is a good chance they know your location better than you. Objectively compare others' information to your actual physical surroundings.

USE PHYSICAL SURROUNDINGS

As experience increases, your physical surroundings will tell you more and more about your location. The map shows a railroad track where you want to turn south. There is no railroad track nearby. You are not where you want to turn south! The map shows a trail on the east, parallel to a stream bed. There are tracks on both sides of the stream. Others before you have been confused too. I would guess the map is correct. Use the trail on the east! The topo shows you turn up hill (increase elevation). This turn leads down hill. It's not your turn! If your resources allow, investigate or drive to a better vantage point. It's fun!

THE INVISIBLE Y

Don't be fooled by the invisible "Y". When you drive up the center leg of this Y, a decision obviously confronts you. The road goes left and right. Now visualize driving down the left arm of the Y. You may not see the right branch coming in when you reach the central point. This branch comes in from behind and depending on its angle, it could go un-noticed. This is particularly true when going down stream or wash. Some tributaries gently intersect the main wash from behind. Remember you may or may not have noted this intersection in your Trip Log on your way in.

UN-NOTED DECISION

Now visualize your return up the Y's central leg. An obvious decision lies before you. Un-noted on the way in, the invisible Y forces an unexpected decision on the way out. Keep your eyes on the rear view mirror for the invisible Y and trails coming in from behind.

LOOK BEHIND

It's a good backcountry practice to occasionally do a visual 180°. See what the scenery looks like going the other direction. I'm continually amazed how different the same trail can appear, depending on the direction of travel.

MOST USED ROAD

On a different Y, you make a guess and travel up the left arm. Surprise, it dead-ends! You now go back down the left arm and continue on the correct, right arm. The next traveler comes to the Y and uses the left arm too. Why? Because it is the most used road. You went in and out on the left arm - two sets of tracks. You only went out on the right - one set of tracks. The old rule to use the most heavily traveled road has its drawbacks. How do you beat it? Allow time to check out such things.

CHECK YOUR RESOURCES

If your resources (personal water, daylight, gasoline, food, weather) are OK, take time to see what's up ahead. I occasionally like to play at being lost. If your resources are critical, gain your composure and do some of the following when lost.

STAY NEARBY TRANSPORTA-TION

Stay with your transportation, particularly if traveling alone. This is an inviolate rule! Cars, motorcycles and even bicycles are easier to find than people. Besides, they contain your survival resources.

USE CB RADIO

Turn your CB radio ON and listen. Turn the squelch so you hear static all the time. With your ignition switch to ACCessories, and other accessories OFF, your CB radio draws very little power. When in real trouble, use the emergency channel 9 and the Area channel (see Chapter 10). Other popular channels are 19 and 21, the highway channels. Channel 14 is the most frequently sold channel. REACT stations typically monitor channels 11 and 12. Try the channel the fellows you passed a while back were on. The Silver Coyote uses channel 1. More on all this in Chapter 7, Survival.

REACT CHANNELS

REACT (Radio Emergency Associated Communication Teams) stations frequently put signs along the paved roads. These real estate size signs tell what channels the locals monitor for emergencies. Useful information if you have a problem.

LOOK FOR DUST

Look for dust. A most probable sign of fellow travelers. Fast moving dust means a good road. Check its distance and direction for triangulation. Also, that's a good time to sweep the CB channels.

LOOK FOR NEW REFERENCES

Look for new references such as railroad tracks, other roads or property boundaries. State Park signs, Federal Forest markers, wild life sanctuaries and cattle guards all indicate property ownership change. Property ownership change on maps is usually shown by a change in color. Find this on the map.

LOOK FOR BIG PICTURE REFERENCES

Look for your big picture landmarks and references. Use your binoculars. Once rediscovered, you can use some of the navigation principles following in this Guide.

TRIANGULATE	Triangulate your position (explained below).
LISTEN	Listen for nearby sounds of nature and civilization. Streams, the highway, chain saws, radios, motorcycles and conversation are encouraging sounds.
SMELL	Smell for campfires or other signs of civilization.
WAIT	Wait for others to pass by. It is very seldom I don't run into others in the backcountry.
USE TRIP LOG	Use your Trip Log.

USE THE TRIP LOG

SHRINK THE MAP

That big map you're giving a blank stare when lost can be pretty intimidating. Consider you are not lost on the whole map, just a small portion, but where is that? Let's learn a technique I call shrinking the map.

MAX MILEAGE CIRCLE

From your Trip Log determine how many miles you've gone since the last known point. A known point is somewhere you confirmed, or were in no doubt about location-wise. With a circle drawing compass, draw a circle whose radius is the above miles and its center at the confirmed location.

REDUCE THE CIRCLE

Without belaboring it, you *must* be within that circle. Other things can reduce the area within the circle further. Have you only traveled south since your known point? This eliminates the northern half of the circle. Does the circle encompass a highway, stream or railroad tracks? If you haven't crossed a particular feature (this would be a new known location), you must be on one side or the other of it! Simple, logical, obvious, practical stuff. Here's a graphic example.

EXAMPLE

Let's say we're lost at 1 PM (see Trip Log on page 34). Our last known point was when we crossed Highway 66 headed south, 1/2 hour ago and 6 miles back. Set the distance between the circle drawing compass point and pen to 6 miles. Place the point at the intersection of the dirt road and Highway 66. Draw a circle. We have not driven more than 6 miles. We have not crossed any paved roads again. We must be within the southern half of that circle. Use this technique to shrink the map, or in other words, locate your general position. Now doesn't that bring that big map down a notch or two?

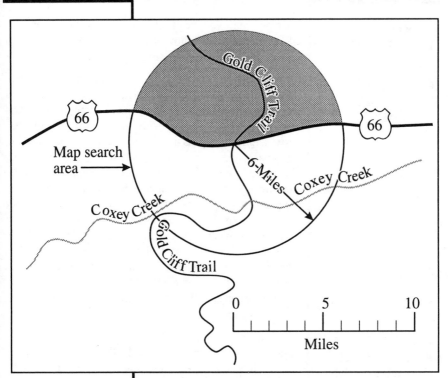

TRIANGULATION & RECONNOITERING

SIMPLIFIED TRIANGULA-TION

The pro's can make this real complicated and frustrating. It doesn't have to be. I make it easier by neglecting magnetic variation (discussed later) and being satisfied with less than exact results. I believe my relaxed methods are justified by the fact that we stay on existing roads and trails, and can cover a fair amount of ground in a relatively short period of time with mechanized travel.

USE KNOWN LAND MARKS

Triangulation is the process of using landmarks and cartographic information (known references) to locate your position on a map, and hence reality. Known references are mountain peaks, railroad tracks, roads, streams, property boundaries, elevation or anything that can be located on the map *and* terrafirma. They are reasonably sound references you can easily identify both places. The certainty of your known references influences the exactness of your triangulation.

NEED TWO REFERENCES

Simply put, you need two references to triangulate. Several examples follow. Use a Riverside County map to follow along on the first two.

ROAD AND MOUNTAIN EXAMPLE

Say we are to the east of Salton Sea, alongside a canal. I can also see Mount San Jacinto. Orient the map as discussed in Chapter 4. In addition, bring the compass body north or N to align with the north on the compass rose and the compass needle. All three, compass needle, compass body, and map north should agree and be pointing in the same direction, north. Find the canal on the map. I can see Mount San Jacinto to the northwest (upper left). I've been keeping track of it since early this morning. Find it on the map too. Stand over the map and project your outstretched arm in the direction of San Jacinto. Get the feel for its direction. Now get back to the map and draw a line from San Jacinto (on the map), at the same angle (direction) as your arm, across the canal. Where that line crosses the canal is your location.

CONFIRM WITH ADDITIONAL REFERENCES

You have taken two visual references, the canal and Mount San Jacinto, and brought them together on the map. Now, look more closely at the map. You may be able to further confirm your location with other landmarks. Isn't that a small town or buildings just about due west? The map confirms that is probably North Shore. There should be a paved road nearby to the west.

SAME AS USING COORDINATES

Triangulation is somewhat similar to using map coordinates, but in this case we use two known references. Use this process with railroad tracks, roads, streams and rivers, wet and dry lakes, mines and industrial sites, beacons and microwave towers, elevation contour lines, and other known references. Small scale maps, ones that cover a large area, are better for triangulation than topos. I quickly learned this years ago, backpacking the Sierra. Topos don't reach out far enough, so I would carry the county and state maps for the big picture.

TWO PEAKS EXAMPLE

Let's do another on the same map, only with two mountain peaks. This requires we draw two lines on the map. One from each peak.

SAME TECHNIQUE

We are somewhere along the aqueduct road south of Joshua Tree National Monument, east of Indio, and north of I-10. We have identified San Jacinto and Rabbit Peak farther south. With the same arm waving technique described above, we draw lines from San Jacinto and Rabbit, in our direction. Where they cross is our location. We have been traveling north for some time and just made a bend to the west. Position confirmed, the map shows our westerly bend in the road!

ROAD AND ELEVATION EXAMPLE

We can also simply use several bits of known information, on a map, without the compass, arm-waving, line-drawing funny business. For example, you've found your road on the topo. You also know your actual elevation by altimeter reading. Locate the contour line on the topo. Where the topo contour and the road cross is your location.

TRAIL AND BOUNDARY EXAMPLE

You could do the same thing with a trail and a property boundary. You're sitting at the State Park boundary sign and you know you're in Tule Wash. Both the State Park boundary and Tule Wash are shown on the map. Any question about your location?

GUESS AT BOUNDARIES

You can take a guess at un-identified property boundaries such as cattle guards and fences. This usually means a transition from public to private property. Again, map color changes usually show ownership change.

TOO EASY

Does all of this sound too easy? Not with practice and persistence. Try it next time you're out. Try it on the pavement first. You don't have to be lost to practice these principles. I hope you're amazed how easy it is to confirm location!

SPEEDOMETER CALIBRATION

USE DISTANCE AND TIME

Remember speed is miles (distance) per hour (time) - how much distance did you travel in how much time. To determine speedometer accuracy, simply drive at a constant rate, measure the elapsed time, over a known distance and divide the latter by the former. That's easier than it sounds.

USE THE INTERSTATES

Use your cruise control to hold speed constant. It also helps to use those long, straight, level, uncongested sections of the interstates so common throughout the southwest. Beside, it's a nice way to while away the miles on a long trip.

USE A STOPWATCH

For accurate time measurement, use a stopwatch. The sweep second-hand on a regular analog watch will do, but it's not nearly as good (or safe) as the stopwatch function on a digital watch. I try to start and stop the time exactly when the mile post passes the front bumper.

USE 1 MILE AT 60 MPH

The easiest way to check your speedometer is use exactly one mile and maintain exactly 60 MPH. Greater distance yields more accuracy, but requires more involved calculations. Beside, most of us are far too impatient to hold 60 MPH for more than a minute or two!

1 MILE PER MINUTE

At 60 MPH you cover 60 miles in one hour (60 minutes), or one mile in one minute. If the measured distance is exactly one mile and it takes exactly 60

MILES PER HOUR		KILOMETERS PER HOUR	
Seconds/mile	MPH	Seconds/km	km/h
55	65.45	40.00	90
56	64.28	39.13	92
57	63.16	38.30	94
58	62.07	37.50	96
59	61.02	36.73	98
60	*60.00*	*36.00*	*100*
61	59.02	35.29	102
62	58.06	34.62	104
63	57.14	33.96	106
64	56.25	33.33	108
65	55.38	32.73	110
66	54.55	32.14	112
67	53.73	31.58	114
68	52.94	31.03	116
69	52.17	30.51	118
70	51.43	30.00	120

seconds to cover that mile, you are traveling at exactly 60 MPH. Easier to use than a formula is the chart on page 42. Remember your test actually gives a percentage error and is only good near the speed at which it was conducted.

COMPASS FUNDAMENTALS

EASY TECHNIQUES

The compass is a fascinating instrument. In years past, I choked at studying orienteering. It seemed so complicated - azimuths and angles, and terms and techniques I didn't understand. Don't let these things scare you off. I've limited this section to basics. As wheeled travelers, we have few techniques to master.

COMPASS PARTS

Some compasses are like Swiss Army knives. They have more bells and whistles than you'll ever use. Let's start with the parts and features of a loaded compass. This will give us the terms for further discussion.

SIGHTING MIRROR UNNECESSARY

The figure on page 44 is a full feature compass without sighting mirror. A sighting mirror allows you to take a bearing while looking directly at a field reference object. It definitely produces more accurate readings. For all practical purposes, a sighting mirror just adds cost and weight, gets scratched, is not as easy to use on maps as a clear body compass and virtually never gets used. I don't use one.

PROTRACTOR

The protractor is used for precise navigation and rough slope measurement. I use the dial, which is also marked off in degrees. To me the protractor is unnecessary.

MAGNIFIER

Use the magnifier to read the fine print. The older I get the more useful this seems. My personal compasses don't have magnifiers. Consider most compasses are plastic and after a couple of trips, the magnifier is too scratched to use. Carry a glass magnifier if you need one.

CLEAR BODY

A clear plastic, see-through body is a must for on-maps usage. Simple pocket-watch type compasses aren't as practical as the rectangular, clear plastic, backpacking type.

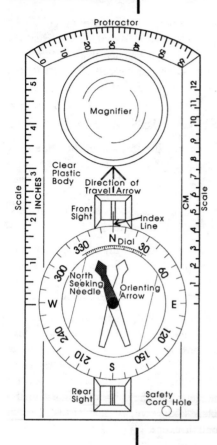

Metric and inch scales are used to scale the maps, but for the maps we use, and the distances we travel in vehicles, they are always too short. I never use them. I usually use my hands or sticks.

Direction of travel arrow is for hikers. When you stay on the roads, you don't need a direction of travel arrow, however, it can double as an index line.

Front and rear sights are not found on all compasses. Nice, but for my unrefined methods, not particularly necessary.

The index line is used to set and read the dial. I can't imagine a compass without one. It is sometimes on the front sight.

The dial is another necessity and must be graduated and turnable. Degrees per division is more a function of eyesight than field usage. Two degrees per division is typical. Don't get hung up on precision.

It's not a compass without a North seeking needle. Make sure you can readily identify the north end and the mark won't come off or fade. The glow-in-the-dark feature is nice, but not necessary. What good is it to see the needle, if you can't see the map too? The needle must be in a fluid-filled vial to settle movement faster.

ORIENTING ARROW

An orienting arrow (and lines) is necessary. If you can offset the orienting arrow from "N", so much the better. With this type you always align the needle over the orienting arrow.

SAFETY CORD

The safety cord hole is if you want to look real outdoorsy and wear it around you neck. Since I carry mine in my pocket and find the cord gets in the way on maps, I don't use this feature.

HAVE THE BASICS

For 99% of all vehicle applications, have at least the clear plastic body, turnable dial and north seeking needle. Everything else is icing on the cake.

HAVE SEVERAL COMPASSES

Compasses are reasonably priced. Consider having more than one. I have several. One for the console in the 4X, one for my survival pack, and another for use at home. Try a couple of different styles and brands to zero in on your exact requirements.

BECOME FAMILIAR WITH YOUR COMPASS

After you buy one, get a feel for it. Read through the instruction manual. Become familiar with the parts. Move the body and watch the needle. Learn how to rotate the dial. Can you move the orienting arrow independently of the dial?

FREE UP THE NEEDLE

Learn this information. Most of us use the compass for only one thing, orienting the map, so any compass will do. Good compass needles are suspended on sapphire bearings, but even a low friction pivot can not compensate for malfunction and poor compass body positioning. Regardless of the type, or what you pay, perform this simple test before every use. Hold the body flat and level, and rotate it a few times slightly clockwise and then counterclockwise. The needle should maintain a relatively fixed position. On a Death Valley trip, while sighting Mount Whitney, our first compass thought north was at one o'clock on the compass body, regardless of the body position. It was obviously broken. Also rock the body slightly to the left and right, and front to back, to insure totally free needle movement. Technically, the needle is not only seeking north in the horizontal (flat) plane, but it's also trying to dip down in the vertical plane. Picture the earth's magnet below the surface. Compass body position must allow for totally free movement. My dad says I hold my mouth funny to get mine just right!

CHECK FOR STRAY FIELDS

The compass needle interacts with any and all magnetic fields. It can't tell one from another. Just bring your compass close to the car door speaker to see the effect. Electric currents produce magnetic fields too. Check this by moving the compass around the car battery with the headlights on and everything else off (including the motor for safety!). The needle will quickly align itself with the field-current in the battery cable. Move it around elsewhere under the hood and you'll see a dancing needle. Other metal parts have subtle fields which also affect needle orientation. When using a compass, you must do your best to insure the needle is not influenced by other magnetic fields.

TEST FOR STRAY FIELDS

Use your compass away from all metal objects and electrical items. This means the car hood is a lousy map table. Using tools as map weights is a no-no too. Even the current to power your flashlight can deceive the compass. Be aware of what's in your pockets. If you're wondering why north is always in the direction of your belly button, check your belt buckle!

ALIGN MAP AND COMPASS

To be entirely useful, a map must be arranged to agree with the physical surroundings. When properly aligned, what's off to the left on the map, will also be off to the left in the real world.

GUESS AT NORTH

Start developing a sense for north - take a guess. Now use your compass to select a good map location and see which way is north. Walk in a straight line for twenty or thirty feet and confirm that north is in one general direction and not centering on some nearby object. Typically, twenty or thirty feet from the car will do fine. How was your guess?

USE ONLY THE NEEDLE

For orienting the map and with no particularly critical readings in mind, simply place the compass over the map's compass rose and twist the map until map north aligns with the compass needle north. You don't even have to move or adjust the compass body or dial. The needle alone provides all the information needed.

MAGNETIC VARIATION

For more precise alignment, you must compensate for magnetic variation. Be aware the North magnetic pole and the geographic North pole (true north) are not located in exactly the same place. Magnetic north moves slightly each year and what's worse, other geographically local fields also influence where the compass needle points.

MAGNETIC NORTH IS NEAR HUDSON BAY

To help bring all this into focus, in California, simply remember the compass needle points more east than expected. It's pointing to a spot near the Hudson Bay, 1,300 miles from the geographic North pole.

CALIFORNIA IS 15°

This offset between the two poles is called magnetic declination and don't worry about the switch in terms from variation above. It's measured in degrees and is always given at the bottom of USGS topographic maps. For Southern California, it's around 14 or 15 degrees. Use whichever is easier to set on your compass.

MAP NORTH IS GEOGRAPHIC NORTH

The other thing you need to know before we get into adjusting for declination is that map-north, the straight up and down vertical lines on a map are virtually always geographic North/South lines. That means when you align your map with the needle, as described above, it's in error by the declination angle.

COMPENSATION NOT ALWAYS NECESSARY

The easy way to handle this small compass error is don't. 99% of all my map usage is done without compensating for declination. However, 15°, over a great distance, introduces considerable error. For example, sighting Mount Whitney, 68 miles from Aguereberry Point in Death Valley suffers from lack of declination correction. Traveling on foot demands correction unless you have a lot more energy than I do!

OFFSET THE ORIENTING ARROW

The second best way to handle this anomaly is buy a Brunton, Lutz or other compass that allows rotation of the orienting arrow independent of the dial. Once set up, you forget it.

TAPE ON AN ORIENTING ARROW

The third best way is to tape your own orienting arrow, offset for declination, to the bottom of the compass. This is the technique I use on my Silva compass.

The way the purists want you to handle it is adjust the dial each time, which really isn't that bad.

ROTATE COUNTER-CLOCKWISE

The objective with all the above is to have the magnetic needle point to the declination angle and not to the N on the dial. In other words, to adjust your compass for magnetic declination, simply rotate the dial counter-clockwise until the 15° mark is exactly at the index mark.

TAKE A BEARING

Another compass talent is locating your destination when potentially in sight. Some roads take near-parallel paths. One leads to your goal, the other just nearby. Knowing the exact location and direction of your destination helps. This is called taking a bearing. The orienteers like the term azimuth instead of bearing. Following is the Coyote method.

NICE SKILL

This skill borders on nice to conquer. Taking a bearing requires the map, compass, straightedge, pencil, knowing you are within sight of your destination and the ability to place yourself on the map.

HOW TO TAKE A BEARING

Orient the map, with declination helps. Draw a line from your current location to the destination. Adjust the compass dial so the "N" is at the index mark and the needle is at the declination. Place the center of the needle (the pivot point) over your current location. Read the degrees where the pencil line intersects the dial. This is your general heading or bearing. It's also the direction to look for your goal. With a little practice, drawing the line will not be necessary - just "eyeball" it.

MOTHER NATURE'S NORTHS

WAYS TO FIND NORTH

When stuck without a compass (shame on you), Mother Nature's your salvation provided you know some of her secrets. The sun, moon, stars, wind and plants bestow potentially lifesaving directions.

THE SUN

Ol' sol still remains the single best daytime reference there is. The principles are few. It rises in the east, sets in the west and makes a more southerly traverse in the winter, in our half of the globe, the northern hemisphere.

BIRDS GO SOUTH FOR THE WINTER

There's an easy way to remember this southerly traverse business. Just remember the birds go south for the winter. They follow the warmth of the sun to southern latitudes. That means the sun's sky-arc is somewhat to the south in winter. In the summer, around our neck of California, it gets almost straight overhead. The sun never goes north of straight overhead in Southern California.

100% RELIABLE SUN

The sun is not perfect, but is 100% reliable. I've had several compasses go bad, but never the sun. While lost in Baja, a friend denied the truth of two compasses and the setting sun! Needless to say, he still won't admit being lost!

MOON TOUGH TO USE

The moon does the same thing - rises in the east and sets in the west. However, without in-depth knowledge of its movement, or daily observations, it's tough to use as reliably as the sun. But again, know its wandering ways and you've got a 100% reliable night beacon.

Here's a method to use your analog watch as a "watch

A WATCH COMPASS

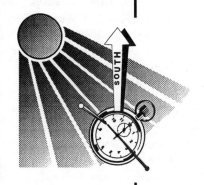

SOUTH'S HALF WAY BETWEEN

ADJUST FOR DAYLIGHT SAVINGS TIME

LEARN ABOUT POLARIS

MOSS ON NORTH OF TREES

compass." From a past *4-Wheeling* newsletter, Walt Wheelock makes simple this useful technique. He dug it out of his 1922 Boy Scout Manual. The best part is this compass is not affected by magnetic variances. Now all I have to do is dig out my old analog watch!

The method takes advantage that the sun, at noon, is in its most southerly position - due south. At six AM, it is due east, and at 6 PM, it is due west.

With the watch-face horizontal, point the hour hand directly at the sun. Due south is now half way between the hour hand and 12 o'clock.

In Walt's own words, "Since you may have a bit of a problem lining up the hour hand with the sun, acquire one of these highly technical devices - a match, a straight straw or even a martini pick will do! Place it vertically over the outer end of the flat-lying hour hand. Rotate the watch slowly until the shadow completely covers the hour hand. South is now half way between the shadow and noon. If you've been raised to be one of those north-thinking people, just do an about face for north."

Remember to watch out for daylight savings time. You've "sprung ahead" for the spring, so place your swizzle stick on the identical spot, one hour behind.

I'll save the stars and moon for another Guide, but be aware there is one star that never ever moves around in the heavens - Polaris, the north star, the last star in the handle of the little dipper, Ursa Minor. It's not always easy to find, but in the unclouded sky, it's always there. It's straight off the end of the cup of the big dipper - Ursa Major. More on stars in another Guide.

All these little tidbits of information seem to fit together and become easier and easier to remember. Mother Nature is not complicated, she simply rewards the observant. Take for example the old Boy Scout trick about moss and the north side of trees - moss grows on the north side of trees. Simple. Remember from above how the sun never gets north of directly overhead? Doesn't moss like a moist, indirectly lighted environment? Moss grows on the north side of trees because it never gets burned by the sun's direct rays. However, moss and the next technique can be fooled, so they are not 100% reliable.

USE BARREL CACTUS FOR SOUTH

The Anza-Borrego Desert Natural History Association should get special credit for this one. I learned it in their volunteer training. Not one library reference mentioned it. Barrel cactus (*Echinocactus acanthodes*), along with many other plants are phototropic - they bend toward the light. Combine this tendency with the southerly path of the sun and you've got a 10 inch diameter, 3 foot high plant pointing south. But again, like the moss on the trees, they can be fooled. And finally, the barrel cactus in not the ready source of water you've been lead to believe in the movies. Don't cut down barrel cactus for water!

THE COMPASS PLANT

There's also the compass plant (*Silphium laciniatum*) in our heartland. Its 10 to 12 inch leaves on a 10 to 12 foot high sunflower-like plant align themselves north and south to shade the gummy stalk. By the way, the Indians used the resinous stem of the compass plant for gum. *Lactuca sirriola*, prickly lettuce, does the same thing.

PREVAILING WINDS

Mother Nature can help determine direction by the prevailing winds too. It's usually my last resort and quite frankly, I've never had to use it. Generally, there is a prevailing westerly wind. Virtually all our weather comes in off the ocean, so simply look which way the dead plants have fallen or which way the trees on mountain peaks are topped. Further, it never hurts, for more than one reason, to check the weather before you leave on a trip. With a current check, you have the latest on the wind's direction.

KNOW NORTH!

Knowing which direction is north is interesting. Knowing what to do with that knowledge comes with time.

ESTIMATING DISTANCE

TWO METHODS

Estimating distance is more complicated, but I'll summarize two methods from an article by Vic Schisler in a past *4-Wheeling* newsletter. The first and easiest is the echo technique. The other involves spherical trigonometry which will be simplified with a table.

ECHO TECHNIQUE

Echo can be used as you walk or drive through canyons and mountains. It simply takes advantage of the speed of sound, and is only practical for short distances. Besides, I feel blowing your horn to determine distance is somewhat of an intrusion into Mother Nature's golden silence. However, it is most useful to estimate the distance of an approaching thunder storm.

ONE-HALF THE SECONDS TIMES 1000 FEET

Sound travels at approximately 1,000 feet per second (easier to remember than 1,130 feet/second). To estimate distance, make a sound, count the number of seconds it takes to hear the echo, divide by two, (the sound makes a trip to the reflector and then back to the source) and multiply by 1,000. For example, we blow a whistle and note eight seconds for the return. Eight divided by two is four, times 1,000 equals 4,000 feet, or about ¾ mile.

USE FOR LIGHTENING TOO

When you see and hear a lightening strike, start counting from the flash and multiply by 1,000. The sound only has to make a single trip from the source to your ear. A strike 5 seconds away is about a mile off.

THE DISTANCE TO HORIZON METHOD

The following calculations start with nautical miles, or 6080 feet and assumes a perfect earth like the smooth sea. To estimate distance, you must know the height of the observing eye and the height of the observed object above sea level. Let's take the average six footer sighting just to the horizon. That's about 3 miles. Put two six footers, with very good eyesight, just over the horizon from each other. They get a first glimpse of each other at about 6 miles apart. Picture their line of sight just skimming the horizon at the same point, from opposite directions.

| USE THE TABLE | The table below is easier to handle than the general equation which is the square root of the height times 1.317 equals the distance to horizon. |

DISTANCE TO HORIZON

Height in feet above horizon	Statute miles to horizon
5	2.9
10	4.2
15	5.1
20	5.9
25	6.6
30	7.2
50	9.3
100	13.2
200	18.6
500	29.5
700	34.8
1000	41.7
1500	51.0
2000	58.9
2500	65.8
3000	72.1
3500	77.9
4000	83.3
4500	88.3
5000	93.1
6000	102.0
7000	110.2
8000	117.8
9000	124.9
10,000	131.7
11,000	138.1
12,000	144.3
13,000	150.2
14,000	155.8
15,000	161.3

| GO PREPARED | For the confident and experienced, getting lost is fun. For the foolhardy and ill-prepared, getting lost is a catastrophe! Keep an accurate Trip Log, go properly prepared and you should never be hopelessly lost! |

CHAPTER 6 TIPS

A BACK ROAD CODE OF ETHICS

On several occasions I've made reference to the *Silver Coyote's book of rules*. The Silver Coyote is my CB radio handle and you've now found his rules. This chapter encompasses resource conservation, safety, fire prevention, trail etiquette, trespass, leadership, and my point of view about rangers and things. I trust it all has a ring of common sense!

RESOURCE CONSERVATION

The following conservation, safety and fire prevention tips are taken, with permission, from the *California OHV Guidebook* which I wrote.

Conservation is tough to address. There are so many things to consider and interests to please, how do you set the guidelines, yet not sound too discouraging? Conservation, safety and fire prevention are more a state of mind than a set of rules.

Mother Nature's world is beyond comprehension. Take the earth and shrink it to the size of a billiard ball. The earth would be smoother! Now imagine a delicate film on the cue ball-size earth. Less than one-tenth the thickness of a human hair will do! This is the biosphere where we live. We definitely walk a thin line on this precious old globe.

Mother Nature controls everything we do. Flip back on your two-wheeler - you passed her balance point; slide out on a corner - you exceeded her coefficient of friction; fail to make a hill - you didn't satisfy her momentum and traction requirements. She puts Einstein to shame about physics, Picasso can't match her kaleidoscope of colors and designs, and the Beatles don't hold a candle to the whisper of her winds or the song of her birds.

MOTHER NATURE IS THE BOSS

Mother Nature is unquestionably the boss. She holds all the cards, sets all the rules, has been playing the game longer than anyone, and will continue to play long after we're all gone! Mess with her rules and she'll kick us off the planet. And she really doesn't care!

WE ARE AN EXPERIMENT

It's not like she doesn't really care. It's more like she'll just make the next experiment a little smarter. She has thousands of ideas just waiting in the shadows to take our place. We are just a brief test in her infinite trials of life. In order to stay around, we have to follow her rules!

MOTHER NATURE HAS NO CONSCIENCE

It sounds rather cruel of Mother Nature to kick us off the earth, but she doesn't make value judgments. She just blindly does her thing without conscience or morals. Think about it. She feeds bunnies to snakes, orchestrates earthquakes, tornadoes and floods that kill thousands, and has foretold of the earth's doom with the eventual death of our sun.

MAN MUST BE MOTHER NATURE'S CONSCIENCE

The same is true for virtually all living creatures: their actions are independent of conscience or consequence. That's why man has such a unique role on earth. We can reason. We can foresee the results of our actions. In essence, we must become Mother Nature's conscience. And that's tough. How much will she take, and will we know soon enough what's right and what's wrong? The right things seem to go along with their surroundings. The wrong things disrupt her system and quickly feel the bottom of her boot. Environmental sensitivity is a learned process. Learn, then teach environmental awareness.

FOOLISH GAME

Picture yourself playing Russian roulette. You know, that dumb game where you put one bullet in a revolver, spin the cylinder, point it at your head, and pull the trigger. Every time we blaze an illegal trail, spin a donut, crush a plant, shoot a sign, speed through camp, build an illegal fire and more, we add another bullet to the revolver of privilege. We're disrupting the system and our surroundings. Sooner or later, we fill the cylinder and do the final deed - lose our riding privileges. If you don't want to play this ridiculous game, don't add ammunition to the revolver.

COYOTE GUIDELINES

GUIDELINES

In this chapter, I offer practical, ecologically sensitive guidelines for backcountry travel, regardless of your mode. Take it as presented: to retain our use privilege.

BACKCOUNTRY PRIVILEGE

Backcountry use of any sort must start with the underlying acknowledgment that use is a privilege. It is not a right. The Constitution does not guarantee access to public lands. Just because your daddy used it before does not mean *you* have a right to now. Our biosphere is thin, but we live an even finer line regarding backcountry privileges. Abuse and we all lose.

STAY ON TRAILS

Stay on existing trails. Plant and wildlife impact is minimized by not blazing new routes. It is illegal to cut trails in all but areas designated for open, off-road travel. You may think your peddle-power-saving short cut doesn't matter, but then your tracks are traced by the motorcycles. The 4-Wheelers now see it as a road while the rangers see it as abuse. Always stay on existing trails and routes.

RESPECT SMALL BARRIERS

That row of small rocks across an apparent trail is not intended to be an unconquerable barrier! It's the rangers' polite way of keeping you on the proper trail. They can't build insurmountable obstacles at every wrong or closed trail. Besides, it seems the bigger the barrier, the smaller the ego required to challenge it. With time and respect, the wrong alternative soon becomes obscure and less likely to be used. Give these subtle hints a chance to take hold. When in doubt, don't use blocked roads and trails.

RESPECT ANIMALS

When wildlife or domestic animals are first spotted, slow down and enjoy their presence. Their unpredictable movement could be a hazard to both you and the animals!

STAY AWAY FROM WATER

Water is vital to wildlife as well as man. Limit your stay near water holes and always camp far away.

DON'T TRAVEL IN WATER

Water ways, their banks and beds are exceptionally fragile. Directly cross the water via the trail and avoid disrupting the surrounding area.

NOISE

Noise is in the ear of the beholder, or should be! That melodious purr of your latest tune-up may be an unwelcome roar to others at midnight. To even others, it may be painful. Hold down speed and noise.

REPORT POACHERS

Poaching, the illegal killing of wild animals, is a dangerous problem. You can help stop this menace to wildlife. Protect your identity and collect sizable rewards by calling WE TIP (1-800-952-5400) with your sightings. But remember, never try to enforce the law, just gather and report information.

HELP RANGERS

Part of backroading is self policing. You can help protect our backcountry privileges by reporting all abuse. The rangers number few and far between, and welcome the help. The key again is to get the facts and leave enforcement to the professionals. In the long run, you are only helping yourself and others interested in responsible backcountry use.

RESPECT PRIVATE PROPERTY

Respect private property. Asking permission to pass enhances the backcountry traveler image.

RESPECT GATES AND FENCES

Respect the intent of fences and gates. Remember to leave gates as you find them or as nearby signs direct. The cows wander off if you leave open a gate that was closed. They can't get back to water if you close a gate that was open.

LIMIT COLLECTING

Public property rules vary. Know the area requirements regarding wildflower, plant, rock, mineral and fossil collecting.

FIREWOOD RULES

Rules vary regarding fires and collecting firewood too. Check with the area manager for current and seasonal requirements.

RESPECT ARTIFACTS

Historical and archaeological sites should be left undisturbed. Artifacts should not be collected. Look but don't touch or take.

HAUL IT OUT

Don't burn trash and never bury it. Simply put, pack it out. Carry a trash bag on the trail and collect the trash of others too. Clean areas seem to stay cleaner.

SHARE THE AREA

Share the area with other recreationalists. Pay particular attention to horseback riders and pack animals. Remember, horses and vehicles are as compatible as their riders want them to be.

BE SENSITIVE

Like the smooth, cue-ball size earth, it's hard to figure the significance of each individual's actions on our environment. On the other hand, the result, whatever it is, can only be the sum of all our behavior. Each positive action, regardless of how (apparently) insignificant, contributes toward a positive overall result. Think and act with sensitivity and responsibility toward our environment.

SAFETY

PRACTICE SAFETY

Practice safety all the time. Travel with other vehicles, never alone. Leave your travel plans with someone at home. If you break down, stay near your vehicle. Make sure you can be spotted from the air. Safely share our environment with Mother Nature and others.

FULL-TIME SAFETY

The safety process is full-time. It kicks off with pre-trip planning and preparation. Keeping your rig and other gear in tip-top shape tunes up the process. Carefully driving to the trailhead moves you farther along. Making contact with the local rangers settles you in. Traveling with others and letting someone know your trail plans keeps the safety process going. Carrying spares and a few survival items maintains the fun, and using only designated areas and trails insures your future return. In the next few paragraphs I offer some practical safety suggestions. But again, when our safe-thinking minds are in gear, the rest comes easy!

PRE-TRIP PLEASURES

Success and enjoyment of most everything revolves around preparation and planning. Besides, excitement and expectation go hand-in-hand with planning! Allow yourself these pre-trip pleasures.

CARRY WATER

Carry and consume adequate drinking water. I recommend one gallon per day per person, or carry at least two gallons minimum. You will probably never die of starvation, but dehydration is a killer. So you don't need to carry water huh, you've got an ice chest full. I learned the hard way an up-side-down 4X and ice chest don't hold water! If you don't carry any other spare, carry water!

DRIVE SOBER

Remember drugs and alcohol don't mix any better with dirt than with asphalt. Drugs, alcohol and egos mix too well! Egos and vehicles typically mix to critical mass - catastrophe! Drive sober.

BE PATIENT

A patient, confident attitude is more important than most spares and skills. Don't injure yourself in a panic to fix your equipment or get unstuck. Don't damage your vehicle in a rush to the hospital with an injury. Patience is a virtue, particularly off the interstates.

ALLOW TRAVEL TIME

Map out the paved route and allow plenty of travel time. Safety starts before leaving home and ends when you're safely back. Let the drive to the area become your unwind time. Arrive fresh and relaxed versus wired and up tight. Calm, relaxed travelers are safe travelers.

USE LISTS

Develop checklists and other guidelines about what to take. Share your experience with others. Some areas have special needs. All Federal, State and most other areas require Forest Service approved spark arresters. Learn and record the unique requirements of each area.

PERSONAL SURVIVAL IS FIRST

It's almost like we should have lists of our lists, and prioritize them! The most important list is for the items you leave home with, or without as the case may be! Personal survival items are more important than vehicle parts, but least often carried. At a minimum, always carry water and a space blanket. The ol' human body can go a long time without food, but not water! There is more than one case of travelers dying of dehydration in a matter of just a few short hours. And drink it when you have it too! The space blanket can serve as shade, shelter, signal mirror or a sleeping bag. For about the size of a tire patch kit, it can save your life! Carry one. Bleached bones throughout the mountains and deserts tell the untold final story, "I went unprepared."

TRAVEL WITH OTHERS

Establish a buddy system. Make it a practice to travel with others and always let someone know where you are going. Tell the ranger where you'll be. Regardless of your capability, breakdowns and falls occur. You may be the best mechanic in the world, but with a shattered wheel and no spare, you're stranded. Traveling with others increases the chance of having a usable spare. They can also go for the part or give you a tow.

SACRED RULE

When you're alone and disabled, there is a sacred rule. Stay with your transportation. It has all your resources and is much easier to spot than a wandering person. Besides, backcountry distances are surprisingly deceptive. What took five minutes to drive or ride can easily take five hours to hike. When alone, stranded, broken down or lost, remember the rule - always stay with your vehicle.

USE ONLY DESIGNATED TRAILS

There are times when areas and trails are closed for safety reasons - a land slippage is eminent, there's a fire or fire hazard, the road is washed out, or there's a rescue operation in progress. Safe backcountry travel means responsible travel. Responsible travel means using only designated areas. And then too, there's always that chance of being cited. When we use undesignated routes and areas, we simply add ammunition for those opposed to mechanized backcountry travel. Backcountry travel is truly a pleasure, but understand clearly, it is a delicate privilege. Abuse the privilege and we lose it. The safest bet is to only use the areas and trails set aside for our travel. We're just shooting ourselves in the foot if we don't!

WATCH THOSE BEHIND

I don't like the permanent sound of lost. As before, let's call it temporarily disoriented. Keep a periodic eye on the traveler behind you. Start this process with the leader and no one gets left behind or separated. Stay on the trails. Look for signs of others. Reserve off-roading for designated open areas only.

WATCH THE WEATHER

Remember to pay attention to weather forecasts and seasonal trends. Snow can easily make your trail in impassable on the way back out. Tropical storms make washes and canyons dangerous in late summer. Blistering heat is always a summer time concern in the desert. Develop a sense about the weather and where you travel.

USE PROTECTIVE GEAR

Regarding motorcycles and mountain bikes, there's not much difference between a pro and casual rider in a fall - provided you're properly equipped. Protective gear saves brains, bones, blood, skin, eyes, lives, and yes, your pride too.

WEAR A HELMET

Helmets are a must for all two-wheeled travelers. But just because you wear a helmet, doesn't mean you can neglect the rest of your body. Eye guard, gloves, boots, and full-body clothes should also be used! Dress for what's appropriate for your use, skills and trail. Safety is a full-time process. Full body protection makes sense too.

FIRE PREVENTION

CAUSES OF FIRE

Fire is pretty tough on the average tree, squirrel, bicycle, motorcycle, 4WD, tent, motorhome, house and person! Virtually nothing survives the heat and smoke of a wilderness fire. And let there be no doubt, all vehicles can cause fires! US Forest Service approved spark arresters go a long way toward preventing fires. Having a little knowledge about what causes fires helps a little more. Vehicles present three possible sources of ignition; hot gases, surface temperatures and sparks.

HOT GASES

Hot gases, the gases coming out of the tail pipe, are the least likely cause of fires. Given enough time and the right material though, exhaust can cause a fire.

HOT PARTS

Surface temperatures, the head at the exhaust port, the header pipe, the spark arrester, muffler, catalytic converter and the tail pipe are more likely to cause a fire than hot gases. When stopped, pick a cleared area; move out of tall grass and other tinder material. Shut off your engine and clear the combustible material away from hot surfaces. Think of it this way; the first thing to go will be your vehicle!

SPARKS

Sparks cause fires! Carbon build up, deteriorating mufflers and other parts can emit fire-causing sparks. These fiery embers stay red-hot long after you leave. If they land on dry tinder, there could be a fire. This is another way the buddy system pays off. Keep an eye on your traveling companion's exhaust and have him check yours. Sparks mean something is wrong. They warn of a faulty exhaust system or failing motor. You are not only saving the wilderness, but a big repair bill by checking your exhaust.

SPINNING TIRES

Spinning the tires can cause sparks too. And don't discount your peddle-power wheel spins either!

OBTAIN PERMITS

Remember to obtain necessary permits and permission prior to building a campfire. Where legal, clear flammable material down to the mineral surface for a minimum radius of five feet. Campfires should never be left unattended and should be extinguished thoroughly by drowning, stirring and feeling.

TRAIL ETIQUETTE

COYOTE ROAD-CODE

Simply put, pavement vehicle code also applies to dirt roads, but things like lanes, intersections, stops and so on are somewhat ambiguous. It helps to know what's right and proper. Following is the Coyote's code for unpaved roads. They are a collection of common practices. Some I've been taught, some I've learned, and others just seem to make sense.

HELP OTHERS

In addition to being self policing, another backcountry traveler responsibility is self assistance. I've got to admit I'm not particularly fond of stopping for someone broken down or stuck. Particularly if it looks like they did it to themselves! I know it will take my time, my equipment, my supplies and I usually end up with dirty hands. What I also know is that when I'm stranded, I want all the help I can get! As a result, I always ask if assistance is needed. Sometimes those in need are too proud to ask. I pay my dues by lending a helping hand. Pay your dues when others need help. What goes around, comes around.

HALF ROAD RULE

I call it the *half road rule*. It has to do with taking breaks and making stops. When stopped, don't block the road. Park half, or just slightly more, off the road. Park such that *you* would be comfortable passing on the remaining half. Parking in the road prompts others to blaze new and unnecessary trails. Parking completely off the road can damage road-side vegetation. Park half off the road, leave room for others to pass, but respect the vegetation.

LOOK FOR OTHERS

I think I've finally overcome my teenage attitude every dirt road is a "chicken alley." I feel most travelers gracefully share the roads too. When I see oncoming traffic, I look for a place to pull off early. Use the *half road rule* when passing too. The closeness offers an opportunity for a quick chat. Inquire of what's in store and tell of what's ahead. Ask how many vehicles in their group. Take a short break for a large caravan. What CB radio channel are they using?

ROAD RIGHT-OF-WAY

If maritime rules applied to the dirt, right-of-away would increase with decreased power and size. Walkers would have it over bikers over motorcycles over 4Xs. Somehow, all this starts with animals at the top. But those high on the totem of trail tranquility should also give-way to those desiring to pass. If you wonder why there's wheels on your heels, check out where you're walking. Right-of-away responsibilities are a two-way track. And mechanized travelers, think about your dust as you go by!

YIELD TO UPHILL TRAFFIC

Yield to uphill traffic on tough climbs. It's easier and safer to start moving down, after a pause, versus up. Further, you have more control backing uphill, out of the way, than backing down. Backing downhill is sometimes necessary, but always dangerous.

DRIVE SLOWLY

Drive slowly. Speed damages equipment and our environment. The plants and animals are sensitive to dust. It's OK to go slow. Plan on it.

FOLLOW WAY BACK

Follow back a hundred yards or so. Following too close is dirty, clouds visibility, is dangerous and usually leads to battered vehicles. Allow extra space when climbing or descending steep grades. If it's particularly steep, wait for an all clear at the top or bottom from the vehicle ahead.

LOOK BEFORE YOU LEAP

When in doubt, investigate. How deep is that water? How steep is that hill? How soft is that mud? It's OK to get out and hike a few hundred yards to check out the road. It's OK to turn around and save that toughie for another trip and specialized equipment.

CHOOSE THE EASY WAY

Consider you may have to travel *every* road in both directions. The first time going in, and upon your return (by choice or when Mother Nature dictates). Choose the harder way for initial exploration. For example, uphill exploration offers an easier, downhill return.

HAVE SPARES

Have a spare tire that holds air and the equipment to change it. Try it at home. A tire patch kit for two-wheelers is a must. Have an air pump too. Take a yank strap (tow rope, chain or cable), fire extinguisher, extra fan belts (at least the one for the water pump) and spare car keys. Carry and use a CB radio. The inexpensive, lunch box size, emergency models are fine. Use your seat belt too.

TAKE TRASH HOME

These overused, but most effective words bear repeating: Haul it in, Haul it out. Practice taking out a little more. That's even better. Shooters recover your cases. Smokers your butts. Drinkers take home your cans and bottles. Fire builders make sure it's out. Haul out your ashes too.

BE FLEXIBLE

Your travel plans and itinerary are your guiding helpers, not your discipline masters. Rigid adherence to plans can spoil a perfectly good trip. If temporary disorientation takes half the day, choose a new campsite. If a breakdown reduces travel time, choose a new destination. Be adaptable and enjoy.

TRESPASS

TRESPASS SUMMARY

Throughout this chapter, I unload about our responsibility toward everything. Regarding private property and trespass, I draw on a past *4-Wheeling* newsletter article by Jonathan Woolf-Willis, Esq. that sums up the legal aspects of this easily misunderstood subject. This material is intended to inform and is not to be used as a basis to enter or not enter any particular property.

WE'VE SEEN THE SIGN

"NO TRESPASSING Violators will be prosecuted to the full extent of the law." As backroad enthusiasts, we all see these types of signs posted throughout the countryside on various gates and fences. What do they mean?

TRESPASS DEFINED

"Trespass" is defined in modern legal terms as both a crime and a tort. The key distinction is that, under criminal law, the trespasser potentially can be arrested, taken into custody by local law enforcement officers and prosecuted by a governmental entity (city, county, state or federal prosecutor). Such criminal prosecution may result in a finding of guilt and the imposition of a fine and/or jail sentence. Under tort law, on the other hand, the trespasser may be sued in a civil action by the private landowner and, if found guilty, may be held financially responsible to that landowner for monetary damages. Generally, they both involve a defendant trespasser wrongfully entering upon another person's land.

California's basic trespass law, dating back to 1872, is Penal Code, section 602, which makes it a misdemeanor (a lesser crime not amounting to a felony) to commit a trespass and is more specifically defined within the twenty sub-sections of PC 602. Relevant to the California backcountry traveler are sub-sections (h), (k), (m), (n), (o) and possibly (r). Essentially, those sub-sections make it against the law to do any of the following:

TRESPASS DATES WAY BACK

TEAR DOWN PROPERTY

1. Open, tear down or destroy any gate, bar or fence of another and willfully leave it open without the written permission of the owner, or maliciously tear down, mutilate or destroy any sign, sign board or other notice forbidding shooting on private property. (Penal Code, section 602(h)).

ENTER CLOSED LAND

2. Enter any land under cultivation or enclosed by a fence which is occupied by another, or enter upon unenclosed land where signs forbidding trespass are displayed at intervals of not less than three to a mile along all exterior boundaries and at all roads and trails entering the lands, without the written permission of the landowner, the owner's agent or a person in lawful possession, and

a. Refuse or fail to leave the land immediately upon being requested by the owner, the owner's agent or person in lawful possession, or

b. Tear down, mutilate or destroy any sign, sign board or notice forbidding trespass or hunting, or

c. Remove, injure, unlock or tamper with any lock on any gate on or leading into the land, or

d. Discharge any firearm. (Penal Code, section 602(k)).

DRIVE ON OTHER'S PROPERTY

3. Drive any vehicle upon property belonging to or lawfully occupied by another, and known not be to open to the general public, without the consent of the owner, the owner's agent or person in lawful possession. (Penal Code, section 602(m)).

REFUSE TO LEAVE

4. Refuse or fail to leave land belonging to or occupied by another and not open to the general public, upon being requested to leave by either a peace officer who

informs the trespasser that he or she is acting at the request of the owner, the owner's agent or person in lawful possession, or by the owner, the owner's agent or person in lawful possession. (This sub-section does not, however, apply to agricultural labor union activists.) (Penal Code, section 602(n)).

ENTER FIRE HAZARD AREA

5. Enter upon land declared closed to entry by the Director of Forestry as a hazardous fire area, if the closed area has been posted with notices declaring the closure at intervals not greater than one mile along the exterior boundaries or along roads and trails passing through the land. (Penal Code, section 602(o)).

NOT PAY FOR USE

6. Fail to leave a hotel or motel where the trespasser has obtained accommodations and has refused to pay for the accommodations, upon request of the proprietor or manager. (Penal Code, section 602(r)).

PENALTIES PROVIDED

In addition to this basic trespass law, in 1989 the California Legislature added Penal Code, section 602.8, which makes it either an infraction (i.e., the most minor criminal offense subject to ticket citation) or a misdemeanor for any person to "willfully" enter upon uncultivated or enclosed land where signs forbid trespass are displayed at intervals not less than three to the mile along all exterior boundaries and at all roads and trails entering the land, without the written permission of the landowner, the owner's agent or person in lawful possession of land. This section goes on to provide for penalties, ranging from a $10 fine for the first offense to imprisonment in the county jail for not more than six months and/or a fine not to exceed $1,000 for the third and subsequent offenses.

GET WRITTEN PERMISSION

Under criminal law a trespassing four-wheeler can be detained, arrested and ultimately tried in a criminal proceeding for such violations. Given the potential penalties discussed above, the wisest course of action is: If it's posted, get written permission first!

CIVIL WRONG DOING

Separate and distinct from the criminal law governing trespass, there exists the civil cause of action known as "trespass to land' as a tort. The concept "tort" simply means a civil wrong which provides the victim with legal redress through the civil justice system, normally, the right to sue the "tortfeasor" (i.e., the wrongdoer) in court, thereby seeking money damages for that wrong.

LACK OF MAL-INTENT IS NO EXCUSE

Generally, trespass is an intentional tort in which the plaintiff (e.g., the landowner) must show that the defendant-trespasser intended to enter upon the land, regardless of the trespasser's specific motivation. Contrary to the popular belief that "trespass" implies some nefarious motive, e.g., the intent to steal goods, to deface property, etc., the legal concept of trespass is broader and carries no such moral connotations. Rather, in early common law, the civil action for trespass could be stated for any unauthorized entry upon another's land as a result of that trespasser's voluntary act. It was no defense that the interloper had accidentally happened upon the land, mistakenly thinking that the entry was authorized or that the land was part of an adjacent parcel. Once the trespass was committed, the defendant-trespasser was legally responsible to the plaintiff-landowner for all harm resulting from that conduct however unforeseeable.

SOME FLEXIBILITY

Under the modern rules of trespass, there has been increasing flexibility in the approach used by the courts by which intentional entries upon another's land are excused. Additionally, with respect to unintentional or negligent intrusions, the earlier theory of strict liability has virtually been eliminated in law. An actor who unintentionally enters upon land in the possession of another is liable now only if that actor is reckless, negligent or engages in an ultra-hazardous activity (e.g., igniting fireworks, dumping toxic waste, etc.). Further, the negligent trespasser is liable only for actual damages suffered as a result of that entry; although, these damages can include all costs to repair improvements (e.g., fences, gates, etc.), as well as any discomfort and arrogance caused by the intrusion.

LIABLE FOR DAMAGES

As for intentional invasions of another's property, that trespasser will still be strictly liable for all damages directly flowing from that trespass. Even in this area, however, the law has evolved to permit more excusable entries upon the land of another. In fact, the cases from recent court decisions in various states recognize over twenty-one separate privileges by which would-be trespassers are excused due to overriding social considerations. The most common example of such circumstances include public necessity and private necessity. Public necessity means that one is privileged to enter another's land if the actor reasonably believes it necessary for the purpose of preventing an immediate public disaster (e.g., to extinguish a forest fire, to sandbag a flooding creek bed, etc.). Private necessity would include the privilege to enter upon another's land when it appears reasonably necessary to prevent serious harm to the trespasser, his land or goods, or to prevent serious harm to a third person, land or goods of another (e.g., to save a stranded hiker, to assist someone with a disabled vehicle, etc.).

SOCIAL UTILITY CONSIDERED

The bottom line, therefore, is that the courts will take into serious consideration the overriding social utility of the trespasser's conduct even when one knowingly enters onto the land of another and absolve that trespasser of any liability if that social purpose outweighs the landowner's interests in ownership of the land.

PROTESTOR MUST KNOW THE LAW TOO

Walt Wheelock, in a follow-up article adds the above was, "well written from the legal point of view, however, it made one assumption that changes the aspect of the problem. It assumes that the person protesting the trespass is either the legal owner, lessee or agent, and knowledgeable of trespass law."

LEADERSHIP

LEADING IS FUN

I've eluded to the pressures and responsibilities of leading in another chapter. With very little energy, a considerable amount of patience, and the willingness to make your first commitment safety, leading trips can be fun.

LEADER SAFETY FIRST

Group priorities are similar to first aid provider priorities. It's not selfishness, it's practical to understand the first priority of the leader is their personal safety. Without a leader, the entire group may be in jeopardy.

GROUP SAFETY NEXT

Second priority is group safety and togetherness. I've experienced leaders who become obsessed with goals and destinations. These are artificial. Group safety is real. Maintaining continuity of the group is real. Like it or not, the group must move at the rate of the slowest traveler. Adjust destinations accordingly.

WITH LEADING COMES PRESSURE

Know where you're going and what you're doing. If that has the familiar ring of planning, then I've done my job. I find the pressures of potential embarrassment distorts my trail sense. Given a half familiar road, a chance to go wrong, and I will. I get anxious and turn too soon, drive faster than I should, or otherwise make less than perfect decisions. Planning and pre-running help a lot! If you're the leader, you must be a planner.

ORIENT YOUR TRAVELERS

The first step in group coordination is to give an orientation talk, preferably at the trail head. Tell who's leading, where you're going, what you're doing, special rules for the area, how to handle breaks, designate your emergency coordination contact, who will be the sweep or last vehicle, and how to use the CB radio.

USE CB RADIOS

Inter-group communication is a must. It's easy to get spread out, separated, someone stops for a picture, and have a spectrum of capabilities that can complicate coordination. I make sure everyone has a working CB radio and knows how to use it.

DO ROLL-CALL ON CB

I use a rolling roll call to test CB equipment and operators. When the sweep gets under way, he chats a bit, describes the vehicle ahead of him and passes the roll call forward. Everyone does this forward to the leader, and radio problems, if any, are worked out as required. Since my tours involve frequent stops, I resolve the radio problem then. On longer trips, we make a special stop to rectify the radio malfunction.

STAY IN TOUCH

As the leader, use the CB to describe the trail and features. If you're instructing, advise when to use 4WD or low range. As a member of the pack (coyotes run in packs, you know), use the CB for questions or to announce brief stops. An announced picture stop puts those about to pass at ease knowing you are not broken down. It's the sweep's job to stay behind until the photographer (or other) is ready to leave. Use the radio to assist with getting unstuck and offer driving instructions too.

SWEEP REPEATS INSTRUCTIONS

My rules require the sweep to echo all trail directions. It may seem useless and unnecessary, but how do you know if everyone heard the instructions? Are you sure your radio is working? Are you sure your transmission reached the end of the pack? Are you sure you gave the correct directions? Those listening may want a second chance to confirm what they thought they heard.

KEEP TRACK OF THE GROUP

They may be in a reception location where the sweep is better able to contact them than the leader. Repeat trail directions.

Another simple practice that helps determine group location is to have the sweep announce when he has completed the last announced trail instruction. Only after you've lead a few trips will the importance and necessity of the above CB practices become evident.

WAIT FOR THE REAR

Speed change can unduly stretch out a group. The leader hits a 30 MPH road after exiting a three MPH section. If he immediately takes off at 30, the last vehicle to exit the snails stuff could be many minutes and miles behind. Wait until you hear the sweep has entered the good road before you move out.

PERMIT INFO

It's important to understand public land use and permits. The best way to do that is get the info from the horse's mouth - the agency responsible for your area of travel. In general, small private groups, where no money changes hands, permits are not required. When money is involved, the group gets large, or the event involves some sort of commercial or competitive nature, a permit is required. Ask and be on the safe side.

RANGERS

THE RANGER'S HERE

I'll share an experience that prompted this section of the Guide. I had a group in Death Valley and we were making our paved way back from a very full day of dirt. From mid-pack comes, "Harry, we just passed a ranger" pause, "Harry, he's pulling out" pause, "Harry, he's following us!"

THE RANGER'S WELCOME

I announced I was glad and continued with the fact that they had known all day where we were, what we were doing and when we were due back. For me, the big green truck was a welcome sight.

RANGER PHOBIA

From who knows where or when, we appear to develop a phobia for uniforms, badges and emblemed cars. We seem to stand at attention and put on our best behavior when "they" are around. We never give a second thought about who's behind the authority figure. They are people. They put their pants on one leg at a time, have their good and bad days, and in the simplest sense, are just doing a job.

**THEY ARE
THE BEST**

I'm envious of their job and apparently quite a few others are too. The competition for ranger positions is intense. As a result, ranger responsibilities are filled by the best, and it's more trying than you might think.

**THEY WORK
HARD**

I've traveled with them. They don't simply count birds, contemplate soil erosion from atop a mountain and spoil your good time with rules. Most of them work far more hours than you or me. They have a paper mill bureaucracy that would drive most of us to ulcers, and they have to deal with the public.

**THEY SHOW
CONTROL**

Think about starting your day by telling some yo-yo he shouldn't chop down the campsite tree for his morning fire, an hour later, pull another dimwit cleaning his motorcycle out of a spring, and by lunch you've had three or four other trying encounters. And then by late afternoon you are expected to approach the guy using the road-side reflectors for target practice like you'd had a perfect day. Rangers exhibit self-control beyond belief!

**THEY TAKE
PRIDE IN
THEIR AREA**

Try this day after day after day understanding their sensitivity, appreciation, enjoyment and pride for their patrol area is more than just a job. It is truly their home, their front yard, their living rooms we mess up. I don't know how they do such a great, patient job year after year.

**THEY NEED
US**

Now take another tack. Their job depends on you and me. Without us, they don't have a job. They are not out there to get us! They are out there to help us. And as Ranger Barb Severson of the San Bernardino National Forest pointed out to me, they are doing the job we pay them to do. Give rangers a hand by acting responsibly. Understand they have a tough job that needs our help and most of all, our understanding.

THE COYOTE SAYS...

THE TRUTH

By now, you've been inundated with preparation, planning, map reading, odometer accuracy, regulations and rules. For me that's part of the fun. It takes the fun out of it for others. What does the Silver Coyote really do? It depends on where I'm going, with whom and for how long. At a minimum, I advise someone where I'm going and when I'll be back. I am a planner. I extensively review the maps at home. However, if I'm going with someone else, I love to follow, never look at a map, and check out my sense of things. Under all circumstances, I carry water, respect Mother Nature and feel confident I'm doing the right thing.

CONFIDENCE

In mind, I'm a hard core, quantitative, analytical engineer. In spirit and heart I allow there are things I do not understand. Years ago, my son tells of throwing sticks and stones into the cholla (the stickeryest of all cactus). He also tells of a jumping cholla attack shortly thereafter. I believe Mother Nature has a scale of justice the US Supreme Court would envy. She gets even and maybe a little ahead! I treat her with great respect. I treat her roads like my driveway, her plants like mine, her animals like my pets and her campsites like my house. I believe she rewards my respect. I have a tremendous amount of experience and skill. I go well prepared. But the hard core basis of my confidence revolves around knowing Mother Nature is on my side. I get lots of sunny days. However, I don't confuse confidence with omnipotence!

GO PREPARED

I started traveling dirt roads when there were fewer travelers, it was more dangerous and we had less reliable equipment. I embark on virtually all trips over prepared. It's my choice and habit. I think it's the only way people should be allowed off the pavement. However, my experience contradicts this. I see travelers in the boonies that I believe shouldn't be permitted out of their driveways, and they do fine! I suspect the whole issue is somewhat like my first backpacking experiences. I was afraid of the bears and snakes. Now, after years of no snakes and bears, I still think about them, but sleep easier. You will tend to go prepared to the degree you're afraid of the *off road boogie men* - lost, broken, stuck. Act responsibly, heed the Coyote's recommendations, carry lots of drinking water and enjoy!

CHAPTER 7 SURVIVAL

FOUR BASIC RULES

Be calm. Carry and drink water. Remain with your transportation. Stay on the roads.

BE CALM

The most significant single obstacle *against* survival is you and your state of mind. Panic, fear, terror, hysteria and anxiety all work against you. They interfere with clear thinking. The better prepared you are, the calmer you will be. Preparation builds confidence which results in calmness. Calmness produces better problem solving. Problem solving "brings 'em back alive!" At it's worst, a calm confident attitude lets you patiently wait until help arrives. Go prepared and keep your head.

WATER IS THE FIRST ESSENTIAL

The most significant physical asset *for* survival is water. Dehydration, heat exhaustion, hyper/hypothermia, exposure, heat stroke, call it what you want, drinking water decreases the chances of it happening. Be it hot or cold, you need water. Most of us can go a week or more without food. On the other hand, we can die in a day without fluids. Although water is best, any consumable fluid is better than nothing. The best place to store water is in your stomach. Consume it, don't horde it. Carry at least two gallons and drink frequently. Here's more on water by Bill Cunningham, MD, from a past RX4 column in the *4-Wheeling* newsletter.

WE CANNOT LIVE WITHOUT WATER

We can not live without water! Actually the human body is made up of about 40% water by weight and has some very sophisticated regulation and control mechanisms to conserve body water. The wise backcountry traveler will understand how the body uses water and will plan for adequate stores and supplies to meet all anticipated situations. The following will help you better understand this need for water and to prepare yourself for travel into environments where adequate water is not readily available. First some facts:

A 70 kilogram (154 pound) male possess about 42 liters (quarts) of water. His normal fluid loss is 1½ to 2 liters

HEAT, FEVER AND ALTITUDE AFFECT WATER LOSS

per day. Of this, the "sensible" loss excreted by the kidneys ranges from 1 to 2 liters per day. "Insensible" fluid losses also occur through perspiration (even in cold climates) and from the lungs through breathing. These losses amount to ½ to 1 liter per day at sea level and in temperate weather. Hot climates, fever or high altitudes can increase insensible loss up to 4 liters per day.

OTHER THINGS AFFECT WATER LOSS

Individuals with certain diseases (particularly heart and kidney diseases) may have a much impaired ability to regulate fluids and should discuss individual needs with their physician before contemplating any extended trips. Certain medications, such as diuretics, lithium (a common type of blood pressure medication) and some antibiotics can also upset the body's fluid balance. Diarrhea, illness and vomiting can cause huge fluid losses resulting in very rapid dehydration unless adequate fluid replacement is achieved.

KIDNEYS REGULATE BODY FLUIDS

The kidneys are the body's main regulator of fluids. Urine volume and color is an excellent indicator of the state of the body's fluid balance. A 24 hour volume of less than 500 cubic centimeters (cc, about ½ quart) of deeply colored urine indicates fluid depletion; a volume of 2000 cc (about 2 quarts) of very lightly colored urine indicates excess hydration.

DRINK WHEN THIRSTY

The earliest indication that you are becoming dehydrated is thirst. The brain responds to the earliest stages of dehydration by producing thirst and by causing the kidneys to produce less urine. As dehydration increases, the urine becomes darker and scantier before stopping completely. Decrease in tears, saliva and sweat are other indicators that the body is becoming dehydrated. Finally, the tissues of the skin and eyes can develop a doughy consistency indicating advanced dehydration.

DEHYDRATION MEANS SALT AND MINERAL LOSS TOO

Body fluids are more than just water. Several salts and minerals are necessary to maintain health. Normal requirements for salt intake is about 5 grams per day which is easily achieved in a normal diet. When large amounts of salts are lost through perspiration, the body's needs can be as high as 15 grams per day. Dehydration which results in loss of salts produces other symptoms including lethargy, confusion, convulsions and even coma. Muscle cramps and heart rhythm disturbances are some other consequences of an imbalance in body salts and fluids. These particular symptoms can indicate a life threatening emergency and medical treatment with rehydration is an urgent necessity. One of the most common mistakes made in a survival situation is replacing the body fluid/salt losses with simple, plain water. When no food is available and dehydration is occurring, drinking only plain water can produce many of these symptoms.

CARRY WATER

What should you do to prepare yourself to survive in exactly this situation? CARRY WATER! Since impure water can be a source of many diseases, great care should be used to obtain (or produce) pure water. Short term travelers are well advised to carry sufficient water to meet their needs. If you need to obtain water from unsure sources, purification is necessary.

PURIFY NATURAL WATER SOURCES

Although there are commercial filters available to purify water, most are expensive and bulky. They do filter out many objectionable solids, including bacteria, however none can remove all infectious agents such as hepatitis A virus particles. This makes their effectiveness less than certain. Boiling water for 20 minutes is the safest method available. Other reliable methods include chlorination (tablets are commercially available) and iodine treatment. Use five drops of two percent tincture of iodine U.S.P. per liter of clean water or ten drops per liter of cloudy water. Remember that commercially available purification tablets and iodine both lose their potency with time. Replacing your stock as part of your pre-trip preparation is a good idea. Stir and let the treated water stand for at least ten minutes before drinking. Using fruit flavored powders after chemical disinfection is one way to improve the nasty taste left by iodine or chlorine tablets. However, do not do this until after the water has been made potable.

PURIFY ALL WATER

Remember that any water going into your mouth can carry diseases. Ice, water used for brushing teeth, and water used to rinse fruits and vegetables must also be purified.

REPLACE SALTS AND MINERALS

A healthy person can drink plain water for routine fluid replacement without any ill effects because they obtain all needed salts and nutrients from their food. However, once dehydration starts, drinking only plain water is not sufficient. This can result in many of the unpleasant and dangerous symptoms described earlier. There are many commercially available oral rehydration formulas that can simply be mixed with purified water for use in rehydration. An improvised mixture consists of two separate glasses: 1) an 8 ounce glass of orange, apple, or other fruit juice with 3 cc (½ teaspoon) honey or corn syrup and a pinch of table salt; 2) another 8 ounce glass of water and 1 gram (¼ teaspoon) baking soda. Drink from alternate glasses to replace fluid losses. Monitoring urine volume and color is a good gauge to know how much replacement to drink.

BEWARE OF DIURETICS

Although coffee, tea and alcoholic beverages are safe in moderation under normal conditions, they all produce a diuretic effect on the kidneys which results in increased fluid losses and more rapid dehydration.

CARRY EXTRA WATER

The prepared backcountry traveler will carry sufficient fluids to meet all anticipated needs. Two liters per day per person is generally sufficient in normal climates and exercise levels. Carry enough additional fluids to meet those unexpected delays and detours. The well prepared traveler will anticipate emergencies and carry materials to purify water when planning to be away from civilization for more than 24 hours. Rehydration materials are good insurance for travelers planning extended trips away from medical support. In an emergency don't overlook "hidden" sources of drinking water. Melted ice in a cooler and rainwater collected and purified may provide just enough to get you out of the situation. However under no circumstances drink salt water (it quickly worsens dehydration) or water from your vehicle's radiator (it is highly poisonous and cannot be purified). And be very clear, barrel cactus are not a ready source of water. The moisture within is undrinkable.

STAY BY YOUR TRANSPORTATION

Rescue parties always find vehicles. They occasionally do not find the occupants. Bikes, motorcycles and 4Xs are easier to spot than people. They are larger and more colorful. The shiny paint, chrome and glass all produce automatic signals for help. When alone, broken down or lost, stick with or nearby your vehicle.

Vehicular rescue parties can cover more ground than those afoot. Roads provide speedy access to large areas.

STAY ON THE ROADS

Leaving the trail opens up a much larger search area. When you stay on the roads you increase the speed and chance of being found. Stay on the obvious roads and trails.

SURVIVAL SKILLS

YOU CAN'T CARRY IT ALL

There was a day when I went prepared for *all* eventualities, or so I thought. I carried a full gasket set, spare starter, pistons and parts beyond imagination. On one occasion a broken crank and on another, a cracked suspension component drove home the fact preparation for *all* eventualities is impossible. To be fully equipped for *every* eventuality means staying home!

PRIMITIVE SKILLS ARCHAIC

I acknowledge specialized survival skills could be useful, but I question the need for resorting to eating plants, making stone tools, rubbing sticks together and trapping animals. I believe primitive survival schools and practices are not compatible with the environment. They lead to abused terrain, destroyed plants and dead animals. In our society, these trainings are more of an experiential bonding thing than an actual teaching and honing of practical skills. It's great to teach resourcefulness, but not at the expense of Mother Nature.

BE PREPARED WITH WATER AND FOOD

Where we travel, the number of other weekend travelers out and about, the reliability of our equipment, and modern communication equipment make primitive survival skills a thing of the past. I'm "out there" a lot and virtually never go without seeing someone, somewhere, every time. Carry water and food. Have other supplies to accommodate reasonable emergencies, and be prepared to signal and wait for help.

SOME SIMPLE SKILLS

A couple of random tidbits that are more useful than learning to make a dead-fall trap or a snow cave, involve simple observation and experience. When you see green, particularly in the desert, it may mean water. Palm trees are a sure sign of year-round water. Remember palm trees keep their heads in the sun, but must always have their toes in the water.

WATER-FINDING SKILLS

Every Boy Scout knows water flows down hill so the ravines, washes and canyons are the place to look for that sparkling fluid, particularly in the mountains. I've also learned where there are wild burros (and other animals), there's water. In Saline Valley I discovered the well worn burro trails reliably lead from waterhole to waterhole. Other animal signs can lead to water. The coyote (not me) is known as the desert's water finder. It will frequently smell moisture, dig for it, and uncover a source for all animals to use.

BEWARE OF GROUND TEMPERATURE

So you're calm, drinking water, with your car, and sitting along side the road. All's well, but it does seem very hot. Get up off the ground! Ground temperatures soar and plummet to unimaginable extremes. Daytime, summer, desert ground temperatures can easily exceed 180 degrees Fahrenheit. Daytime, winter, mountain ground temperatures can be colder than the air. Don't sit on bare ground in either extreme heat or cold situations. At face-level it may be 100°, but a foot off the ground it can be 130°. Do what you must to insulate yourself from the ground in extreme temperature conditions.

USE SHELTER

If you have access to good shelter, use it. In the heat, open the car doors and windows. Make shade over the car and sit inside. If you're in the shade of a cliff or tree, consider sitting on the roof of the car to evade the ground heat. In the cold, close the doors and windows, provide some ventilation by cracking the windows, and sit inside. Cover the windows with your space blankets or other material to prevent heat loss. Running the 4X motor and heater can be dangerous due to carbon monoxide. Use any available shelter or make your car a shelter.

CARRY SURVIVAL RESOURCES

Cars have many resources. The ones you carry: water, food, sleeping bags, firewood and so on. Put a space blanket permanently in your transportation. These fist-size marvels have many uses: shade from the sun, warmth from the cold, reflection for signaling, shelter from the rain and wind, gathering rain water and more.

4X PARTS ARE SURVIVAL RESOURCES

Other resources are built into the car: the shelter it provides, or the lights and horn for signaling. Some may mean sacrificing sacred components. When deflated, used far from the car, and constructed in a safe area, the spare tire is a day and night smoke-signal fire. The headliner, carpets and hood noise-insulation materials make great blankets. But beware some are itchy fiberglass. Remove a rearview mirror for signaling. Foolishness? What is your life worth? More than a mirror? When serious about survival, everything around you is a survival resource!

RADIO MAYDAY

**HAVE AND USE
2-WAY RADIOS**

The common denominator to put the backroad boogie men under the covers, is two-way radio service. The most readily available is citizens band radio service (CB). In time of need, do the following.

**YOUR MAYDAY
MESSAGE**

Adjust the squelch on the CB radio so you hear static all the time and start listening. The radio is now at its most sensitive position. Use this procedure. Transmit the following on the international emergency channel, number 9. Identify yourself (your name and vehicle description) and give your last known position. Be as specific as possible. State your needs (need medical help, need water and food, or no immediate emergencies - stuck in the sand). Advise if you are monitoring another CB channel or have other radio communication equipment - amateur (ham) radio or cellular telephone. Sign-off with the current time and the next time you will broadcast. Make this transmission one minute long and repeat it every four minutes, night and day. Follow this schedule religiously and accurately. Use the four minute interval to listen for help. Respond if you hear someone acknowledging your "Mayday". Since you are following the good safety practice of traveling with others, do this on other channels too. Coordinate your transmit times so you don't interfere with each other.

**BE
CONSISTENT**

This is boring stuff, but what's your salvation worth? Write out the message and assign shifts to your traveling companions. You are on a strict schedule so rescuers can confirm your signal is no hoax or fill in missed information. Your schedule is frequent so those with radio triangulation equipment can zero in on your position. There are literally thousands of CBers "reading the mail". They are listening for your plea for help. Give them a chance to do their thing by transmitting a rescue request.

TRY MANY CHANNELS

Other frequently used channels are 21, 19, 14, or the channel the last group you passed were using. Channel 21 is the highway channel. Those who frequently use the highways use channel 21 to exchange road information. Channel 19 is the truckers' channel. They exchange road information, highway patrol location and weigh station activity. They typically have very powerful, capable radios too. Channel 14 is the most frequently sold channel in the United States. You will find recreational vehicle caravans on this channel because their economical, one-channel radios only have channel 14. Give all a periodic try with another radio.

LOCAL OR FAR, GIVE THEM A CALL

CB range is hard to predict. I have been unable to reach the end of my group a couple of miles away and talked to Australia at the same time. Your help could come from out of state or out of the country. Try calling whomever you hear, regardless of their location. Keep the CB on and use it, particularly channel 9.

SAVE YOUR BATTERY

Eliminate all but essential battery usage. Open doors mean dome light drain. Key "ON" means ignition, AM/FM radio, air conditioning/heater fan and other accessory drain. Foot on the brake peddle means stop light drain. Hood up means hood light drain. Same for the trunk or tail gate. Head lights for making camp are a catastrophe! Selectively pull fuses to eliminate unwanted drain.

RECHARGE YOUR BATTERY

Periodically run the motor to recharge the battery, but be aware of potential carbon monoxide poisoning. Don't put yourself in the catch 22 position of needing to start the car to charge the battery and the battery being too dead to start the car. With a good battery and only CB drain, twice a day for about 15 minutes will do fine, provided the charge meter shows in the plus. Given a hard to start car, it may be self-defeating to run the starter too long.

RADIO SPARES

CARRY RADIO SPARES

The next few paragraphs are from an article I did for the *4-Wheeling* newsletter. Radio spares are frequently neglected. I learned the hard way that an upside down 4X is at least antenna-less, if not more. Following are installation, maintenance, and spares recommendations for two-way radios. Although I discuss CB radio, by no means are other services exempt from the need for spares. For a relatively few dollars, you can be prepared for most radio problems.

ANTENNAS

The most common backcountry radio problem is antennas. The solutions are simple, available, and relatively inexpensive. First on the list is the lost mast. This long metal part is in essence your connection to the outside world. The masts fall out because the set-screws were improperly tightened or worked loose. Don't over-tighten and strip the set-screws. Use loctite to keep the screws from coming loose. The K-40 antenna, in particular, suffers two design deficiencies. It has only one mast-attach set screw and unpaved use fractures the top of the base coil housing. The constant rough-road whipping stresses the skimpy metal cone/coil-housing interface, and sooner or later, either breaks the coil housing or completely falls out. And beware, the manufacturer typically refuses to replace defective units. I prefer the Wilson 1000 series of antennas.

SPARE MAST

A simple trick for the lost mast is to carry a spare. Have the original and spare mast standing-wave-ratio (SWR) matched and scribe a small mounting-depth mark on both so either the replacement or recovered original unit can easily be reinstalled in exactly the correct position. I carry spare set screws too.

SWR MATCH THE SPARE

You can also carry a completely matched magnet mount spare. This will not only serve your needs, but can also help your traveling companions. Have this SWR matched, but be aware the match is only good to the original transceiver. Without belaboring this SWR thing, consider scribing all of your masts with the match for your backup radio too. That's why CB radios with a built-in SWR meter position are invaluable. You can match the replacement antenna on the spot.

CABLE CONVERTERS

Yet another approach is to use your emergency CB radio antenna. This requires you carry the proper adapter. This is an off-the-shelf PL259-to-RCA female adapter. If you want to go the other way - use your regular antenna with your emergency radio - use the RCA male-to-SO239 adapter. This is useful when your regular radio fails and you want to take advantage of your better, permanent mount antenna. But note the need for a coax extension. Chances are, your in-car antenna cable is too short to reach up to your driving position.

TWO MORE TRICKS

As you can see, there is no excuse for lack of radio communication due to antenna problems. And before we leave the subject, I'll share two more tricks.

BEWARE OF CROSS THREADING

Cross-threaded antennas, particularly the NMO2700 variety, spell eventual disaster to the antenna, the vehicle mount, and more subtly, the radio transmitter itself! To avoid screwing up removable antennas, when installing, place the antenna in as near perfect alignment position as possible. Next, and believe me it works, turn the antenna counter-clockwise until you hear or feel a faint click. This indicates the two threads are properly aligned and ready for the next step. Keeping the antenna properly aligned, change rotation to clockwise. I use two hands to maintain mast alignment. There should be no resistance until you reach full engagement. Repeat this counter-clockwise/clockwise technique until you achieve success.

CLEAN THE BASE

On several occasions while traveling the beaches of Baja, I've noticed signal degradation. I discovered simply washing the base of the antenna with fresh water cures the problem. I suspect the salt accumulates and shorts or attenuates the radio signal.

EMERGENCY RADIOS NICE

Moving on down the antenna cable, complete radio failure is not that uncommon. Although the solution to this communication stopper is a little more costly, you may already have the answer in your garage. In my lectures, I recommend you get started with the emergency-type CBs. These are the plug-in-the-cigarette-lighter, magnet-the-antenna-on-the-roof, General Electric HELP, or equivalent, type transceivers. They serve as an acceptable backup when your main radio fails. But even this economical and readily available unit does not handle all eventualities. Auto electrical system power or cigarette lighter failure stops all non-portable radios.

PORTABLES ARE BETTER

There are a couple of nice CBs that fulfill not only the backup function, but are portable as well. These are equally useful and practical for motorcycles and mountain bikes. Uniden's PRO310e and Maxon's 27-SP are excellent candidates for your backup radio. These units can be powered from the vehicle's cigarette lighter (cable supplied) or a slide-on battery case, making them completely independent of the vehicle electrical system. In the 4X power mode, both are little more than mike-sized, and very convenient to use. With the battery pack attached, they are still smaller than conventional handheld units. And needless to say, without fresh batteries, all portables are useless. Both are also supplied with a sturdy magnet-mount antenna.

BEWARE OF NICKEL CADMIUM BATTERIES

If you are a nickel cadmium battery fan, the 27-SP also comes with a 10 cell ni-cad, slide-on, battery case, and trick, vehicle charger option! My preference is alkaline batteries. The care and feeding of ni-cads is another subject.

CIGARETTE TO RADIO POWER CONVERTER

Another power accessory I've built for my primary vehicle radio is a cigarette lighter power plug adapter. I sometimes find myself traveling in another vehicle and still want the superiority of my radio. This adapter, along with my magnet mount antenna, give me the best of both worlds. To wrap-up the power subject, it goes without saying, carry spare fuses, but don't try to cure a bad radio with a larger fuse!

SPARE MICROPHONE

I suppose to be complete, I should mention I also carry a spare microphone. A failed primary mike means you go to your backup radio. Summarizing the above, a radio spares list follows.

- Antenna mast and set screws
- Magnet mount antenna
- PL259 to RCA female cable adapter
- RCA male to SO239 cable adapter
- Six foot antenna cable extension with female to female splice
- Back up radio with antenna and power cable
- Portable battery pack
- Spare batteries
- Cigarette to primary radio power cable adapter
- Spare microphone

CELLULAR TELEPHONE USEFUL TOO

Don't overlook your cellular telephone for emergency communication. Cellular coverage is expanding and worth a try in an emergency. If you're a couple of miles from a highway where there are emergency call boxes, there's cellular coverage in the area. Emergency call boxes work on cellular telephone links.

CODELESS AMATEUR LICENSE

Amateur radio service is another desirable communication resource. Elimination of Morse code and easing of technical requirements has put amateur radio service within the reach of anyone willing to take a day at a licensing school. Repeaters, unmanned mountain top radio links, are everywhere. The code-less technician license makes two meter amateur radio a viable alternative to CB radio. For about the size of a portable telephone, you can have metropolitan areas and 911 at your fingertips. Roger Vargo (N6YDT) provides the following repeater locations and frequencies.

AMATEUR RADIO REPEATERS

Amateur radio usually provides more reliable communications than CB radio. Keep a current copy of one of the major repeater directories handy. The *ARRL Repeater Directory* (American Radio Relay League, Newington CT 06111) is published yearly and covers the entire US. Karl Pagel's *Original Repeater Location Guide* (P.O. Box 6080, Anaheim CA 92816,) is published twice each year and covers just Southern California. Several wide-coverage repeaters are:

NAME	FREQ	LOCATION
KELLER PEAK	146.985 <->	In San Bernardino National Forest
BIRD SPRINGS	146.085 <+>	At Bird Springs Pass
SANTIAGO PEAK	145.220 <->	In Orange County
HAUSER PEAK	146.730 <->	Near Palmdale
MOUNT LAGUNA	147.150 <+>	In San Diego County
MOUNT PALOMAR	146.730 <->	In San Diego County
MAGIC MOUNTAIN	147.735 <->	In the Angeles National Forest
MOUNT DISAPPOINTMENT	145.300 <->	On Mount Disappointment

SIMPLEX FREQUENCIES

The national 2-meter simplex frequency is 146.520. Silver Coyote packs use 146.535 for in-group simplex communication in all areas.

FIRST AID

From another RX4 column by Dr. Bill Cunningham, in the *4-Wheeling* newsletter comes the following.

TWO PARTS TO FIRST AID

Backcountry first aid is actually a two element thing. Knowing what to carry is half the battle. How to use it is of equal importance. I will treat assembling a first aid kit for backcountry travel. Most important is enrolling in a training class. A first aid kit, no matter how complete, is of little use unless the "operator" is trained and practiced in its use.

FIRST AID DEFINED

The American Red Cross defines first aid as the immediate and temporary care given to a person who has been injured or becomes suddenly ill.

REFERENCE BOOKS

There are many excellent books available that can be consulted for information concerning treatment of specific injuries or illness. I have included some samples in the following reading list.

HANDBOOK OF FIRST AID AND EMERGENCY CARE, The American Medical Association, Edited by Stanley Zydlo, MD and James Hill, MD. Published by Random House.

BASIC EMERGENCY CARE OF THE SICK AND INJURED, Guy S. Parcel. Published by C.V. Mosby Company.

EMERGENCY HANDBOOK, Peter Arnold and Edward Pendagast, MD. Published by Doubleday and Company.

EMERGENCY FIRST AID, Charles Mosher, MD. Published by Beekman House.

THE OUTWARD BOUND WILDERNESS FIRST-AID HANDBOOK, Jeff Isaac, P.A.C. and Peter Goth, MD.

CUSTOMIZE YOUR KIT

A first aid kit really serves several different purposes. The traditional concept is that it is a collection of medical supplies and equipment to be kept sealed-away in anticipation of medical emergencies. However, most people will also want to carry supplies for treatment of annoyance conditions such as sunburn, insect bites or traveler's diarrhea. There are also those personal prescription items for treatment of your individual medical conditions. Here are some general comments on putting together a kit, then the list follows.

FIRST AID MANUAL IMPORTANT

First, include an up to date and comprehensive first aid manual. The American Red Cross standard and advanced version First Aid Manuals are an excellent start. Other texts I have found particularly useful include *Medicine for Mountaineering* edited by James A. Wilkerson, MD; *Wilderness Medicine* by William W. Forgey; *The Pocket Doctor* by Steven Bezruchka; and *Mountaineering First Aid* by Dick Mitchell.

KEEP THE ELEMENTS OUT

Second, make your kit rustproof, dustproof, waterproof and easily accessible. Self sealing Tupperware style containers and zip-lock plastic bags are ways to keep your supplies clean and dry. Other ideas include plastic tackle or tool boxes with trays and dividers. The new, small, soft-pack/six-pack, ice chests work well too. While surplus ammunition cases are waterproof and macho, they are not particularly space efficient, they rust, and they scratch and mar the car's interior or nearby objects.

CHECK SHELF LIFE

Next comes the issue of "shelf life". Take a look at the medicines and supplies that you purchase. Many will have expiration dates listed on the package. After this date, the supplies should not be used. Potency and effectiveness of drugs may diminish and sterility not be preserved. You should have a system to periodically review and restock these items. A simple list inside the kit, with expiration dates will suffice. And at least a yearly review is recommended. This list can also serve as a reminder to replace materials that have been used on the trail.

HAVE A SMALL KIT TOO

Finally, I recommend that you put together a smaller, portable kit that can be carried away from your transportation. I keep mine in a "fanny" pack.

"FIRST, DO NO HARM."

To put together the following list of supplies, I reviewed literature from medical and first aid texts as well as popular articles written in general interest magazines. The size of the kit and amount of materials to include will vary with your degree of medical training as well as with the distance and time you intend to be out of touch with civilization. Don't carry equipment or medications that you are not qualified or trained to use. "First, do no harm," is as appropriate for the first aider as it is for the MD!

PERSONAL ADDITIONS

If you are planning extensive excursions, check with your personal physician about carrying antibiotics, more potent pain medications, medications to treat Giardia, an anaphylaxis kit and personal prescription items.

WOUND and TRAUMA CARE

- 4" X 4" Sterile Dressing Pads (4 ply absorbent pads)
- 3" X 3" Adaptic or Telfa Pads (non-adherent, won't stick to wounds)
- Vaseline Impregnated Gauze (occlusive dressing) 8" X 10" ABD Pads (for large bleeding wounds or burns)
- Kling or Kerlix Roll Bandages 4" X 5 yards (Stretchy gauze roll for bandaging or securing splints in place)
- 2" Athletic Adhesive Tape (easier to use than 1" and can be torn when needed. Useful for taping joints and even equipment repair)
- Butterfly Skin Closures (for lacerations instead of suture)
- Tincture of Benzoin (applied to skin around wound makes adhesive stick more securely and longer)
- Betadine or Povodine (liquid antiseptic for wound disinfection, Mibiclens is an alternative that won't stain)
- Triple Antibiotic ointment (for skin infections)
- Band Aids (you can never have enough of these in various sizes)
- Sterile Eye Pads
- Bar Soap (for daily cleansing of cuts, abrasions, burns)
- Elastic Bandage (ACE Wrap good for wrapping sprains or applying compression to large bleeding wounds)
- Triangular Bandage (for sling, turban bandage or to secure a splint)
- Safety Pins
- Tongue Blades (useful for small splints) Inflatable splints (indispensable with a fracture)

MEDICATIONS

- ASPIRIN (one of the best all around medications to relieve pain, reduce fever and decrease inflammation). Do not use in children as aspirin has been associated with Reyes Disease. TYLENOL is a preferred substitute for kids. IBUPROFEN is an aspirin substitute.
- MAALOX, MYLANTA, or alternative antacid preparation.
- DRAMAMINE 50mg for motion sickness. MECLAZINE 25mg is an effective single dose alternative. TRANSDERM SCOPOLAMINE patches are a nifty prescription item that works wonders to prevent motion sickness.
- BENEDRYL 25mg to control itching from poison ivy and other allergic reactions. It is also a sedative so don't drive while taking this preparation.
- MICATIN OR LOTRIMIN Athlete's Foot Fungal Preparations
- HYDROCORTISONE 0.5% Topical Steroid Cream is a good choice.
- DONNAGEL OR IMMODIUM Anti Diarrhea Preparations are good choices for symptomatic relief. KAOPECTATE is good alternative.
- METAMUCIL laxative (bulk product not an irritant like EXLAX)
- Cough Syrup (Preparation with DEXTROMETHORPHAN is most effective at decreasing coughing.)

ANTI ANNOYANCE ITEMS

* Moleskin 4" x 4" (also Spenco Second Skin or Mole Foam)
* Sunscreen (at least SPF 15)
* Sun block (Zinc Oxide is most effective)
* Lip Balm
* Insect Repellent (those with DEET are most effective)
* Eyewash (sterile drops for irrigation)
* Q tips
* Solarcaine (for sunburn relief)
* Calamine or Caladryl (for poison ivy relief)
* Domboro Tablets (mix with water for BURROUGHS solution)

ADDITIONS TO CONSIDER

* Snake bite kit
* Stethoscope and Blood Pressure Cuff
* Cold Packs
* EMT Scissors
* Tweezers
* Rescue Blanket
* Water purification tablets
* Disposable razor
* Penlight/Flashlight
* Pencil/Paper
* ... and the ever-present need for toilet paper

TRANSPORTABLE KIT

* Antiseptic Solution or packaged disposable wipes
* 6, Adhesive Bandage Strips (Band-Aids)
* 4, Skin Closure Strips (Butterflies)
* 4, 4" X 4" Sterile Gauze Dressing
* 3, 2½" X 2½" Elastic Bandages
* Waterproof Adhesive Tape
* Waterproof Matches
* Triangular Bandage and Safety Pins
* Pain Medication (ASPIRIN, TYLENOL or IBUPROFEN)
* Rescue Blanket
* Signal Mirror

EASY CAMERA REPAIR KIT

CAMERA SURVIVAL

Camera survival is important for enjoyable treks. Once again, I draw from Vargo's Variety column in the *4-Wheeling* newsletter. Roger is a professional photographer for the LA Daily News.

A basic camera repair kit doesn't take much space and may resurrect an otherwise "dead" camera. Build your camera tool kit around: battery failure, vibration, and dust. Pack the kit in whatever container is appropriate. It need not be carried in your camera equipment bag.

CAMERA SPARES

BATTERIES - Pack an extra set of camera, motor drive, and flash batteries. Unless you have a portable charger, replace rechargeable batteries with alkaline cells before going on an extended trip. If a critical battery is of the hard-to-find-at-home variety, bring two as they will be impossible to find in remote stores.

SCREWDRIVERS - A set of assorted jewelers screwdrivers (flat and cross point blades) is adequate for most repairs. Check to see the blades fit the types of screws on your equipment.

PLIERS - Grabbers such as a hemostat, needle nose pliers or a pair of tweezers are great for holding tiny parts and making minor adjustments to battery terminals.

SCREWS - Those tiny screws used in cameras get lost under the best of conditions. Obtain some extras from your camera repair shop. Some of the screws used in eyeglass repair kits may be adequate in a pinch.

ADHESIVE - Clear nail polish is used to prevent screws from vibrating out of their holes. It also can be used to secure trim items and sometimes as a plastic adhesive.

LENS WRENCH - Lens filter wrenches. These plastic hands can remove a stubborn lens filter without damaging the optics.

BLOWER - A blower-brush, ear syringe or "canned air" provides the motive force for dust removal. Be careful around camera shutters and lens iris parts.

BRUSH - An inexpensive nylon paint brush works well for removing dust from exterior camera surfaces, but don't use it on the optics.

LENS FLUID - Lens cleaning fluid and lens tissue are best for cleaning lenses.

HEAD CLEANER - Head cleaning fluid and cleaning swabs are needed for video cameras. But don't attempt to clean camcorder heads unless you are familiar with the procedure. The pros also tell me plain newspaper is best. It leaves no fibers or threads.

BAGS - Zip lock bags are excellent for storage of lenses and small items against dust and moisture.

ANTI-STATIC - Cloths or chemicals can be of benefit if used carefully. Do not use them on optics.

MISCELLANEOUS - There are lots of little parts that, if lost, won't ruin photographic equipment, but having spares takes up little space and can make picture taking more convenient.

- Camera strap fasteners.
- Viewfinder eyepiece.
- Front and rear lens caps.
- Flash sync cable.
- Extra tripod bolt. A 1/4-20 nut and bolt may also work.
- Acrylic marker that (Marks-A-Lot or Sharpie brands) will write on film and most any surface.

RICK RUSSELL RECOMMENDS

BETTER LISTS

EQUIPMENT PREP IS IMPORTANT

PACK FOR WHAT YOU'RE DOING

THREE ASPECTS

CARRY WHAT YOUR 4X USES

VEHICLE SPARES

I thought I would draw on the experience of Rick Russell, publisher of Sidekick Off Road Maps regarding what tools to carry. Rick has more hard core miles on his roll bar than I have on my tires. And by the sound of the first sentence, he welcomes the opportunity!

The Silver Coyote's first edition of the Glovebox Guide was a little light on addressing what to carry in your 4WD. But that issue will be resolved in the next few paragraphs.

Factors such as the weather, the environment and length of time you'll be gone affect your personal gear. But what about your vehicle, break downs and getting stuck (unstuck)? Will you spend twice as long having a "good time" as planned? Are you prepared to handle the unforeseen situations?

Take as much time with vehicle preparation as you do with yourself. My recommendation is simple: pack the vehicle for each trip based on the difficulty of the route and the remoteness of the trail. As the level of difficulty increases, so should the items you carry. An EASY trip in 2WD to the local mountains for a picnic lunch, requires fewer items than the John Bull challenge rated at MOST DIFFICULT.

After I define each level of trail difficulty, I discuss three aspects of vehicle preparation: maintenance; equipment and supplies; and vehicle upgrades. Each of these items is cumulative - the EASY items should be included with the MORE DIFFICULT lists and so on. It makes even more sense to pack for a MORE DIFFICULT trip and do an EASY one! And it goes without saying, water is required on every trip.

Basic to all lists is understanding you must carry what your vehicle uses. A bright and shiny new SAE socketset is of little value to the foreign (metric) car owner. By having what your rig uses, even if you're not mechanically inclined, a passer-by may be able to assist because you have the necessary tools. Also be aware the lists are only recommendations and must be supplemented by your particular vehicle, personal experience and requirements. The following is only a beginning.

TRAIL DIFFICULTY SYMBOLS

EASY

I use the symbols shown in the margin to indicate trail difficulty on my Sidekick Off Road Maps. Maybe the Coyote will come around someday and use them too!

EASY 4WD TRIPS: Two wheel drive is usually acceptable with good ground clearance. Using four wheel drive makes the trip safer and there will be less tire spinning. Always travel with others!

Maintenance Check

- Fuel tank - full
- Engine oil
- Transmission oil
- Brake fluid
- Metal top or roll bar
- Tire air pressure (including spare)
- Tire wear - 40% or less wear
- Windshield wipers and fluid
- Hoses
- Fan belts
- Radiator coolant
- Lube job
- Seat belts

Equipment and supplies

- Basic tools (see below)
- Spare tire
- Tire jack
- Tow strap
- First aid kit
- Duct tape
- Spare keys
- 40 channel CB radio (emergency type OK)
- Air pump (12 volt DC type desired)
- Shop manual
- Air pressure gauge
- Tire sealer/inflator
- Shovel
- Fire extinguisher
- Pay phone coins
- Flashlight and batts

Vehicle Upgrade - none required for EASY trips.

MORE DIFFICULT 4WD TRIPS: Four wheel drive, lower tire pressure, and some 4WD driving experience is best. For experienced motorcycle and mountain bike riders only.

Maintenance Check - same as EASY plus:

- Front/rear axle oil
- Wheels and lug nuts
- Exhaust system components
- Transfer case oil
- Shocks

MORE DIFFICULT

Equipment and supplies

- Expanded tools
- Tire star wrench
- Extra flashlight
- Engine oil
- Grease
- Brake fluid
- Tire repair kit
- Spark plug wires
- Radiator stop leak
- Bungie cords
- Fuel line
- Fuses
- Assorted nuts & bolts
- Rags
- Full size shovel
- Gloves
- Power steering fluid
- WD40
- Jumper cables
- Valve stems/cores
- Electrical wire
- Radiator hoses/clamps
- Extra gas & funnel
- Tie wraps
- Electrical tape
- Lug nuts
- Hand cleaner

Vehicle upgrade

- Tire size and quality upgrade
- Adjust air pressure
- Lift kit only if required for larger tires
- Front tow hook
- Rear hitch or tow hooks
- Transmission/transfer case/gas tank skid plates
- Rear closed differential recommended
- Upgraded CB plus hand-held back up unit
- Auxiliary lights desired

MOST DIFFICULT

MOST DIFFICULT 4WD TRIPS: Four wheel drive with a closed differential in the rear is preferred. Closed differentials in the front and rear are ideal. Low air pressure, experience and buddy-vehicles are important. For advanced mountain bike and motorcycle riders only.

If you desire to equip your vehicle for the MOST DIFFICULT routes, always travel with three or more well-equipped vehicles.

Maintenance Check

- Motor mounts
- Fuel tank & lines
- Suspension bushings
- Loose bolts and nuts
- Inspect brakes & hydraulic lines
- Inspect frame & body for cracks
- Steering components
- Wiring harnesses
- U-joints

Equipment and supplies

- Winch kit
- Coil & ignition parts
- Water pump fan belts
- Starter & solenoid
- Front hub or flange
- Axles & drive shafts
- Cotter pins
- Crimp connectors
- Hi-lift jack
- Electric fuel pump
- U-joints
- Alternator
- Loctite
- Come-along
- Silicone (RTV)
- Special nuts
- Chain with hooks on both ends and shackle
- Anything that has broken two times or more

Vehicle Upgrade

- Tire Upgrade to 33" - 35"
- Lift kit as required
- Rocker panel protection
- CB radio, with sideband for maximum range
- Skid plates under spring pads
- Rear closed differential required
- Front closed differential recommended
- Winch desired

TOOLS

Tools should be carried on all trips. Tools are separated into two groups: Basic Tools that everyone should carry; and Extended Tools.

BASIC TOOLS

- 3/8" & 1/2" drive sockets
- 3/8" & 1/2" ratchets
- Spark plug socket
- Crescents-several
- Pliers
- Wire cutters
- Openend/box wrenches
- Screwdrivers-slot & Phillips
- Extensions
- Vice grips
- Channel locks
- Allen wrenches
- Hammer
- Knife

EXTENDED TOOLS

- 1/4" square drive ratchet and sockets
- Hacksaw
- Chisels
- Deep sockets
- Very large hammer
- Valve core remover
- Large crescent wrench
- Tube wrenches
- C-clamps
- Voltmeter or test light
- Part retrieval magnet and mirror
- Battery terminal cleaner
- Files
- Breaker bars
- Torx bits and sockets
- Special large sockets
- Valve stem installer
- Tire irons
- Large channel locks
- Pipe wrenches
- Hydraulic jack

BE CREATIVE WITH STORAGE

I'm sure the next question on your mind is where do I store all these things? There are storage boxes built for most 4WDs. Large, multi-purpose, plastic camping boxes work well too. They make segregating supplies into trail level difficulty boxes easy. Be creative with under-seat and otherwise forgotten areas.

BEING RESCUED

MULTI-MODE SEARCH

When you've done your job by leaving the homebody with your return time and they report you missing, the search will come via many modes. Hikers, horses, vehicles and airplanes are all used by search and rescue teams. White is the easiest color to see unless you're in the snow. If you can't move the car to a good location for visibility from above, put markers out which can be seen from the air. Be prepared to signal with mirrors, lights and noise. Make yourself easy to spot.

SURVIVAL IS ATTITUDE AND PREPARATION

Survival is more a matter of attitude and preparation than skills and training. Attitude gives you the patience. Preparation gives you the resources. Staying on the trails gives you passerbys and makes you accessible. Drinking water keeps you alive. Now just be calm and confident it will all come together. That's all there is to it!

CHAPTER 8 PICKING PLACES

Before we move on, I'd like to talk trail philosophy and backcountry boogie men.

FEAR, ANOTHER F WORD

I work as a volunteer at a state park along with many others. Most are retired and live in the immediate area. On one occasion, a ranger was leading a natural history association 4WD tour and I was working as sweep. After completing a relatively mild drop-off, a 22 year resident professed he was glad he had finally done the drop-off. With typical Coyote lack of tact, I asked why he hadn't done it sooner and what he was afraid of. With clenched waving fist, he immediately and emphatically told me he spends lots of time in the outback, has a great deal of experience, knows what he was doing, and wasn't *afraid* of anything! Somehow, I couldn't bring 22 years in the area and all this experience together with no fear and the first time over the drop-off. I suppose you can look at *fear* as another one of those four letter F words - no one likes to use it; no one admits it; but everyone feels it.

FEAR IS GOOD

Our fears serve good purpose and are not without sound basis. They help us survive, make rational decisions and introduce an element of caution. These things offset the other side of the spectrum - our ego, our concern of being the only one who didn't make the hill, getting stuck in the sand and so on. Most fear for their life, and that of family and loved ones. A most practical consideration! Fear keeps us back a safe distance from the edge of the cliff or off thin ice. Another fear has to do with our transportation - will I hurt my 4X or get stuck forever? Good stuff again! It keeps your foot off the floorboard and the 4X out of deep water. There's also the concern for the environment - will we damage the terrain? This one sometimes needs to be taught! But fear is the word we find hard to use, so let's treat a couple of backcountry travel *considerations*!

REALLY OUT THERE

On another occasion, I was helping an automobile manufacturer introduce a new model. We left the Hilton (really), went a mile or two down the pavement, made a turn into the woods, and within a couple of hundred yards my high-roller rider white knuckled the sissy bar and exclaimed, "Well, we're *really* out there now!" I could still see pavement! To be *really* out there in Southern California is *really* stretching it. When you heed the precautions and follow the practices recommended in this Guide, the chances of being threatened by being *really* out there are just about nil.

LEARN TO CRAWL BEFORE YOU RUN

What I understand is *really* out there is really relative to your experience. The first time out, like the sales manager, out of sight of asphalt is trying. With time, you become more and more comfortable with greater and greater distances from civilization. Typically, it's not too long before most adventurers are pushing the envelope of our local mountains and deserts. My philosophy is learn to crawl before you walk before you run. Don't try to jump into the Superbowl in shorts and tennis shoes! Give yourself a chance to get in shape, equip yourself properly, and learn what it feels like to be really out there. Now I'll treat some of my past fears.

NARROW ROAD TO NOWHERE

How about the road that leads forever to nowhere and narrows down to the point where you can't turn around? One where you have to back all the way out? They don't exist! You may be temporarily inconvenienced with a short distance in reverse, but I've never had to back *all* the way out any road.

CAN ALWAYS TURN AROUND

I hope you are pleasantly surprised how little road-width it takes to turn around. I've backed my mud flaps off in a narrow, vee-ravine, but have always found a way to turn around. The old timers call it a three point turn, and maybe you'll have to make it a five pointer, but there's always a way. That's where you zig-zag more or less in one spot until you've done the 180. When the chips are down, most adventurers are happy with their creativity and the capability of their 4X.

CAN ALWAYS FIND ROOM TO PASS

Here's another one - you meet someone on a trail where you can't pass. Another myth. Consider I've conducted tours with up to 40 vehicles in a string and have always found a way to pass. If you practice the advice of Chapter 6, Tips, and think about passing and oncoming traffic ahead of time, you'll always find room to pass.

SEÑOR STUCK

Next, we worry about - excuse me - other people worry about the off-road boogie men. There's Señor Stuck. He puts you in a place where extrication is impossible. You know, stuck forever! I've never seen a 4X stuck forever. I've seen some pretty foolish acts and irresponsible situations, but all have been recovered. That's not to say a total wreck can't stay at the bottom of a canyon for years, but what I'm addressing is reasonably rational behavior. Stay on the roads and trails, travel with others, look before you leap, and Señor Stuck will only be something for others to worry about.

BLACK BART BROKE

Black Bart Broke is another self defeating goblin. Eight years of conducting tours has given me a tremendous data base regarding vehicle reliability. I have never had to leave anyone in the field for any reason. This speaks well for modern equipment and what slow and easy does to Black Bart. Time and again I hear the same horror stories as you, but they don't happen on my tours. Black Bart Broke preys on victims - those unwilling to take responsibility for their actions. If you're inclined to drive off the cliff because, "That curve just came up too fast", break an axle when, "That rock wasn't there the first time I went by", or bust your equipment trying to make a hill, then Bart will find you. Drive slowly and responsibly, and ol' Bart will go hide under a rock.

LITTLE LAD LOST

Little Lad Lost is a state of mind. If I demand to know my exact position to a fraction of a foot every second of my outings, I'd be lost more than I'm not! That's why I like the term temporarily disoriented. With sufficient resources - water, time and gasoline - it's pretty hard to be lost in Southern California for more than half a day. An anxious state of mind is Little Lad's prey. Confusion sets in and then you drive in circles or not see the road or not hear the train or not smell the campfire or overlook other obvious signs of a better way. Weekend travelers are everywhere. Give yourself a chance to find them.

BOOGIE MEN PREY ON FOOLISH ACTS

The backroad boogie men prey on procrastinating planners and irresponsible practices. Plan your trips well, drive slowly, act responsibly, and the boogie men only surface around campfires and tale telling!

YOUR CHOICE OF TRAILS

The trails you pick are obviously up to you. Where you live, how much time you have and many other factors influence your choice of adventures. There are three ways to arrange the Guide's trails: alphabetically, geographically and trail-to-trail. I chose alphabetically for Chapter 10 which means it is two-thirds wrong for those who want it another way. This is no help when trying to pick a trip nearby home or combine trails in a given area. The *QUICK-LOOK* locator map inside the front cover helps with the geographical arrangement. The *REMARKS* section of each trail-text page tells of nearby trails to put them together. Below I explain how to use the trail description and map *identifiers*. These help you pick trails close to home. All of this helps you arrange several adventures into longer and more personalized excursions. More often than not, you'll find the alphabetical arrangement used most often as you want to get to familiar trails or tell a friend about one you want to do.

THE IDENTIFIERS

QUICK-LOOK LOCATOR

The first, biggest and easiest way to locate a trail is inside the front cover. This is the *QUICK-LOOK* locator map. It outlines Southern California and designates all of the trails except Baja and Death Valley. Get a feel for your general location from the major highways and towns shown on this map. Use the inside back cover and the trail reference number to determine the trail name and applicable page number. Inside the front cover gives you the big picture. Inside the back cover gives you the name and page number for any trail.

You can also thumb through the trail pages and use the smaller *CALIFORNIA LOCATOR* map on each page. The *CALIFORNIA LOCATOR* is the Southern California outline in the upper right-hand corner of each trail-text page. The general location of the trail is shown by an area manager symbol within the California outline. A bear means the State of California manages the area. A triangle represents the Bureau of Land Management and the Forest Service is shown by their shield. Other areas are shown with a star. When a trail falls within several jurisdictions, I use the manager with the most miles within the area.

GET TO KNOW HOME TURF

Get to know the approximate location of home turf on the *QUICK-LOOK* map or the area map on page 100. By simply flipping through the trail pages, specific locales will stand out. Once you locate a trail or two, you can then use the *AREA* designation and the index to discover neighboring trails. The *REMARKS* paragraph in the text portion also designates nearby trails.

AREA DESIGNATIONS

Each trail in Chapter 10 has an *AREA* number on the trail-text page. For example, the **Mormon Rocks** and **Lytle Creek** trails are in area 4, Angeles. Go to the index and look up AREA 4. You will find all the trails in this area listed under this heading. The same is true for all other areas. The *AREA* designation and *QUICK-LOOK* map help you determine trails nearby each other.

USE THE AREA MAP

The areas obviously have common borders with each other. The Angeles Area, is bordered on the north by the Mojave Area, Big Bear to the east, Saddleback to the south, and Los Padres to the northwest. When traveling an area's borders, use the Area Map on page 100 to identify adjacent areas.

USE TRAIL-TEXT REMARKS

The trail-text pages list nearby trails in bold type under *REMARKS*. Bold type shows the word is a trail in the Guide. For example, the **Lytle Creek** trail lists **Mormon Rocks** as a nearby trail. You will gain more insight into a trail's attractions, and information on getting there, if you read about nearby trails too.

THE AREAS

Following are the names and descriptions of the ten areas used in the Guide. I've used highways as borders to define the areas. An exact understanding of the areas is not that important. Better than words is the area map on page 100.

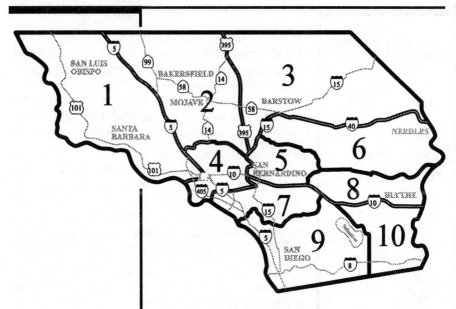

AREA 1
LOS PADRES

San Luis Obispo County's northern border is Area 1's northern border too. Interstate 5 on the east, the Pacific Ocean on the west, and I-10 on the south define the other three edges. It is named after the Los Padres National Forest within. It offers mostly mountain and forest environments, with a few surprises around Hungry Valley.

AREA 2
MOJAVE

Kern County on the north, Highway 395 on the east, Interstate 5 on the west, and Highways 138 and 14 on the south define Area 2. It contains the town of Mojave and some of the Mojave Desert, hence the name Mojave. I've just barely touched the surface regarding trails in this area.

AREA 3
ZZYZX

Area 3 encompasses San Bernardino County on the north, the California border on the east, Interstates 40 and 15 on the south, and Highway 395 on the west. It's pronounced "zi - zax", it's in the middle of the area, the last trail in the Guide, so why not name the area Zzyzx? You learn about its name in the trail description.

AREA 4
ANGELES

The Pacific Ocean, Interstates 10, then 5, and finally Highways 14 and 138 define the western and northern borders of Area 4. Interstate 15 and the 91 freeway, plus an imaginary line farther west to the ocean complete the eastern and southern boundaries. So close to Los Angeles, it contains the Angeles National Forest, the name should obviously be Angeles.

AREA 5
BIG BEAR

Area 5 gets more attention than most others. Interstate 15, and Highways 18 and 247 on the northwest and northeast respectively define the top limits. Interstate 10 and a small piece of Highway 62 are the southern limits. Named after the biggest attraction in the area, Big Bear Lake is right in the middle. This area defines two distinctly differing biological zones - mountains and high desert.

AREA 6
ESSEX

Interstates 15 and 40 on the north, the California border on the east, Highway 62 on the south and Highways 247 and 18 on the southwest put Area 6 smack dab in the middle of California's biggest desert. "S - X" is the name and the area should not be neglected. It contains California's own little Carlsbad-type caverns.

AREA 7
SADDLEBACK

This is about the point where it's easier to trust the map, and forget the words. Area 7's northern border is easy - Interstates 10, 15 and the 91 freeway. Now it gets complicated. It has Highways 74, 371 and 79, Interstate 15 and then 74 again to the ocean on the southeast and south. The Pacific Ocean is on the southwest. Saddleback is the name, after the mountain in Orange County.

AREA 8
JOSHUA TREE

Area 8 includes the magnificent Joshua Tree National Monument, the namesake for the area and my introduction to desert beauty. The northern edge is defined by Highway 62. The east is California's border and the south and west are contained by Interstate 10.

AREA 9
ANZA-
BORREGO

Area 9 has the same complicated border as Area 7's southern border. On the east is Highway 111 along the northeastern edge of the Salton Sea. The Mexican border and the Pacific Ocean clearly identify the south and west edges. Check out the number of trails and you will see why the Anza-Borrego Desert State Park is my all time favorite in California and how I came up with the name for the most southern area.

AREA 10
SAND HILLS

Interstate 10 on the north, California and Mexican borders on the east and south respectively and Highway 111 on the west are the limits of Area 10. Naming this area the Sand Hills is my tribute to the 40 miles of sand dunes that deserve more recognition and respect than they currently get.

USE THE INDEX TOO

The index has plentiful entries. Use it. To find the trails in a given area, look up that area number in the index. To find an area's surrounding areas, look at the area map on page 100, then look in the index.

MORE SENSITIVE DESCRIPTIONS

Without making excuses about editorial style and poetic liberties, the first edition of this Guide used less than becoming words to describe some trails. Worthless, God forsaken, nothingness and so on may have added color, but they did an injustice to some of California's unique features and attractions. My environmental insensitivity was showing. While reviewing the second edition maps, some governing agencies very clearly brought this to light. Thank you for waking me up.

WORDS FROM PUBLIC LAND MANAGERS

No one knows a particular area better than those who deal with it on a daily basis. I thought why not let these folks tell you what they have to offer and how they want their area treated. It goes along with picking places to know what's there and how you're expected to act. If there appears to be a common thread, it's only because they have an important common message. I've given you the Coyote's words, now here are a few from those who manage California's public lands.

Happy trail hunting.

ANZA-BORREGO DESERT STATE PARK

HAVE A PLEASANT STAY

Welcome to Anza-Borrego Desert State Park. We wish you a pleasant and rewarding visit. The best means of ensuring a pleasant visit and preserving the unique beauty of Anza Borrego is by planning ahead and being aware of a few simple rules. Remember that you make a difference.

600,000 ACRE PARK

Anza-Borrego Desert State Park is the largest unit in the California State System. The park's 600,000 acres are comprised of areas of great biological, cultural, geological and paleontological significance. The park is home to an endangered population of Bighorn Sheep or "borrego" from which the park takes its name.

PATROLLED ON FOOT, 4Xs AND AIRPLANE

The park is patrolled by park rangers in four wheel drive vehicles, on foot and by airplane. They are happy to render needed assistance and provide information about the park and its resources. They are empowered to enforce State Park Rules and Regulations, and other state laws as well.

USE ONLY DESIGNATED ROADS

Vehicles may travel only on designated routes of travel, either the paved roads or the park's 500 miles of primitive roads. Cross country driving damages the desert. Leaving the roadway is prohibited.

STREET LICENSED VEHICLES ONLY

All vehicles must be highway legal and all drivers must be licensed. Underage and unlicensed drivers may operate vehicles at adjacent Ocotillo Wells State Vehicular Recreation Area, but not within Anza Borrego.

WEAPONS NOT ALLOWED

Loaded weapons of any type (guns, crossbows, bows and arrows, slingshots, etc.) are not allowed in Anza-Borrego Desert State Park. Weapons must be incapable of being discharged and must be encased or kept within a vehicle or temporary form of lodging.

REMOVE OR DISTURB NOTHING

All features of the Park are fully protected. Nothing may be removed from its place or disturbed. This includes wildflowers, dead wood, rattlesnakes, potsherds and arrow heads. Wild animals are a part of the park's natural world. Rattlesnakes, in particular, are common throughout the park. By taking a few simple precautions they can be avoided. Wear rugged foot wear, watch where you put your feet and hands, and use a flashlight at night.

NO OPEN GROUND FIRES

Open ground fires are not allowed in Anza-Borrego Desert State Park. Campfires are permitted only in metal containers such as Bar-B-Ques and metal drum halves. Bring your own fuel. Dead wood helps enrich the soil and may not be gathered. Take your ashes and other trash home with you too.

PETS NOT ALLOWED IN THE BACK COUNTRY

Park staff do not recommend that pets be brought into the park. The desert can be a very dangerous place for your pet. If you decide to bring your pet, it must be kept under your control at all times. Dogs must be kept on a six foot leash and confined to a vehicle or tent at night. Dogs are not allowed in the backcountry or on foot trails.

VEHICLES STAY ON THE ROADS

When camping, your vehicle may not be parked more than two car lengths from a roadway. You may not disturb any vegetation or remove rocks or boulders to move your vehicle to the camp site.

ROADS FOR PLEASURE, NOT A CHALLENGE

Roadways within the park are intended as a means of viewing the park's many features and getting places to enjoy the tranquil beauty that the desert offers. The park's roadways are not meant to be viewed as challenges to be conquered. Some roads may be very rugged and challenging to even the most experienced driver or rider. Know your route beforehand and plan accordingly. We strongly recommend you visit the park's Visitors Center at the west end of Palm Canyon Drive in Borrego Springs. Information about the park and its many features is available.

HELP PRESERVE OUR PARK

Anza-Borrego Desert State Park was set aside as a desert preserve many years ago by that almost passed generation for the enjoyment of the present generation and generations yet to come. It is only through our efforts that the desert's natural beauty will be preserved and its natural processes allowed to continue relatively undisturbed. We hope that you will enjoy the park in a safe and responsible manner. Only with your help may we, as custodians of the land, safeguard it for the future. Enjoy the satisfaction of being a responsible visitor and explorer of the desert wilderness of Anza-Borrego Desert State Park.

Dave Van Cleve, District Superintendent,

Colorado Desert District

DEATH VALLEY

FASCINATING NAMES

So are you up for adventure in a place with names like Starvation Canyon, Coffin Peak, Funeral Mountains, and Hell's Gate? Welcome to Death Valley National Monument!

3200 SQUARE MILES

Established in 1933 and now encompassing about 3200 square miles, this National Park Service area can offer you some 287 miles of gravel and dirt roads to explore.

COLLAGE OF PLEASURE

Those of you who have been here before know of the rich collage of backcountry delights this relatively pristine corner of the Mojave Desert can offer; the dramatic show of summer thunderstorms building up over wildly twisted mountain ranges; the crisp, cool fall mornings broken by the harsh cry of a passing raptor; the breathtaking sparkle of winter-white constellations in a dark winter sky; the patchwork of spring colors when cacti, creosote, and coreopsis bloom.

GET HOOKED ON DESOLATE BEAUTY

Those of you who are intrigued, but put off by the macabre name of the valley, rest assured, with proper prior planning and common sense, you can survive, even get hooked on this beautiful desolation, protected for all to enjoy.

REGULATIONS TO CONSERVE FOR GENERATIONS TO COME

Visitors to public lands administered by different agencies sometimes say that our national park areas are too regulated. Perhaps after reading through our backcountry regulations, all of which it is your responsibility to know and obey while in the Monument, you will agree. However, keep in mind that the whole reason behind national park areas is "to conserve the scenery and the natural and historic objects and the wildlife... by such means as will leave them unimpaired for the enjoyment of future generations." This is a noble task articulated over three quarters of a century ago when the National Park Service was established. "Getting away from it all" is becoming more and more important these days, but making sure that there is always a place to get away to is what our backcountry is all about.

Briefly highlighting some of the regulations that may be different from your usual weekend haunts:

STAY ON THE TRAILS

1) Driving or riding any vehicle, bicycle, or motorcycle off-road is prohibited throughout Death Valley National Monument.

NO BACKCOUNTRY CAMPFIRES

WEAPONS NOT ALLOWED

REMOVE OR DISTURB NOTHING

STREET LICENSED VEHICLES ONLY

LIMITED CAMP- ING ALLOWED

REPORT VIOLATORS

CALL FOR CURRENT INFO

ENJOY DESERT WILDERNESS

2) Campfires are allowed only in the grates provided in the frontcountry auto campgrounds, but are prohibited in the backcountry. Wood collection is not permitted anywhere in the Monument.

3) All firearms need to stay unloaded, cased, and inaccessible while traveling in the Monument. All shooting, even target shooting, is prohibited.

4 Collection of anything (except souvenir cigarette butts, gum wrappers, or roadside trash) is illegal. Leave the rocks, plants, animals, and historic artifacts for the next backcountry adventurer to enjoy.

5) Dirt roads are still official roadways, hence park rangers enforce all vehicle code regulations, including helmet laws, seatbelt laws, open container laws, and DUI (driving under the influence) laws.

6) Camping is allowed only in specific areas. Check with the visitor center or a ranger for details.

Remember, violation of Monument regulations can lead to severe fines, even imprisonment, so play by the rules and recreate responsibly! If you happen to see someone breaking the law, please let a park ranger know. Use our confidential toll-free phone line: 800-438-PARK (7275), which may lead to a $1000 reward for you. Although it is the Park Service's job on paper to preserve and protect, an extra set of eyes and ears to help identify poaching, vandalism, or drug trafficking problems is always welcome.

Several of the dangers of Death Valley are heat exhaustion, car breakdowns, mineshaft hazards, or flash floods. If you'd like more information to help plan your upcoming trek, please call us at (619) 786-2331. Once here, feel free to stop by the Visitor Center at Furnace Creek for the latest road conditions, weather reports, and special instructions.

All in all, the extremes of Death Valley command respect, but invite exploration. Enjoy this desert wilderness.

Edwin L. Rothfuss, Superintendent,
Death Valley National Monument

written by Ranger Maya Serephin

NATIONAL FORESTS

EXPERIENCE YOUR NATIONAL FORESTS

I would like to extend an invitation to visit your National Forest and experience for yourself some of the excellent opportunities that await you with your four wheel drive, motorcycle or mountain bike. Whether you are using your chosen means to find that special trout stream, to get to that secret hunting spot or to just drive through and experience our magnificent scenery, I invite you to come and enjoy. While you are here, I only ask that you help us protect these national treasures that are your National Forests.

FOUR SOUTHERN CALIFORNIA FORESTS

Before you visit, it might be helpful to know a little about the Forest Service and the dedicated people who help manage the Forests. National Forest lands in California are divided into 18 different National Forests. Four, the Angeles, Cleveland, San Bernardino and Los Padres are located in Southern California and offer the closest opportunities for you to visit. Overall management of each National Forest is the responsibility of a Forest Supervisor. The Forests are further subdivided into Ranger Districts. The District Ranger has the management and decision making responsibilities for the District. For current maps and updated information on open routes and restrictions, you should contact the Ranger District office. After your trip, I encourage you to let the Ranger or their staff know about your experiences, the good times and the bad, any problems you encountered, trail repair needs you identified, or any other suggestions you might have for changes that would make future visits more enjoyable.

RANGERS THERE TO ASSIST

While you are out on the trail, you may encounter some of our patrol personnel. These hard working people are there to ensure that you and other visitors have a safe and enjoyable visit. While they may, from time to time, be called upon to enforce some rule or regulation which is being violated, they also have other duties such as maintaining the trails, cleaning recreation facilities or fire fighting. If you need assistance when you are in the field, call on them—they are there to help.

THEY HAVE MANY JOBS

Most people in the Forest Service have a variety of job responsibilities. In addition to recreation, the District Rangers and their staff have the responsibility to manage all resources on the National Forest, including fish and wildlife, soil and water resources, vegetation and grazing. Managing all these resources in a balanced manner to ensure that they are available for future generations can be a complex job. This is further complicated by the heavy population pressures in Southern California. It is a difficult job, but it can be done if you help by doing your part when you are out in the forest with your vehicle. One way to enjoy the Forest and protect the resources is by learning and following the principles contained in the Tread Lightly program.

WE'RE WORKING HARD FOR YOU

Here in the Pacific Southwest Region of the Forest Service, we recognize off-highway vehicle (OHV) use as a legitimate recreational use of public lands in a managed situation. We are attempting to provide a wide range of opportunities for 4-wheelers from the tough and challenging John Bull trail to the miles and miles of less difficult routes that provide access into the remote backcountry. This is being accomplished through the efforts of a lot of people in the Forest Service, but more importantly, it is also being done through a series of partnerships with clubs and organizations, manufacturers, and the State of California OHV Program (the Green Sticker Program). Without the help and support of these valuable partners, we could not succeed. I urge you to get involved, join a club or organization, and see that your non-street legal vehicle has a Green Sticker. Let's all work together to make National Forest OHV opportunities all they can be.

TRY OTHER RECREATIONS

When you come to visit, I would also encourage you to bring your fishing pole, binoculars and your tent to experience some of the other excellent opportunities the National Forests have to offer. Again, I would like to emphasize that your comments and suggestions are important to us. You can send them to any of our Forest Supervisor or Ranger District offices, or to me.

ENJOY

I sincerely hope you enjoy your visits to the National Forests, America's Great Outdoors.

Ronald E. Stewart, Regional Forester

HUNGRY VALLEY AND OCOTILLO WELLS

OFF-ROAD AREAS

In addition to the off the pavement opportunities available at Red Rock Canyon and Anza-Borrego Desert State Parks, there are two other areas operated by your California Department of Parks and Recreation for off-road exploring.

TWO NEARBY

One of these, Ocotillo Wells State Vehicular Recreation Area (SVRA), is adjacent to Anza-Borrego Desert State Park off Highway 78. The other is Hungry Valley SVRA located about halfway between Los Angeles and Bakersfield next to I-5 at Gorman.

OPERATED BY OHMVR DIVISION

Both of these areas have been acquired and are operated by the Department's Division of Off-Highway Motor Vehicle Recreation (OHMVR) with the "Green Sticker" Fund. This fund receives gas tax revenue when you operate your vehicles off the pavement, so these are your areas; you have helped acquire and maintain these areas.

OCOTILLO WELLS

Ocotillo Wells SVRA, at 40,000 acres (62.5 square miles), is the largest SVRA in the State (there are 6 others throughout California). It is chock-full of places to explore: Barrel Springs, Shell Reef and Blow Sand Hill to name a few. Drop in at the ranger station on Highway 78 before you venture off the pavement for a free map and suggestions of things to see and do. In the future we have plans to expand Ocotillo Wells by another 30,000 acres to the east of the present facility.

HUNGRY VALLEY

Hungry Valley SVRA is our other area you should check out. It is located right off I-5 at Gorman and is almost 19,000 acres in size (additional exploring opportunities abound on the adjacent Los Padres National Forest). Hungry Valley stands in stark contrast to Ocotillo Wells. With elevations from 3,000 to 5,000 feet, it gets snow in winter and there are many different vegetation types. Keep your eyes open while in the area for you just might see a deer, bear, bobcat, mountain lion or possibly even a condor. Stop by the ranger's station on your way in for a free map and then seek out the remote areas of Freeman Canyon for some neat exploring. For a change of pace, ask for directions to the Hungry Valley Oak Woodland Natural Preserve. You'll have to hike in (no

ENJOY CALIFORNIA'S SVRAs

vehicles allowed) where you can wander among a stand of immense valley oaks and native grasses. This particular plant community exists nowhere else in California.

Whichever areas you visit, please remember these are especially set aside for your use and for future generations to explore. Rangers are available to assist in emergency situations. Both areas provide extensive space for primitive camping too, if you wish to extend your stay. Enjoy yourself at California's SVRAs, and remember to "Tread Lightly!"

Donald W. Murphy, Director

California Department of Parks and Recreation

JOSHUA TREE NATIONAL MONUMENT

WELCOME TO TWO DESERTS

Welcome to Joshua Tree National Monument. These lands have been set aside to preserve a portion of the California desert in its natural condition for all time. This 560,000 acre Monument includes portions of both the Colorado and Mojave Deserts. The area is rich in biological diversity, containing a richly variable mixture of plants and animals from high and low desert regions. The interrelationships of all organisms are seen here in their natural state with relatively little impacts from human activities.

MOJAVE DESERT

In the Mojave Desert portion of the Monument one finds the habitat of the Joshua Tree, a variously shaped tree, that may often provide a nesting site for ladder-backed woodpeckers, Scott's orioles, or red-tailed hawks. Actually a large yucca, the Joshua Tree is a member of the agave family. One theory for the name is that early Mormon pioneers, traveling across the desert viewed the limbs of the Joshua Trees as the raised arms of the prophet Joshua, leading them on to the promised lands.

COLORADO DESERT

The lower Colorado Desert portion of the Monument is a drier more sparsely vegetated region. Here the creosote bush appears to be one of the best survivors, along with burrow bush, scattered ocotillos, and palo verdes.

PROTECTED LANDS

All lands within Joshua Tree National Monument are protected. Park Rangers with law enforcement responsibilities patrol the park lands, protecting against natural and cultural resource damage or loss. Removal of anything is prohibited. This will permit those who come in the future to enjoy this park as you have enjoyed it.

PROTECTED WILDLIFE

All wildlife (including snakes and scorpions) is protected. Feeding coyotes, ground squirrels and other animals weans them away from their natural food and causes problems of over population. For these reasons feeding of animals is prohibited. Observe animals from a safe distance and be careful where you put your hands and feet when traveling through the desert.

NO WEAPONS

Weapons of any type (guns, bows and arrows, air pistols, etc.) are not allowed in the Monument.

FIRES PROHIBITED

Gathering wood or building fires in unauthorized areas adversely affects the life cycle of the desert. Plants in the desert depend upon recycled organic materials. Unnatural fires may leave unsightly scars and adversely impact other organisms. Collecting of any vegetation, living or dead is prohibited. Leave all vegetation where you find it.

NO PROSPECTING

Prospecting, including the use of metal detectors, is prohibited, as it removes formations other visitors would enjoy seeing, disturbs plant and animal life and leaves unsightly scars.

USE ONLY EXISTING ROADS

Motor vehicles (including motorcycles and bicycles) must be operated only on the park roads. The desert ecosystem is fragile. Vehicles driven off of established roads destroy vegetation, uprooting and smashing plants, destroying shelters and homes, and altering food and water supplies; collapse rodent dens and tortoise burrows; and leave scars that will last for centuries. State vehicle laws apply in the Monument. All motor vehicles and drivers must be licensed. Over 80 miles of paved roads and over 100 miles of dirt roads are available for travel in the Monument. About 40 miles of the dirt roads offer four wheel driving opportunities.

CAMPING AVAILABLE

Certain areas are set aside as campgrounds. They are planned to provide an attractive setting for overnight visitation, while disturbing the natural environment as little as possible. To minimize human impacts, all overnight stays (except backcountry travel) are restricted to the developed campsites. Backcountry users are required to depart only from designated registration and parking sites, camp at least one mile from any developed areas, and fires and pets are prohibited in the backcountry. All backpackers are required to register before starting their trip in order to be aware of any special regulations designed to preserve the natural scene and resources and to assure a safer experience.

People are an unnatural addition to the original environment of Joshua Tree National Monument, however the park has been established to preserve the environment and provide for the enjoyment of this and future generations. As humans we can control our impact on

PETS DISCOURAGED

the natural environment to some degree. Pets add another uncontrolled element. The waste products of your pet may force a native animal to leave its territory, thereby reducing their chance for survival. Your pet may also chase rodents, and lizards. You may also find your pet in the middle of a cactus patch. Your pet may also be an annoyance to other visitors. For these reasons it is required that all pets be kept under physical restraint while in the Monument (tied or on a leash) at all times. Pets are prohibited on trails and must remain in developed areas, not being taken beyond 100 feet from campgrounds or designated roads.

RESTRICTED AREAS

Certain areas within the Monument are designated as restricted or day use only areas. Entering restricted areas is strictly prohibited. Because of the historical sensitivity of the Desert Queen Ranch, for instance, visitors to the area must be part of a conducted tour group. Ranger lead tours are offered, and people are encouraged to obtain the schedule of tours before visiting the Monument. Other restricted areas are privately owned or they protect critical wildlife areas. Day use areas are set aside to protect sensitive populations of wildlife and are closed during hours of darkness.

ILLEGAL SUBSTANCES

All State and Federal regulations pertaining to the possession, use, and sale of liquor or drugs are applicable within the Monument.

HELP THE RANGERS

Be sure to report to a Ranger any incidents of injury or property damage as soon as possible.

HELP PRESERVE OUR PARK

The Monument preserves some of the most interesting and still natural features of the Colorado and Mojave Deserts, massive rock formations, natural fan palm oases, natural washes and arroyos, desert bighorn sheep and other significant wildlife. The area was set aside to preserve these natural features as well as the significant cultural resources associated with the mining and ranching activities that occurred in the region. With your cooperation, these resources can be observed and enjoyed now and left for others to see in the future.

David E. Moore, Superintendent

written by William G. Truesdale, Chief Interpreter

CHAPTER 9
PRODUCTS AND SERVICES

ANSWERS TO YOUR QUESTIONS

This chapter came about as a result of you, my readers and followers. In classes, on tours, and via mail and telephone, I am frequently asked where to buy products or secure services. This chapter answers some of those questions.

INFORMATION FOR INFORMED DECISIONS

Let there be no doubt it is paid advertising, but according to Coyote specifications. I ignored the pleas of my pocketbook to fulfill your need. My intent is to entertain and inform; to provide information so you can make better decisions regarding the companies you deal with. I think the history of long standing institutions in the industry is interesting. Their stocking philosophy or simply their promise to do a good job is worth knowing. They've taken a chance on my approach by letting me control what went into the Guide. If you like the approach, tell them. If you don't like it, tell me. It is not in the strictest book-publishing tradition to include advertising, but I'm interested to see how it works and what you think.

BACKCOUNTRY YELLOW PAGES

Those of you who have motor oil in your veins know where to buy parts and accessories, but what about maps? On the other hand, the people with an altimeter on their wrist know about maps, but want for vehicle info. Some sources are obvious and others are real gems to discover. As you sit around the campfire planning your next tire purchase, or to have the maps so you won't get lost tomorrow, consider this chapter the backcountry yellow pages. I trust it will be put to good use.

QUALITY DEATH VALLEY ACCOMMODATIONS

GREAT LOCATIONS

The Furnace Creek Inn & Ranch Resort, located in the heart of the Death Valley National Monument, offers two great properties in one great location.

COMPLETE FACILITIES

Furnace Creek makes the perfect base for exploring the back country of Death Valley. First, there is a General Store full of everything you need to prepare yourself for the day's activities. Next, there is a Service Station which can provide AAA services if needed, or patch a flat. You may wish to spend a few minutes at the Monument Visitor's Center discussing your trip with the Park Rangers, and checking on road conditions.

DINE IN COMFORT

When you return after a full day of back country bouncing, the Resort offers two cocktail lounges in which to refresh yourself, as well as a great variety of restaurants, ranging from dressy-casual Northern Italian Cuisine, to a Wrangler Steak House, Señor Coyote's Mexican offerings or a Pizza to satisfy your appetite.

RECREATION ACTIVITIES

Of course, our accommodations are spacious and comfortable, and are located near our natural, spring-fed swimming pools. We offer many activities for our guests. You may golf on our championship 18 hole golf course, "The World's Lowest Golf Course." There are six lighted tennis courts for your enjoyment. We also offer horseback riding, haywagon rides and there are hiking and biking trails for your exploring enjoyment.

CALL FOR INFORMATION

The Silver Coyote uses the Furnace Creek Resort for all of his Death Valley tours. We invite you to experience our Resort too! Call us at (619) 786-2345 for information and reservations.

THE DICK CEPEK STORY

As a not-so-famous ex-president once said, "wellll". I guess you have gotten through just about enough of this highly informative, extremely exciting, heart pounding Glovebox Guide to be a real threat to anyone off-roading!

READY TO GO!

It's more like you're all keyed up and throttle stompin' ready to go, but don't know where to get the goodies you need to survive your next adventure.

FAMILY BUSINESS

The Dick Cepek Company was started in 1961 by Dick, Dot and Tom Cepek as a family business. We were involved with the likes of the "Fast Camel" and the "Sierra Al-Jamal" (circa 1960), yet had no place to get trail-tough accessories. We were in the same boat as you!

EXPERIENCE COUNTS

We learned, like you, by paying our dues. We got stuck about umpteen quadrillion times and then decided all this knowledge was a salable commodity! Particularly at a time when there was basically one size tire and two sizes of wheels! After installing what by today's standards are only moderate size tires, Dick got branded as "never get stuck again" Cepek. The next thing we knew our garage was up to the rafters with big black donuts and lots of wheels.

WORLDWIDE COMPANY

The rest, as they say, is history. We now have nine retail locations, three major warehouses, one in Nagoya, Japan, and worldwide distributors. We ship to more than 38 countries!

EXTENSIVE PRODUCT LINES

All of this is supported by a 340 page, full color catalog, 140 dedicated employees practicing the fine art of off-roading, and over 400 product lines that go beyond imagination! Let me name just a few - Dick Cepek tires and lights, Rancho, Superlift and Trailmaster suspension, Warn and Ramsey winches, Hi-Lift jacks, BF Goodrich tires, True-Trac differentials, Detroit lockers, Dana/Spicer hard parts, Bestop Jeep tops, Cragar, Centerline, Ultra and Weld wheels, Smittybilt bars and bumpers, Bushwacker fender flares and cut-outs, and more. Did I say just a few?

FREE HAT

Bring in your Glovebox Guide and I'll give you a Dick Cepek hat for saying hello! Call (310) 527-5888 for the outlet nearest you.

THE Solder Joint

TWO-WAY RADIOS NEEDED	Off-roading has its inherent dangers, among them the possibility of getting stuck in the middle of nowhere, far from the nearest telephone.
SUMMON HELP VIA RADIO	Carrying reliable radio communications equipment with you into the mountains and deserts allows you to summon help immediately.
FOR INTER-GROUP TALK TOO	Beyond that, it's nice to be able to communicate with others in your caravan without having to stop and get out of the vehicle, or use sign language.
HERE TO HELP	The Solder Joint in Orange can help you outfit your off-road vehicle with a communications system that will solve these problems for you.
18 YEARS EXPERIENCE	Mark Foster, owner of the Solder Joint, has 18 years of experience with mobile communications systems. He served eight years as chief of the technical staff for Uniden Corp., the largest manufacturer of CB radio equipment in the world, and one of the world's largest mobile radio equipment manufacturers.
CB, HAM OR BUSINESS RADIOS	At The Solder Joint, Mark and his staff can discuss your communications needs and help you choose the right CB, Ham or business-band two-way radio equipment for your off-road needs, including antennas and professional installation.
CELLULAR IS LIMITED	Don't be caught in the wilds without communications. Your cellular phone probably will be well out of range, so you can't depend on it.
FACTORY AUTHORIZED SERVICE	The Solder Joint sells and services a complete range of mobile communications equipment. With factory authorized warranty service, the Solder Joint is a one-stop center for all of your communications needs.
CHECK US OUT	For a free consultation, call for an appointment or stop by The Solder Joint at 808 N. Tustin Ave. in Orange. Telephone (714) 997-8535. The Silver Coyote uses The Solder Joint.
CONVENIENT HOURS	The store is open Monday through Friday, 9 a.m. to 6 p.m., and Saturday from 9 a.m. to 5 p.m. Visa, MasterCard and American Express cards are welcome.

OFF ROAD GENERAL STORE

ESTABLISHED IN 1983

We're Southern Orange County's oldest and largest store for Truck, Mini-Truck, and Four Wheel Drive accessories! We opened way back in 1983 in order to provide the residents of Southern Orange County with a convenient place to outfit their rigs for safe and enjoyable 4Wheel'n.

INSTALLATION AVAILABLE

At Off Road General Store, our goal has always been to offer our customers quality products at competitive prices with professional installation! We offer a wide assortment of quality name-brand truck accessories competitively priced with other truck accessory stores in Southern California. We offer our customers as many choices as possible since everyone has different ideas as to how he or she wants to have her or his truck look and perform. Our staff is trained and ready to install most of the accessories we sell. However, if your prefer to Do-It-Yourself, we can offer free advice and hints to make your installation easier and trouble-free.

NAME-BRAND ACCESSORIES

A few of the many quality product lines offered at Off Road General Store include suspension components from Rancho Suspension, Trailmaster Suspension, Heckethron Offroad Products, Super-Lift Suspension and Rugged Trail Suspension; Tube Products from Smittybilt, Hobrecht, Con-Ferr, and Grizzly; Street-Legal and Offroad Lights from Dick Cepek, KC Hilites, PIAA, Hella and Delta; Wheels and Tires from BF Goodrich, Dick Cepek, Mickey Thompson, Centerline, Ultra-Wheel, and Progressive Custom Wheel; as well as accessories from Warn, Deflecta-Shield, Polaris, Energy Suspension, Lecarra, and many others!

FREE TRAIL MAP

Stop by with your Glovebox Guide and receive a FREE Sidekick Off-Road Trail Map with $50.00 minimum purchase!

TOLL FREE NUMBER

We're easy to locate at 23052 Lake Forest Drive, Suite B4, Laguna Hills, California 92653, just off the San Diego (I-405) Freeway. Call us at **800-628-3303** or 714-770-9300 and we'll gladly give you directions to our store.

**FULL-COLOR
TOPOGRAPHIC
MAPS**

**DIRT ROADS
AND TRAILS**

**UNBEATABLE
DETAIL**

**SMALL
LAKES AND
STREAMS**

**FORESTS,
SCRUBLAND,
SAND AND
MORE**

**THE SILVER
COYOTE SAYS,
"I SWEAR BY
THEM."**

FILLING the MAP GAP

Southern California offers untold opportunities for backcountry travel. For a long time, the only problem was finding maps showing where those opportunities exist.

Fortunately, there is now a collection of full-color topographic maps covering the entire southern half of the state, from Death Valley east to Santa Cruz and south to the Mexican border.

The *Southern & Central California Atlas & Gazetteer,* published by DeLorme Mapping of Freeport, Maine, offers the most detailed, up-to-date maps available for the area it covers. A companion publication, the *Northern California Atlas & Gazetteer,* maps the rest of the state.

Two features make DeLorme's California atlases unique. First, they provide comprehensive topographic coverage in convenient book form. Second, they show virtually all back roads, including dirt roads.

The result: maps that are indispensable for 4-Wheeling, motorcycling and mountain biking. They are great for trip planning and as take-along guides.

Besides back roads and elevation contours, the maps show even the smallest lakes and streams, as well as forests, wetlands, scrubland, sand, lava fields, military reservations, railroads, airfields, powerlines, mines, campgrounds and much more.

In addition, the comprehensive gazetteer sections are packed with information on places to go and things to do, from family outings to wilderness treks. One gazetteer category is devoted entirely to vehicular recreation.

There is also an invaluable place name index that lists everything from major cities to country crossroads.

Available wherever books, maps or sporting goods are sold, or order from Harry Lewellyn's newsletter. The Silver Coyote says, "I swear by them."

Similar atlases are available for Alaska, Colorado, Idaho, Oregon, Washington, Utah, Wyoming and 14 other states.

For a free catalog, write to DeLorme Mapping, P.O. Box 298-5505, Freeport, Maine 04032, or call toll-free **1-800-227-1656**, ext. 5505. Phone orders gladly accepted; Visa, Master Card, American Express welcome.

COMPLETE MAP STOCK

Let Map Link be your single-source supplier for all your maps. Map Link has the most comprehensive stock in the world, featuring thousands of titles.

USGS TOPOS

Map Link stocks hundreds of thousands of United States Geological Survey topographic maps in our Santa Barbara warehouse. We have complete coverage of the lower 48 states and Hawaii at 7.5' (1:24,000) and 1:250,000 scales. We also have most 15' (1:63,360) and all 1:250,000 scale topos for Alaska. Because of customer demand we have re-printed many of the 15' topos of the Sierra Nevadas in California. Some original 15' series stock is still available for western states. In addition, we stock the 1:100,000 scale topos for the western US, New England and Texas. USGS topo indexes are available at no charge.

OTHER MAPS

Map Link carries a complete selection of United States and international maps, including road and street maps of every country and major city in the world, trail maps and wall maps. Map Link stocks all BLM Desert Access Guides, United States Forest Service visitor maps and

FREE CATALOG

Trails Illustrated National Park maps, too. Please contact us for a free catalog of our top map titles.

FAST SERVICE

Map Link ships all reasonably sized USGS orders within three working days; overnight service is available for an additional priority service fee. Priority orders received before 2pm Pacific time will be shipped the same day.

COMPETENT STAFF

Our staff can assist you in locating the correct maps for your project or travel needs.

SHIPPING

All maps are shipped and billed from our Santa Barbara warehouse.

RETURNS

Please order carefully. Map Link will not accept returns of improperly ordered maps.

PAYMENT AND ORDERING

Map Link accepts Visa, MasterCard and American Express over the phone or fax. UPS or Federal Express COD service is available for an additional fee. Please check stock with us first if sending a check or money order. Call or write Map Link, 25 East Mason Street, Santa Barbara, CA 93101, Phone (805) 965-4402, Fax (805) 962-0884.

FROM THE SILVER COYOTE

PROTECT YOUR FAVORITE RECREATION

Right about now, I feel like one of those PBS TV campaigns. I'm torn between my enthusiasm for my favorite recreation, my need to get your serious attention and a compulsion to declare some guilt. I watch the shows and contribute little.

DON'T PASSIVELY SIT BY

Most of us sit back on our high morals and attitudes, talk about what should be done, and do nothing. It takes too much time, too much energy, too much money, too much commitment, to act! We passively watch what's happening and righteously profess what's prim and proper!

TREAD LIGHTLY! NEEDS OUR HELP

Fortunately, there are those who act in our behalf. In the Individual Membership brochure with this Guide, Cliff Blake modestly says "...the US Forest Service established **Tread Lightly!**" The fact is he did it while a forester, then moved from the warmth and security of a long and successful Forest Service career to follow his commitment. He is **Tread Lightly!** and he has put together a professional, quality organization that will be around for years and years to come. . . with our support!

As with any private, non-profit corporation, he needs our assistance. Tread Lightly will only prosper and achieve its goals with your and my help.

IT'S A BARGAIN

Seriously consider an individual membership. Look at it this way: you enjoy your recreation at literally no trail-related costs. The average family spends more on one trip to the movies than a year's **Tread Lightly!** membership! Tread Lightly is a bargain!

JOIN NOW!

Whether you do it for yourself, the Silver Coyote or the environment, show **Tread Lightly!** you care. Join **Tread Lightly!** now! Use the enclosed Individual Membership brochure to join today.

TREAD LIGHTLY! ™
ON PUBLIC AND PRIVATE LAND

AMERICA'S PUBLIC AND PRIVATE LANDS NEED YOUR HELP!

Most outdoor recreationists have a respect for the land, but there are still those who damage the environment.

STARTLING STATISTIC

Over the past 15 years, 42 percent of our public lands have been restricted or closed because of environmental abuse. Closures continue! This startling statistic, combined with an increase in outdoor recreation, has made the **Tread Lightly!** message a crucial one.

TREAD LIGHTLY!

Tread Lightly! incorporated as a non-profit public service corporation in October, 1990 and is a national education program dedicated to increasing awareness on how to enjoy public and private lands without causing damage. Guidelines are offered for various modes of outdoor travel.

EDUCATION PROGRAM

Through educational materials, editorial coverage, and manufacturer-generated advertising and promotions, **Tread Lightly!** urges outdoor travelers to be responsible toward the environment and help preserve future opportunities for outdoor recreational travel.

ENHANCE OUTDOOR RECREATION IMAGE

By joining **Tread Lightly!** you'll encourage environmentally responsible activity and advance and enhance the image of various forms of outdoor recreation. You will join the ranks of prominent corporations, clubs, associations, and many individuals who find our concepts worthy of their sponsorship. Your membership helps **Tread Lightly!** achieve its educational goals.

JOIN NOW!

An Individual Charter Membership is $20.00 per year and it's tax deductible. Upon joining, you'll receive our Charter Member packet and quarterly newsletter.

CALL 1-800-966-9900

Help us promote responsible off-highway vehicle use! Call 1-800-966-9900 for club or corporate membership information, or better yet, mail your membership to **Tread Lightly!**, Inc., 298 24th St., Suite 325C, Ogden, UT 84401.

Cliff Blake,
Executive Director

TRACTION KING
(ARB) AIR LOCKER

HAVING TRACTION WHEN IT COUNTS

FOUR-WHEEL-DRIVE? NOT REALLY

Traction, or the lack thereof, is the biggest hindrance to 4x4 *and* 2x4 unpaved travelers! The frustration of spinning tires is compounded by the common misconception that four-wheel-drive vehicles are always driven by four tires. The Coyote calls it diagonal teeter-totter-you sit still while your 4x4 furiously spins one tire on each axle!

TRADITIONAL PRODUCTS

In reality, when the going gets rough, stock 4Xs only drive two tires! Aftermarket manufacturers offer "limited-slip" and "locking" differentials to help, but these traditional "lockers" exhibit less than optimum street/ trail manners.

LIMITED PERFORMANCE

Limited-slips provide limited power transfer under certain conditions. True lockers provide 100% power transfer to both tires even when not desired. Both cause uneven, accelerated tire wear and can cause handling problems.

PERFECT, PUSH-BUTTON PERFORMANCE

The best traction-enhancing device is the new Australian-made ARB Air Locker. It works normally, like a conventional differential, but locks the left and right tires together, on demand, at the push of a button! To the racers, it turns that axle into a spool.

AIR OPERATED LOCKING DIFFERENTIAL

Activating the ARB Air Locker sends compressed air from the on-board compressor to the special locking device inside the differential. The Air Locker instantly locks both wheels on that axle into one driving force. Even if one wheel is hanging in the air, the other will provide full driving power. Push the button a second time and the Air Locker disengages, returning the axle to its stock behavior; no corner-hop and uneven tire wear.

WRITE FOR FREE INFORMATION

ARB Air Lockers are the ecological approach for those seeking the ultimate in traction. The Silver Coyote uses one. They reduce tire spin and produce less trail erosion. For more information and a free brochure, write, ARB-USA, 564 Valley St., Seattle, WA 98109; or call 206/ 284-5906, FAX 206/284-6171.

**ENJOYABLE
BAJA TRAVEL**

**INFORMATIVE
NEWSLETTER**

**INSURANCE
SAVINGS**

**OTHER
DISCOUNTS**

**ADVENTURE
TRIPS**

**RESOURCE
CENTER**

JOIN   NOW!

**TOLL-FREE
NUMBER**

BRINGING YOU THE BEST OF BAJA

The DISCOVER BAJA Travel Club is committed to making your Baja travels easier, cheaper and more enjoyable. We offer members more benefits, assistance and information than has ever been available to Baja travelers.

With our exciting monthly newsletter, *Discover Baja*, you'll know what's happening around the mysterious peninsula. We've got the names, numbers, rates and dates that make your trips to Baja more interesting, fun, and most of all, economical.

Take advantage of up to 80% discounts on insurance provided through Oscar Padilla Mexican Insurance Company. Their reputation for service and integrity is outstanding and there are no lower rates!

You'll also enjoy savings of 10-30% on hotels, RV parks, restaurants, resorts, sportfishing and other services throughout the peninsula. These discounts stretch your budget so you can afford to go to Baja again and again.

In the comfort of small groups, we offer special adventure trips with experienced Baja guides. They share their knowledge and literally show you things you've never seen, no matter how often you've journeyed south.

Our DISCOVER BAJA Resource Center in San Diego carries Baja reference materials, books, maps, videos, permits and special travel supplies ... your one-stop-shop for all your Baja needs.

Annual membership is just $39. You'll probably save more than that the first time you use the Club's discounts on insurance, lodging, dining or supplies.

No matter where you're going in Baja, you're spending more money than you need to, unless you're a member of DISCOVER BAJA Travel Club. Write or call toll-free to join, or to request a free copy of our newsletter today: DISCOVER BAJA Travel Club, 3065 Clairemont Dr., San Diego, CA 92117, **(800) 727-BAJA**.

SOUTH SHORES
INSURANCE AGENCY

SAFE RESPONSIBLE DRIVERS

IMPORTANT INSURANCE IDEAS

PREMIUM SAVINGS

EXPERIENCE COUNTS

FREE QUOTE

TOLL FREE NUMBER

QUALITY 4X VEHICLE INSURANCE

We endorse and support the Silver Coyote's 4X safety program for unpaved adventures.

- Plan your trip carefully in advance - get accurate maps.
- Figure off road mileage - start with a full gas tank.
- Have another vehicle with you. Advise someone at home where you will be.
- Maintain a trip log with miles and remarks.
- Carry drinking water.
- In the event of an emergency or temporary disorientation, stay with your vehicle.
- Respect our environment. Haul it in. Haul it out.

Review your insurance annually. Each individual's situation changes - new Driving Distance, New Cars, Home Replacement Cost increases, Purchase New Property, Young Drivers, Jobs and benefits change. Meet with your Insurance Broker to take advantage of the best new products that meet your changing individual needs. Spend your premium dollars wisely to best protect your assets in the event of major disaster. With our 30 years experience, we can help you purchase adequate insurance protection at the best value.

Take advantage of all possible discounts - Good Student Driving Distance - Highest Practical Deductibles on home and auto. Accurately review your annual premiums and coverage.

Let us use our 30 years experience to help you review your insurance. We represent excellent companies - Safeco - Mercury - Aetna - Cigna - American States.

We would be glad to provide information for Auto - Home - Business Insurance. Our offices are conveniently located in Huntington Beach and South Orange County. For Vehicle and Home Insurance please call David Smith, CIC, or for Business Insurance, Steve Holden, CIC, at 714-963-5647, FAX (714) 965-0637 or call toll free **1-800-350-5647**.

Steve Holden, KD6LVI

FAIRWAY FORD

ESTABLISHED 1965

The Fairway car and truck dealership was established in 1965 in Los Angeles and moved to the current Placentia location in 1966. Fairway was one of the first Orange County dealerships to regularly customize RV and 4WD vehicles for sale to the public.

FIRST TO CUSTOMIZE RVs

Among the packages that Fairway has offered over the years was the first camper special packages, lifted 4x4s, lowered 4x2s, functional race-prerunner trucks, turbo-charged 4x4 motorhomes, and specially modified performance Mustangs.

TRUCK/RV SERVICE CENTER

The Truck/RV Center was added in 1971. They continue to offer custom modifications, parts and accessories. They have a ten bay service department offering installation and repairs of virtually all standard and custom accessories.

IN-DEPTH STOCK

Everything from hub sockets and dash covers to complete suspension systems and street legal superchargers are available at Fairway. Regularly stocked product lines include Vortech superchargers, Bilstein gas shocks, Rancho suspension, J&J stainless steel accessories, Paxton superchargers, Banks turbochargers, Pendaliner bedliners, Doetschtech shocks, Colgan bras, GTS buggards, Stull grilles, Borla performance exhaust systems, Bell Tech suspension, Cibie lighting, Saddlebags, consoles, and much more. Products for all popular makes are sold, with Ford being our specialty.

SUPERCHARGER SPECIALISTS

Among the hot new items is the street legal supercharger for the Explorer/Ranger 4L V-6. Power and performance are increased, with no adverse effects on idle, fuel economy, or driveability. Similar systems are available for Ford's 302, 351, 460, and the GM 305 and 350.

TRY US!

FAIRWAY FORD is loated at 1350 Yorba Linda Blvd., Placentia, California 92670 (714) 524-1200.

Mexico West Travel Club

17 YEAR RECORD

Mexico West Travel Club is an exclusive International club with a seventeen year record of providing information, service and savings to over 10,000 members worldwide.

MONTHLY NEWSLETTER

Members receive a monthly newsletter that provides them with the most up-to-date Baja California and west coast Mexico travel information. Specialized current tips including fishing reports, interesting stories and articles, and insight into an overall view of activities and destinations to help in planning a first or 50th excursion.

INSURANCE DISCOUNTS

Through International Gateway Insurance Brokers in Chula Vista, members are offered considerable savings on their Mexican auto, boat, aircraft and RV insurance for their travel. International Gateway Insurance Brokers represent ASEMEX, the largest insurance company in Latin America. Members usually handle their insurance needs over the phone and enjoy 20% savings on short term insurance and 50% on yearly coverage.

OTHER DISCOUNTS

Members of Mexico West enjoy discounts at hotels, resorts, RV parks, restaurants, fishing fleets and on vacation packages to popular destinations.

CALL OR WRITE

The club maintains a supply of other materials required of the traveler, such as Mexican fishing licenses, boat permits, tourist cards and numerous books and maps. Call Mexico West at (619) 585-3033 or write to us at P.O. Box 1646, Bonita, CA 91908.

Amateur Radio Training Service

RADIOS ARE IMPORTANT IN OUTBACK

Most off-roaders know the importance of having a CB radio on board while exploring so you can summon help from nearby friends or other four-wheelers when trouble strikes.

CB RADIOS LIMITED

But most people who have used CB radio know its considerable limitations: It's short-range communications and not always reliable — especially when you really need it.

CONSIDER NO-CODE HAM RADIO

Now, there's an answer to your two-way radio needs beyond the limited capacities of CB. Consider the FCC's new No-code Technician Class Amateur Radio license. Created in February 1991, this new type of ham license allows you to get on the air by passing just a 55-question written exam given by volunteer examiners. You no longer have to learn the Morse telegraph code!

REPEATERS THROUGHOUT THE SOUTH-WEST

Using ham radio, you can talk via mountaintop repeaters from almost anywhere in California to other hams up to 100 or more miles away. You can even make telephone calls from your vehicle's mobile radio, or a small handheld transceiver about the size of a pack of cigarettes. Calling for help is never easier than with ham radio, especially when you're out of range of the limited cellular-phone network.

BETTER 4X TO 4X LINK TOO

You'll also find that talking vehicle-to-vehicle with others in your group is better and more reliable with ham radio than with CB.

EASY, ONE-DAY, NO-CODE CLASS

So how can you get that new No-code Technician ham license with a minimum of effort? Amateur Radio Training Service of Garden Grove offers regular ONE-DAY classes for the No-code license. You'll learn all you need to know to pass the FCC test in one day, and you will take the test in class at the conclusion of the instruction period, so you won't forget what you've just learned.

TRY *ARTS*

For information about the One-Day No-Code classes, call **Amateur Radio Training Service** at (714) 895-3345 or (714) 551-0305.

BFGoodrich Tires

1976 - BFG INTRODUCES LIGHT-TRUCK RADIALS

It began in 1976, when Fritz Kroyer's buggy introduced the world's first light-truck *radial* to the off-road racing world. It was the BFGoodrich, Radial All-Terrain T/A. Kroyer wasn't victorious, but BFGoodrich learned the tire would not only survive, it would thrive and perform very well in hostile terrain.

The tire has turned a lot of miles since its introduction. It's accumulated more miles on the road than off, but what makes it survive race environments is exactly what makes it a safe on or off road sport-utility tire for your vehicle or truck.

THREE PLY SIDEWALL

The Radial All-Terrain T/A starts off with a three-ply carcass. That's more than just jargon. Many other tires have only two plies in the sidewall of the carcass. The more plies, the stronger the tire and the better the puncture resistance.

TWO STEEL BELTS

Atop the base of these three plies are two additional belts. They are steel! Steel provides extra puncture resistance, but that's not all. Flexible enough to conform to the terrain on or off the road, steel belts hold their shape when deflected, so the tire is stronger and less likely to deform.

COMPUTER GENERATED TREAD PATTERN

Then there's the tread pattern. The Radial All-Terrain T/A has a lot of biting edges for extra grip in sand, gravel or mud, but the tread also gives a quiet highway ride and even wear.

The Radial All-Terrain T/A has won a lot of races since 1976. But it's more important that the ones on your vehicle get you to wherever you're going. Depend on it! The Silver Coyote does.

THREE TIRES TO CHOOSE FROM

By the way, the T/A family of light-truck radials offers three outstanding choices. At the head of the lineup is the Baja T/A, a super-duty radial. The All-Terrain Radial T/A is for people more serious about getting off-road. The Mud-Terrain is for those who need the ultimate in rock grabbing, self-cleaning backcountry rubber.

CHAPTER 10 TRAILS

2000 MILES OF TRAILS

This chapter contains 101 trails throughout Southern California plus selected trails in Baja and Death Valley. It also tells how to use the trail maps and text. From San Luis Obispo to the Mexican border, it identifies more than 2000 miles of unpaved roads. Some of the trails offer places to go and things to see. Others are just drives in the backcountry. The trails are public and private roads on which to use your street-legal 4WD, motorcycle or mountain bike.

PLANNING IS IMPORTANT

I want to encourage the good habit of proper planning and preparation. The descriptions are best reviewed before you leave home. This is also an opportunity to combine and personalize the excursions to fit your style. Throw in a five miler on the way to grandma's. Check out **Painted Canyon** while vacationing in Palm Springs. Combine **Mineral Hill** with your weekend at the Apple Festival in Julian and so on. Under all circumstances, make sure you can see what I'm talking about from paved road to paved road on your navigational map. Look for map gate symbols and the like. This means you'd best check with the keeper or risk disappointment. Travel with others and leave your written itinerary with someone not traveling with the group.

HARD TO FOLLOW DIRECTIONS

Back road directions are typically hard to follow and I've learned, even harder to write. Proper preparation is essential. Car odometers differ. See Chapter 5, Navigation, for information on determining the accuracy of yours. Qualitative terms are subject to interpretation. It's just a little ways or it's not too rough may mean one thing to me and another to you. Calibrate your information source. The roads change. Mother Nature can easily rearrange a road to the point of leaving you no choice but to go her way - turn around. The rules change. The statutes, the authorities and private property owners all have the option and right to regulate road usage. Follow their directions. And most frustrating of all, road designations and routes differ, disappear and even vary from map to map and reality. Sometimes,

AMBIGUOUS DIRECTIONS

going without a map is downright foolish. Reality is what you see on the spot. It must be dealt with realistically and responsibly. In the final analysis, you must deal with what is actually before you, not what your buddy told you, what ought to be, or what used to be. Determine who has jurisdiction where you will travel (under *AUTHORITY* in the trail-text) and talk with them. Get the most current information.

PLANNING AND PREPARATION IMPORTANT

There are enough trail instructions in this Guide to have successful trips. The maps and text however, do not provide exact mile by mile route descriptions. By leaving more questions than answers, I hope to encourage proper planning and spark individual exploration. For me, personal discovery is far more exciting than being lead by the hand. After all, isn't that part of what you are out there for, a little adventure? Consider my trail yarns like rallies and scavenger hunts. They require reading between the lines and bottom line is, there is no substitute for proper planning and preparation. Chapter 3 covers planning.

AN INACCURATE SCIENCE

INACCURATE MAPS

There are no 100% accurate maps. John Skinner, the Automobile Club of Southern California dirt road mapper, and I went over all the maps in this Guide. In a back issue of the *4-Wheeling* newsletter he did an article (The Exact Science of Mapping) on making maps. In essence - maps can be inaccurate. The mere fact that time has elapsed between the physical survey and printing the map means potential changes (errors). Sometimes the field mapper's notes are misinterpreted by the cartographers resulting in map errors. Other times, things just don't fit the way they actually are, so designations and symbols are mis-located on purpose. Don't be surprised by roads in the field that aren't shown on your map and vice versa. Some map publishers choose to not include perfectly good roads. Others include roads that have long since been removed or closed. Consult more than one map to be sure.

NAME CONFUSION

Confusion abounds about using maps and trail descriptions. The number of Main Streets in Southern California is amazing. The number of Tule, Coyote, Cottonwood and other Canyons, Mountains, Creeks, Washes, Points, Hills, Flats, etc. is staggering too! There is name duplication even on the same map. Make sure you have the one you want.

SYNTACTICAL AMBIGUITY

Syntactical ambiguity is confusing. Huh? Take your choice. 5 times 1 plus 3 can equal 8 or 20. Follow along. 5 times 1 (is 5), plus 3, equals 8. How about 5 times (1 plus 3) 4, equals 20. These damn engineers! Trail and route descriptions suffer from the same disease. They can be interpreted in more than one way. Dennis Casebier's *Mojave Road Guide*, works out to be about one page per mile. I've had reports of people still get temporarily disoriented using his book. Yes, he covers history too, but his trail descriptions are far more complete than mine. At his ratio of miles to pages, this guide would be 2433 pages thick. Hardly a Glovebox Guide™! That's why it's important to take an evening and properly plan any trip regardless of whose books or maps you use. You are in essence planning every trip from scratch.

INACCURATE DISTANCES

Distances printed on maps aren't always accurate. The professional field mapper is only a little more sure than you which road he is on when logging distance. He may have a choice of several approximately parallel roads. They all lead to and from the same points. With the same choice, you can't be sure which one he mapped and measured versus the one you are traveling. To me, the exact road is not that important. What is important is that I'm safely and responsibly having a good time. Have a good time with my trail descriptions and maps.

USING THE TRAIL PAGES

GUIDE MAPS LACK DETAIL

The *TRAIL TITLE* on the *TRAIL MAP* page names the specific trail. The map shows the suggested travel route, some branch trails and nearby paved roads and towns. The *TRAIL MAP* does not however, include every route, twist, turn, track, trail, thoroughfare, bend, detour, access, approach, artery, and alternative (get the picture!) you will encounter. I specify better navigational maps in the *MAPS* paragraph on the trail-text page. Navigational maps provide more detail, but they too lack every detail encountered on the trail.

GUIDE MAPS SHOW TRAIL LOCATIONS

F

GUIDE MAPS HAVE NO SCALE

AREA DEFINITION MAP ON PAGE 100

TRAIL-TEXT PAGES

CALIFORNIA LOCATOR

Again, the trail maps are not intended for navigation. They are intended to show the general area, access to the trail head, and the start and finish. They give enough detail, when used in conjunction with the listed *MAPS*, to travel from point to point. They also indicate the start and finish for each trail with the symbols shown in the margin. For dead-end trails, the finish is shown at the recommended turn-around point.

Also recognize two other important aspects about the Guide's trail maps. My maps have no scale. I may have compressed border areas to bring significant paved roads and interstates on to the map. This provides more surrounding information on each map. More importantly, the top of the *page* is not always north. Check the compass rose on each trail map for north. The legend is on the inside back cover for easy reference for any trail. This keeps the map area bigger and less cluttered. The symbols are kept to a minimum and after a couple of times, you won't need the legend.

The Southern California area definition map is on page 100. As the **AREA** numbers help you identify trails within the same area, the area definition map helps you identify surrounding area borders. Use it to combine trails in border areas.

The trail-text pages, to the right of each trail map, contain a *CALIFORNIA LOCATOR, AREA NUMBER,* the recommended *CB RADIO* channel, and the following paragraph headings: **DESCRIPTION, MAPS, MILES, AUTHORITY** and **REMARKS**. Use each of the above as follows.

In the upper right-hand corner of each trail-text page is a *CALIFORNIA LOCATOR*. It locates that particular trail within Southern California by an area manager symbol. A bear means the State of California, a triangle represents the Bureau of Land Management, the Forest Service is shown with their shield and a star means others. When a trail falls within several jurisdictions, I use the manager with the most miles within the area. Learn to quickly flip through the map pages to locate trails near home or points of travel.

AREA NUMBER

The *AREA NUMBER* identifies the area within which the trail falls. I have also assigned a *CB RADIO* channel for each area. Listen for fellow Guide users on this channel. Area channels are best used to make new friends, but can also be used to assist with breakdowns and disorientation.

DESCRIBES THE TRAIL

DESCRIPTION describes getting to the trail head, the trail route, points of interest and suggested activities. It lists trail names and numbers, landmarks or other helpful information, but not every turn and alternate trail. That is why a Trip Log (see Chapter 5) is so important.

LISTS APPLICABLE MAPS

MAPS lists more detailed maps to use for navigating as explained above. The first map listed is the *principal reference map*. It is used in the *DESCRIPTION* when I refer to trails and points of interest by coordinates. Other usable maps are also listed, but the coordinates in the *DESCRIPTION* apply only to the *principal reference map*. The other listed maps only give the start and finish points coordinates. These coordinates are in parentheses behind each map in the *MAPS* paragraph. DeLorme Atlas references also list the page number. p... designates the page for that atlas. When a particular map or series of maps is omitted, I felt it lacked sufficient detail to be used for effective navigation.

COORDINATES APPLY TO PRINCIPAL MAP

All coordinate are shown in parentheses "( )". When you see (A5), it means look on the *principal reference map* at coordinates A-5 as you learned in the chapter on maps. When you see (A/B5), it means look near the A, B division and 5. This provides a little finer resolution and is intended to speed the location process. Same is true for (A5/6) - look near the 5, 6 division line. My apologies for "(T7N,R20W)" and the like. These more accurate coordinates are used on some federal maps. We have no choice on those.

TELLS MILES OF DIRT

MILES first tells if the trail is a loop or dead-end. Dead-end trails cover the same ground twice. It is recommended you go in and out the same route. Loop trails start and finish at different spots. Next, *MILES* gives the trail distance from point to point. Side trip miles are typically not included. The *MILES* along with the distance from your home will help you plan how much time, provisions and gasoline will be needed.

TELLS WHO'S IN CHARGE

AUTHORITY gives the local governing authority. Both address and telephone numbers (when available) are provided. Where there are several authorities, they are all listed. Use this information to get the current maps, conditions, information and required permits.

OTHER INFO

I use **REMARKS** to suggest the best season for a trip, special equipment or personal needs, and other tid-bits that don't logically fall into any of the above categories. I also list nearby trails by name in bold print.

TRAIL DIFFICULTY

In my college classes and lectures, I'm frequently asked, "How hard is the trail?" That's the most difficult question I have to answer. How high is high? It depends on three things: 1) your experience; 2) the vehicle you are driving; and 3) what Mother Nature has done recently. Hard to some is not hard enough for others. Use your navigational maps for an indication of road difficulty. The Sidekick Maps use very specific symbols to designate EASY, MORE and MOST DIFFICULT. My intent is to provide places and trails to appreciate and enjoy Mother Nature, not thrill rides. However, some of the routes are very difficult, challenging and dangerous. Heed my cryptic words of caution. I only warn of trails that are known to be rough! Don't bite off more than you can chew, particularly on your first outings. Most first-timers have no concept whatsoever how rough a trail can be. And remember, the law, both man's and Mother Nature's, has the last word! Respect both.

ENJOY

Enjoy safe, responsible and ecologically compatible backcountry travel.

17 Palms

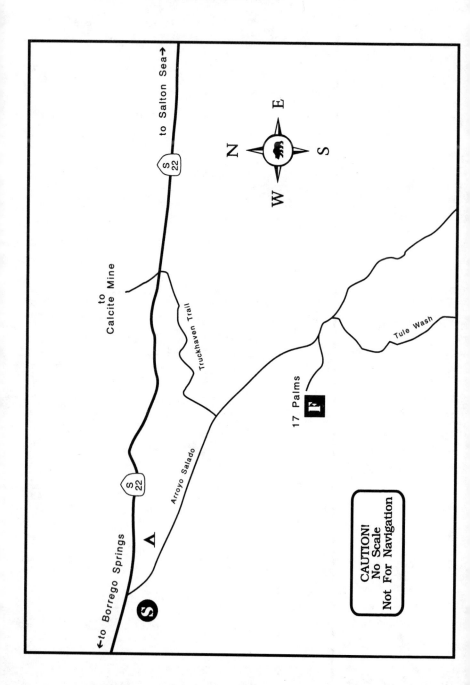

to Salton Sea→

to Calcite Mine

Truckhaven Trail

Tule Wash

17 Palms

Arroyo Salado

←to Borrego Springs

N E
W S

CAUTION!
No Scale
Not For Navigation

Area 9
CB-36

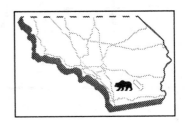

17 PALMS

DESCRIPTION: A sensitive watering hole for the locals (desert life that is) and a mail stop for the early prospectors during the 1800's, **17 Palms** Oasis isn't a Hollywood set, but worth the experience to find. As with other ABDSP trails, first get to Borrego Springs (C12). About 9 miles east of Peg Leg Smith Monument (C13), on HWY S22, is the Arroyo Salado primitive campgrounds on your right (south). Turn in and use the road through camp to a sign (sometimes down) for a hard right (west) to the oasis. Neither park in the palm trees nor spend the night, but find the mail barrel in the trees. The trace of surface water will tell you why the area is so sensitive. Home is back the way you came in.

MAPS: ACSC San Diego County (C14/15). Anza-Borrego Desert State Park map (C/D6), Desert Access Guide #19 (E3/4). Highly recommended is Lindsay's *The Anza-Borrego Desert Region* (ISBN 911824-67-7) book and map (trip 3B). DeLorme p116 (B/C1), trail shown but unnamed, USGS 33116.

MILES: Dead-end. 8 miles in and out from HWY S22.

AUTHORITY: Anza-Borrego Desert State Park, P. O. Box 428, Borrego Springs, CA 92004 (619) 767-5311.

REMARKS: First stop should be the visitor center where you can get the Park map. Remember, look, but don't take anything from the Park. **Pumpkin Patch, Vista Del Mal Pais, Fonts Point, Cut Across Trail** and **Calcite Mine** are nearby.

Mike Smith

Afton Canyon

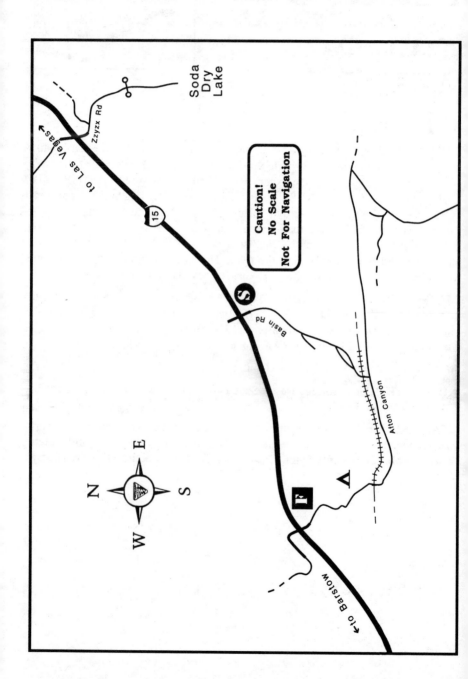

Area 3
CB-7

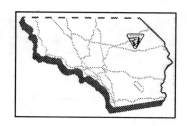

AFTON CANYON

DESCRIPTION: **Afton Canyon** is a beauty. Best to get a copy of Dennis Casebier's *Mojave Road Guide* (ISBN # 0-914224-13-1) to make sure you don't miss a thing. Go north on I-15, past Barstow (a stop at the BLM Way Station wouldn't hurt) to the Basin Road off ramp. Use it right (south) and you're on your way. Once you come to the RR tracks, go right (west) on the main road all the way back to I-15. Simple as that, except lots of side roads to both explore and confuse. Also be aware that many routes in **Afton Canyon** are closed, so watch for signs. Plan on spending the night if the wind's not blowing too hard. At I-15, south takes you back to Barstow and home.

MAPS: ACSC San Bernardino County (D6). DeLorme p69 (D6, D5). USGS 35116, Desert Access Guide #9 (G/H6/7).

MILES: Loop. 14 miles from Basin Road to Afton Canyon at I-15, but plan on more to thoroughly enjoy this area.

AUTHORITY: BLM, California Desert Information Center, 831 Barstow Road, Barstow, CA 92311 (619) 256-8313.

REMARKS: The tours of the area are self guided so you won't need to make any arrangements. Also consider combining with **Zzyzx**.

Ty Prettyman

Agua Escondido

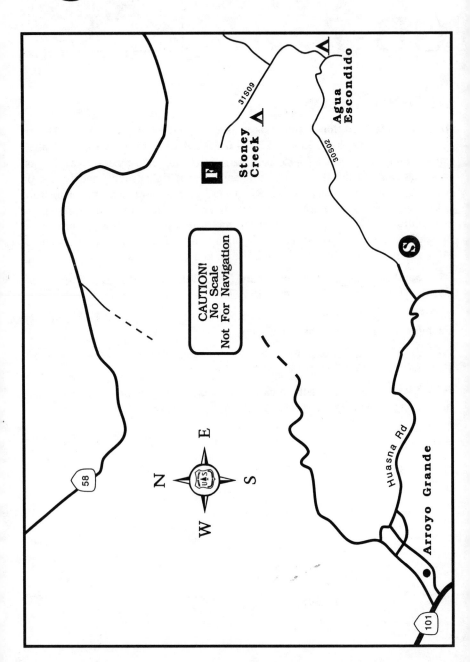

Area 1
CB-1

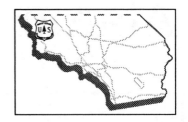

AGUA ESCONDIDO

DESCRIPTION: Here are a couple of year-around campgrounds that are far enough out to give you some privacy, but close enough for a weekend. After passing through Santa Maria (J8) on HWY 101, start looking for Mill Road in Arroyo Grande (H7). This runs into Huasna Road which you follow east to either the **Agua Escondido** (30S02) or Stony Creek Campgrounds (31S09). How do you get out? Retrace your route in. Beware of some jeep trails between **Agua Escondido** and Stony Creek. They can lead to some tough stuff!

MAPS: ACSC San Luis Obispo County (H8, G9). DeLorme p60 (C2). Forest Service Map, Los Padres National Forest (E12, F11), USGS 35120.

MILES: Dead-end. 38 miles to the locked gate past Stony Creek Campground.

AUTHORITY: Los Padres National Forest, Santa Lucia District, 1616 Carlotti Dr., Santa Maria, CA 93454 (805) 925-9538.

REMARKS: **Hi Mountain** and **La Panza** are nearby. No water at **Agua Escondido**. Best done the first time with someone who knows the area.

Alamo Mountain

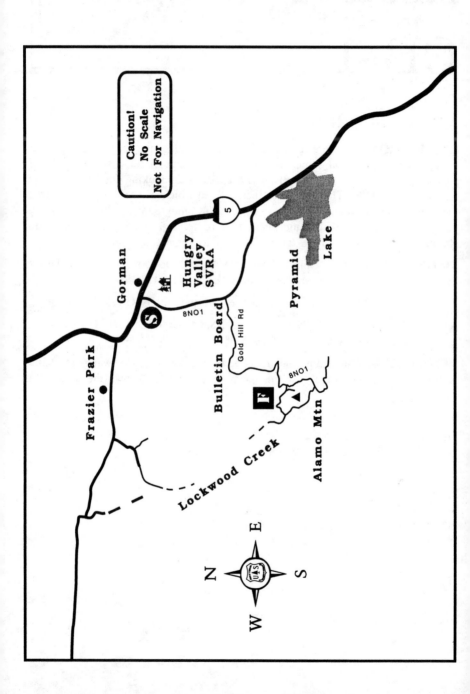

Area 1
CB-1

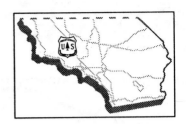

ALAMO MOUNTAIN

DESCRIPTION: This area is dangerous for two reasons. One, wrong turns lead to very tough roads. The other is the area is also used by ORVs. Be on the look out for them at all times. The first time you pass a trail sign designation board, take time to study it. This will help you determine trail difficulty. Use I-5 north to Gorman exit, go west under the freeway to a right on Frontage Road. Then go left into the Hungry Valley SVRA about 1.5 miles north of Gorman. Follow Hungry Valley Road, which is actually 8N01, and loop **Alamo Mountain**. There is a public bulletin board at an easily missed right about 4 ½ miles from the gate. This right is intermittent paved road. Your final stream crossing sends you up and around the mountain. There is no easy way down the mountain other than the way you came in. At the hard to see right (public bulletin board), either right or left will lead you out to I-5 and home.

MAPS: Mount Pinos Ranger District ORV Map (T7N, R20W). Use the detail map in the lower right hand corner to get through the Vehicular Recreation Area. ACSC LA and Vicinity (B1). ACSC Ventura County (E/F7). DeLorme p77 (C6). USGS 34118.

MILES: Dead-end. From Hungry Valley gate (paved), one loop around **Alamo Mountain** and back, 38 miles. Signs are sparse. Allow time to explore.

AUTHORITY: Mount Pinos Ranger District, Chuchupate Ranger Station, Frazier Park, CA 93225 (805) 245-3731. 24 hour recorded message (805) 245-3449. Also Hungry Valley State Vehicular Recreation Area, P. O. Box 1360, Lebec, CA 93243-1360 (805) 248-6447.

REMARKS: Beware of Miller Jeep Road, **Lockwood Creek**, Piru Creek and Yellowjacket Canyon unless you like body damage! **Lockwood, Liebre Mountain** and **Warm Springs** are all nearby trails. Subject to winter closure.

Ty Prettyman

Apache Canyon

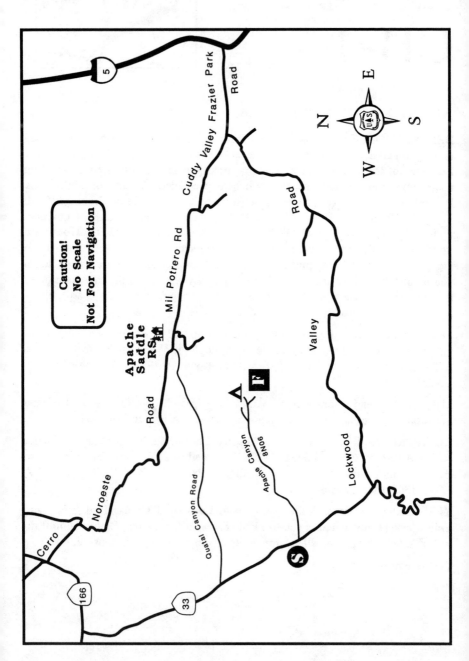

Area 1
CB-1

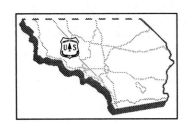

APACHE CANYON

DESCRIPTION: This is another dirt road that gets more challenging as you go along. However, water is available at Nettle Springs Campground at the end. Like **Quatal Canyon**, use I-5 headed toward Bakersfield and just beyond Gorman use the Frazier Park turn off west (C8). Follow Frazier Mountain Park, Cuddy Valley and Cerro Noroeste Roads to HWY 166/33 or use the shortcut described in **Quatal Canyon**. When you hit HWY 33, go south (left) down the road 6 miles past Quatal Canyon Road. This is the entrance to **Apache Canyon** Road (8N06) to your left (east). Since it dead-ends, your way out is behind you. Home is back either Lockwood Valley Road and I-5 or use HWY 33 all the way to HWY 101.

MAPS: ACSC Ventura County (D2, C/D3). DeLorme p76 (C2, B3). Mount Pinos Ranger District ORV Map (T8N, R24W to T8N, R23W), Los Padres National Forest Recreation Map. USGS 34118 and 34119.

MILES: Dead-end. 9 miles to the campground and the same back out to paved HWY 33.

AUTHORITY: Los Padres National Forest, Mount Pinos District, Chuchupate Ranger Station, Frazier Park, CA 93225 (805) 245-3731. Recorded message at (805) 245-3449.

REMARKS: The main road is paralleled by 4WD sandy washes designated trail 103 on the above Forest map. Give the sand a try, but don't get suckered into the motorcycle only trails that some of 103 turns into. **Quatal Canyon, Grade Valley, Santa Barbara Canyon** and **Reyes Peak** are nearby. This area is subject to flash floods. Please reclose all gates after passing through them.

Brian Wolsky

BarnettOpalMine

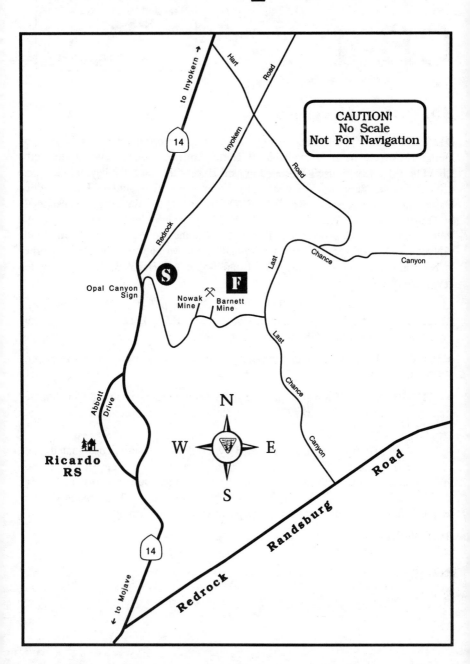

Area 2
CB-4

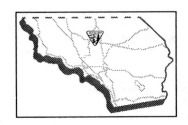

BARNETT OPAL MINE

DESCRIPTION: Not all desert mining is limited to gold and silver. Gemstones, such as fire opals, can be found if you know where to look. The Barnett and Norwalk fire opal mines give weekend gem hunters a chance to try their luck. Take Highway 14 north from Mojave (fill up on fuel and provisions before leaving town) through Red Rock Canyon State Park about 33 miles to Abbott Road at the north end of the park. Continue north past a roadside elevation sign on your right (east) and exit the highway at the "Opal Canyon" sign near the top of a four-lane uphill section. The dirt road is well traveled and marked with a series of arrows or "opal" signs. Follow the signs correctly and you will end up at the Norwalk Mine (lower claims) in about three miles. The Barnett's mine is about a mile further. Follow the signs to "upper claims and Barnett's". Dick and Shirley Barnett have a collection of polished fire opals that they can usually be persuaded to display. They are exceptionally helpful in showing first-timers what to look for and how to dig. Mining fee is $2 per person. The mines are open weekends only. Camping is permitted at the mines with owners' permission, and on BLM lands surrounding the claims. Bring your own drinking water and tools. Suggested tools are: hammer, chisel, small shovel, diagonal wire cutters (for removing opals from rock matrix), gloves, bucket or sack for opal bearing rocks and a small container for the opals. Home is back out the way you came in.

MAPS: ACSC Kern County (D18/19). Desert Access Guide #7 (A2). Hileman's #1 (no coordinates), DeLorme p65 (A7) and mine symbol not shown at Barnetts. USGS 35117.

MILES: Dead end. 4 miles from HWY 14 and back.

AUTHORITY: Bureau of Land Management, 300 South Richmond Road, Ridgecrest, CA 93555 (619) 375-7125.

REMARKS: More El Paso Mountain adventure. Camping is permitted on public lands but no water is available and a fire permit is required. Nearby trails are **Steam Well**, **Last Chance Canyon** and **Burro Schmidt's Tunnel**.

Roger Vargo

150

Blair Valley

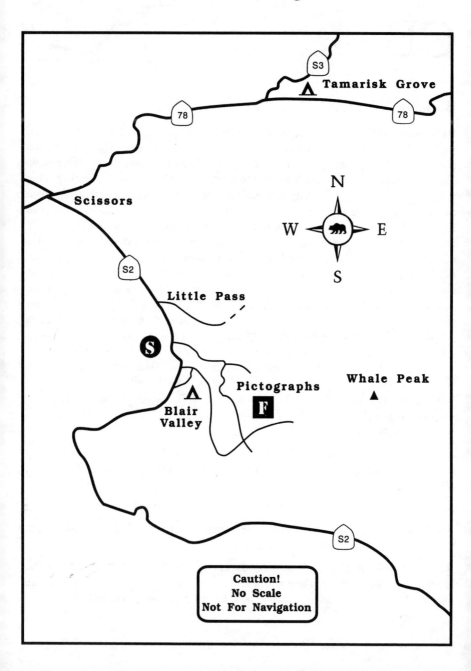

Area 9
CB-36

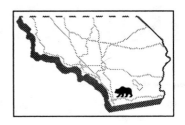

BLAIR VALLEY

DESCRIPTION: How about towing the 4X with the motorhome, setting up a nice camp and exploring from there? If this sounds like your thing, **Blair Valley** is for you. The abandoned Marshall South home, bedrock mortars, pictographs (now mostly vandalized), the Foot and Walker Pass where stagecoach passengers had to help push the stage over the pass, and a foot trail to Whale Peak are all accessible from here. I'll lead you from Borrego Springs (C12), but it's easier to find your way directly there from Julian. South out of Borrego Springs on HWY S3, to right (west) on HWY 78, to left (southeast) on HWY S2. seven miles out S2 is the turnoff left (east) into the massive Little Pass campground. I'll give no specifics, but within a five mile arc to the east are all of the above. You're camped so close to the road, you know the way back.

MAPS: ACSC San Diego County (F12). Anza-Borrego Desert State Park map (F3/4). Highly recommended is Lindsay's *The Anza-Borrego Desert Region* (ISBN 911824-67-7) book and map (trip 4B). DeLorme p115 (D5). Desert Access Guide #19 (B/C6). USGS 33116.

MILES: Loops and dead-ends. 11 miles of trails in the area.

AUTHORITY: Anza-Borrego Desert State Park, P. O. Box 428, Borrego Springs, CA 92004 (619) 767-5311.

REMARKS: First stop should be the visitor center where you can get the Park map. Late spring is best since early spring can put you in a very wet, Blair Dry Lake. Remember, look, but don't take anything from the Park. I hesitate to tell you the very dangerous **Pinyon Mountain** is nearby.

Dick Cumiskey

Box Canyon

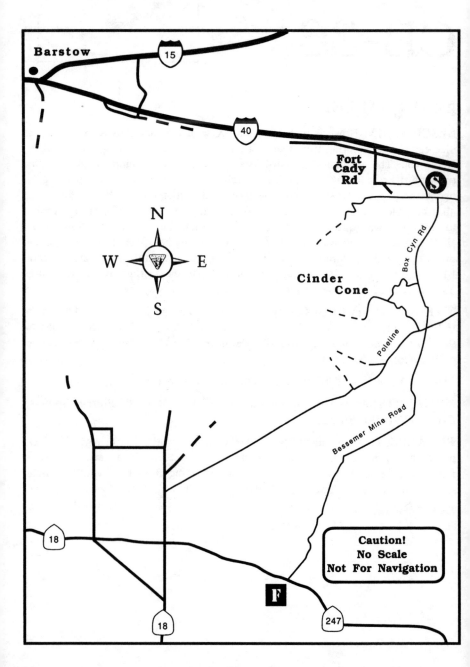

Barstow

15

40

Fort
Cady
Rd

S

N

W E

S

Cinder
Cone

Box Cyn Rd

Poleline

Bessemer Mine Road

18

Caution!
No Scale
Not For Navigation

F

18

247

Area 6
CB-17

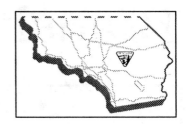

BOX CANYON

DESCRIPTION: If you were successful on **Cinder Cone**, you'll like this. It's just rough enough to be fun. Remember there are five trails to help you learn Lucerne Valley. This one familiarizes you with the northern section. Best to go out I-15, refuel in Barstow (E3), then go east on I-40 to Fort Cady Road. Use old HWY 66, south of the freeway, east for about three miles to a dirt road south. In two miles you intersect a better dirt road for a dogleg (that's a quick left then right) onto Box Canyon Road south. About eight miles down this road you come to a rock with silver paint on it. This identifies a not-shown-on-any-map turn off up to the **Cinder Cone** area (F5). We continue on south, under the power lines, past the old Bessemer Mine, and 6 miles after the lines you merge with several other roads. You want to go southwest on what is now Bessemer Road which takes you out to HWY 247. Right on 247 to straight on HWY 18 leads to I-15 in Victorville. Home is south.

MAPS: ACSC San Bernardino County (E5, G5) and they left "Box" off Box Canyon. DeLorme p83 (B4), p96 (A3). USGS 34116 and 34117, Desert Access Guide, start on #11 (E3) and finish on #14 (C/D2).

MILES: Loop. 32 miles from paved HWY 66 to HWY 247. Plan on more.

AUTHORITY: San Bernardino County, private and BLM, California Desert Information Center, 831 Barstow Road, Barstow, CA 92311 (619) 256-8313.

REMARKS: **Stoddard Well Road, Cinder Cone, Camp Rock Road** and **Dry Lake Loop** are the other 4 trails in Lucerne Valley. Go well prepared for extra time and miles in this area. Use the many microwave towers for orientation. Do not enter the Twentynine Palms Marine Corps Base property to the east of the pole line road.

Bradshaw Trail

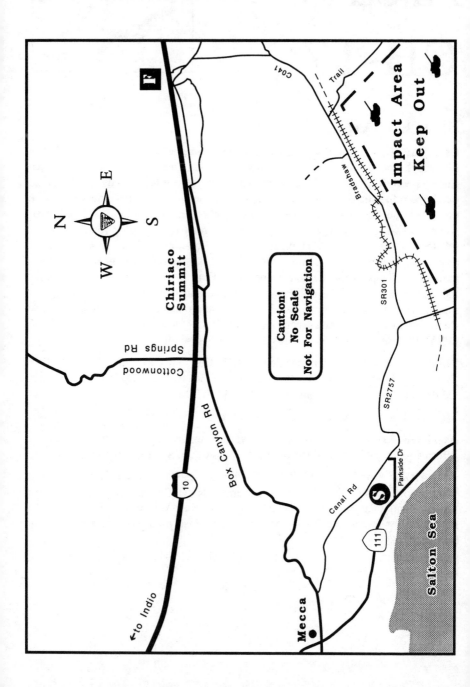

Area 10
CB-39

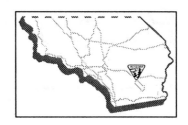

BRADSHAW TRAIL

DESCRIPTION: The **Bradshaw Trail** was the quick way to get from San Bernardino to the Colorado River gold rush area in 1862. We aren't going for gold and we won't use the entire trail, but we'll have fun! Like **Painted Canyon**, go out I-10, pass up Palm Springs, and in Indio take HWY 111 southeast to the Salton Sea Park Headquarters entrance. Across from the park headquarters entrance sign is Parkside Drive. Go left (east) on Parkside for 1½ miles then left on Desert Aire for ½ miles to the Canal Road. Turn right (east) on the Canal Road and go approximately 10 miles to Drop 24 (Drop 24 is painted on the bridge). You pick up the **Bradshaw Trail** after crossing Drop 24. About 100 yards up the trail is a BLM **Bradshaw Trail** Marker (SR310) and if you cross the RR tracks on Canal Road, you are about a mile too far. Several trails work. You're on the right one when you pass under the RR tracks twice, at about 3 and 5 miles. In 11 miles get off the **Bradshaw Trail** by not making its right. Don't cross the RR tracks here. You should be swinging up to the northeast and not southeast. Stay with the RR tracks all the way to I-10 at Red Cloud Mine Road. The BLM calls this C041. Home is to the west (left) on I-10.

MAPS: ACSC Riverside County (F/G16, E19). DeLorme p108 (D1), p109 (C5), Sidekick (Orocopia) with no coordinates. Desert Access Guide #18 (A6, D5). USGS 33115.

MILES: Loop. 32 miles from Parkside Drive to I-10.

AUTHORITY: BLM, Palm Springs-South Coast Resource Area Office, 63-500 Garnet Ave, P.O. Box 2000, N. Palm Springs, CA 92258-2000 (619) 251-0812.

REMARKS: On this trip, check out where you might think the toughy **Red Canyon** is. Be aware the property to the right of the Bradshaw Trail is an active gunnery range. Keep out. **Coachella Canal, Painted Canyon, Corn Springs** and **Red Canyon** are nearby.

Burro Schmidt's

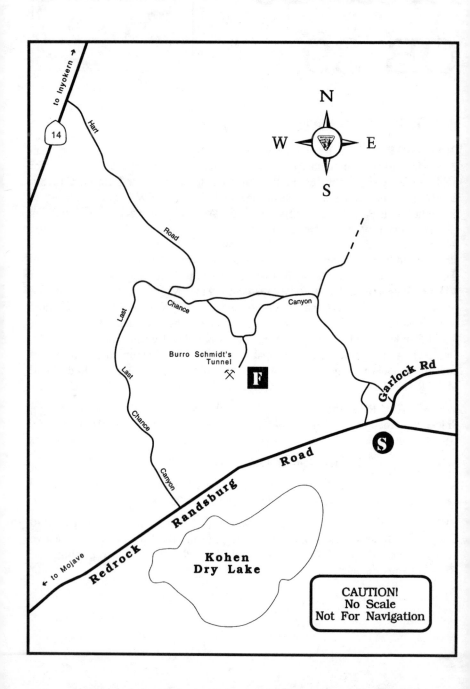

Area 2
CB-4

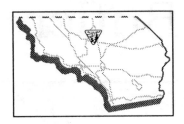

BURRO SCHMIDT'S TUNNEL

DESCRIPTION: William Henry Schmidt came to California in 1894, supposedly with only a short time to live. After prospecting for a time on the Kern River, he eventually moved to the El Paso Mountains, lived another sixty years and managed to dig a 2087-foot tunnel through a mountain. Schmidt used hand labor and a team of burros in his work and acquired the nickname of "Burro" Schmidt. His tunnel, now owned by Tonie Sieger, is open to visitors. Like many sites in the El Pasos, there are numerous routes to the famous tunnel. The easy route, suitable for many 2WD vehicles is from Mesquite Canyon, eleven miles east of Highway 14 off the Redrock-Randsburg Road, then the Garlock Road. Follow the "Tunnel" signs up the canyon to Schmidt's place. If you're in the El Pasos, find the Last Chance Canyon signpost, then go east about a mile and take the right, signed, fork of the road. Follow this road gradually uphill another 1.5 miles and make a right turn at a pair of 55-gallon drums also marked "tunnel". The parking lot, Schmidt's cabin and tunnel are less than a mile beyond. A small donation, though not required, is appreciated to help Tonie maintain the property. Bring a flashlight if you plan to explore the tunnel interior. Home is back the way you came in or on to explore more of the area.

MAPS: ACSC Kern County (D/E19/20), Desert Access Guide #7 (B/C2). Hileman's #1 (no coordinates). DeLorme p66 (A1) and mine symbol not shown. *Exploring the Ghost Town Desert* by Roberta Martin Starry (book, p108). USGS 35117.

MILES: Loop. 16 miles from Garlock Road via Mesquite Canyon. From Last Chance signpost to tunnel, 3.5 miles.

AUTHORITY: Bureau of Land Management, 300 South Richmond Road, Ridgecrest, CA 93555 (619) 375-7125.

REMARKS: Schmidt's tunnel is just one excuse to visit the El Paso Mountains. Camping is permitted on public lands but no water is available and a fire permit is required. Nearby trails are **Steam Well**, **Last Chance Canyon** and **Barnett Opal Mine**.

Roger Vargo

Butler Peak

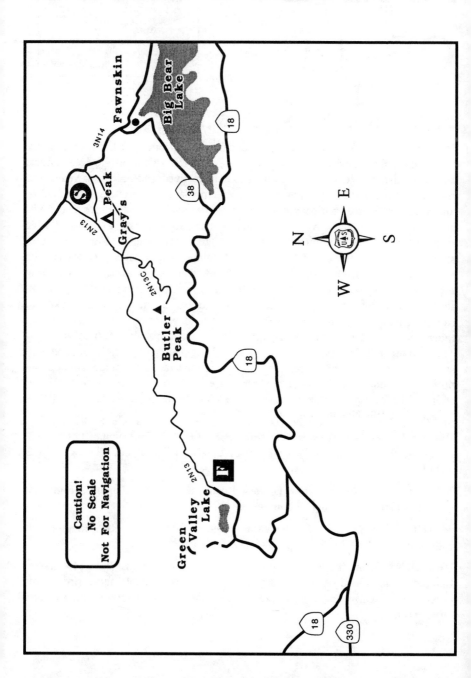

Area 5
CB-14

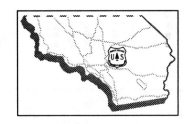

BUTLER PEAK

DESCRIPTION: For a short drive, the lookout at **Butler Peak** offers a 360 degree view of the San Bernardino Mountains. It's only topped by a few mountains to the southeast. Hiking is required to reach the top. Take all your maps and navigational equipment and allow about half a day to figure out what's what. At the north side of Big Bear Lake is Fawnskin. Starting out paved, take 3N14 to either 2N68 or 2N13 west. Best to follow Rim of the World Drive signs. Your objective is to pass Gray's Peak Campground and make a left (south) on 2N13C which leads to the lookout. Back down this road to where you made the left leaves you the opportunity to go back the same way or take more of 2N13 right (west) to pavement at Green Valley Lake. Just follow the traffic down hill for home.

MAPS: San Bernardino National Forest, San Bernardino Meridian (G2/3, F3). ACSC LA and Vicinity (E17, E/F16). DeLorme p96 (B1), p95 (B/C7). Sidekick (Big Bear Lake) with no coordinates. Desert Access Guide start on #14 (A4), finish not shown on Desert Access Guides. USGS 34116 and 34117.

MILES: Loop. 18 miles from Fawnskin to Green Valley Lake including the paved start and finish, and the trip to the peak.

AUTHORITY: San Bernardino National Forest, Arrowhead District, P. O. Box 7, Rim Forest, CA 92378 (909) 337-2444. Also, Big Bear District, P. O. Box 290, Fawnskin, CA 92333 (909) 866-3437.

REMARKS: Best avoided during ski season. Snow makes a trip to the peak dangerous. Carry chains. **Holcomb Creek** and **Holcomb Valley** are nearby and cautiously check **Crab Flats**.

Cajon Mountain

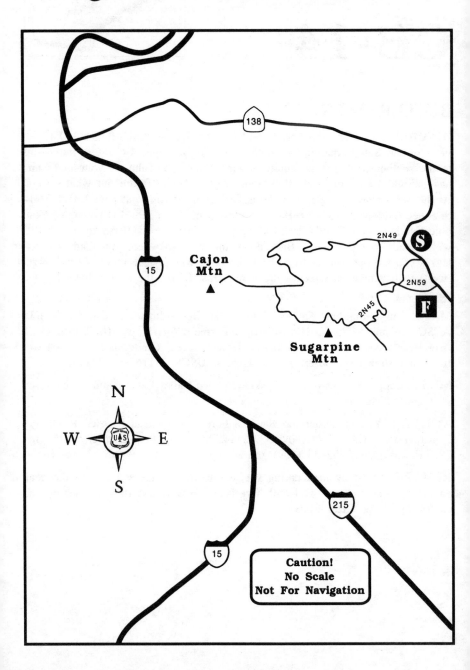

Area 5
CB-14

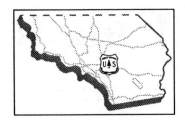

CAJON MOUNTAIN

DESCRIPTION: With this and the other two listed below, you will be real clear on the difference between the Cajon Pass, Cajon Summit and **Cajon Mountain**, if that's important to you. Go toward Vegas on I-15 and then east on HWY 138. Just as you drop down into the streambed, before the entrance to Silverwood Lake, turn right (west) on 2N49. About half way through the trip, take the optional trip to the top of **Cajon Mountain**. Just past the **Sugarpine Mountain** peak, take the left on 2N45. At the confusing intersection of 2N49, 2N45 and 2N59, continue on down 2N59. This completes the trail at paved 138 only about 2 miles from where you left it. Home is, gosh, let's just spend the rest of the day at the lake!

MAPS: San Bernardino National Forest, San Bernardino Meridian (C/D2/3). ACSC LA and Vicinity, no trail shown, peak at (E13). DeLorme p95 (B5). USGS 34117.

MILES: Loop. 16 miles from paved 138 to 138.

AUTHORITY: San Bernardino National Forest, Cajon Ranger District, Star Route Box 100, Fontana, CA 92335 (909) 887-2576.

REMARKS: Although described as 3 trails, use this one along with **Cleghorn Mountain** and **Sugarpine Mountain** to fill a very long day. **Pilot Rock** is also nearby.

Calcite Mine

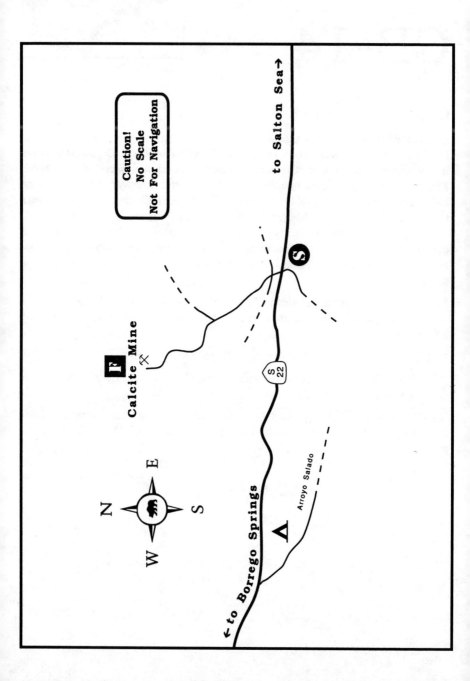

Area 9
CB-36

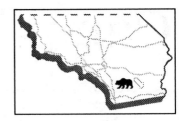

CALCITE MINE

DESCRIPTION: Some bad info about the WW II Norden bomb site and calcite keeps 'em coming into this steep, cliffy drive. 4WD, low, low recommended. Repeating from other ABDSP trails, just get to Borrego Springs (C12). About 12 ½ miles east of Peg Leg Smith Monument (C13), on HWY S22, is the not so obvious dirt road to the **Calcite Mine** on the left (north). If you get confused on the drive in, remember you don't want to drive in a wash. You are up and down, in and out of the washes. When you're there you won't know it because the mines aren't mines, just slices into the hill. The calcite is the thick, more or less clear, glassy, mica looking stuff. If you're spending the night in Borrego Springs, home is back west on S22. Otherwise, go east on S22 when you exit the **Calcite Mine** to HWY 86 left (north) to I-10 for home.

MAPS: ACSC San Diego County (C15). Anza-Borrego Desert State Park map (C6). DeLorme p116 (B1). Desert Access Guide #20 (A3). Highly recommended is Lindsay's *The Anza-Borrego Desert Region* (ISBN 911824-67-7) book and map (trip 3C). USGS 33116.

MILES: Dead-end. 4 miles, S22 and back.

AUTHORITY: Anza-Borrego Desert State Park, P. O. Box 428, Borrego Springs, CA 92004 (619) 767-5311.

REMARKS: First stop should be the visitor center where you can get the Park map. Remember, look, but don't take anything from the Park. **Fonts Point, Vista Del Mal Pais, Cut Across Trail, 17 Palms** and **Rockhouse Canyon** are nearby.

Mike Smith

Camp Rock Road

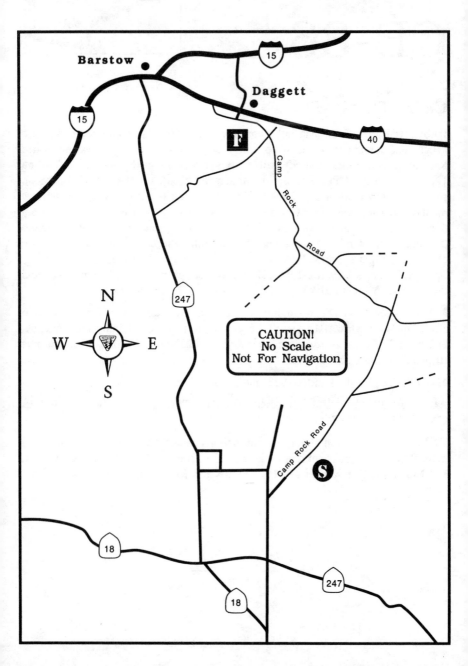

Area 6
CB-17

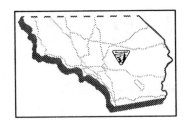

CAMP ROCK ROAD

DESCRIPTION: This trail is another of the five that helps you learn Lucerne Valley. It goes through the center. Check out the Roy Rogers, Dale Evans Museum in Victorville (F2), off I-15 before you head east on HWY 18. Use HWY 247 east to paved **Camp Rock Road** left (north). Be sure to catch the bend in **Camp Rock Road** at Harbor Road. About 2 miles out it turns to dirt which you follow to the I-40 on ramp in Daggett. Be alert to the abrupt left turn (northwest) the road makes 13 miles out the dirt. Also, the name changes to Pendleton Road near the on ramp. Home is west on I-40 to a south turn on I-15.

MAPS: ACSC San Bernardino County (F4, E4). DeLorme p82 (D2, B1). Desert Access Guide #11 (B/C6, B2). USGS 34116 and 34117.

MILES: Loop. 30 miles from the start of dirt on Camp Rock Road to I-40 in Daggett.

AUTHORITY: San Bernardino County, private and BLM California Desert Information Center, 831 Barstow Road, Barstow, CA 92311 (619) 256-8313.

REMARKS: Consider these trails spring-time adventures. The summer-time is hot, dry and windy. **Stoddard Well Road, Box Canyon, Cinder Cone** and **Dry Lake Loop** are the other 4 trails in Lucerne Valley.

Camuesa Road

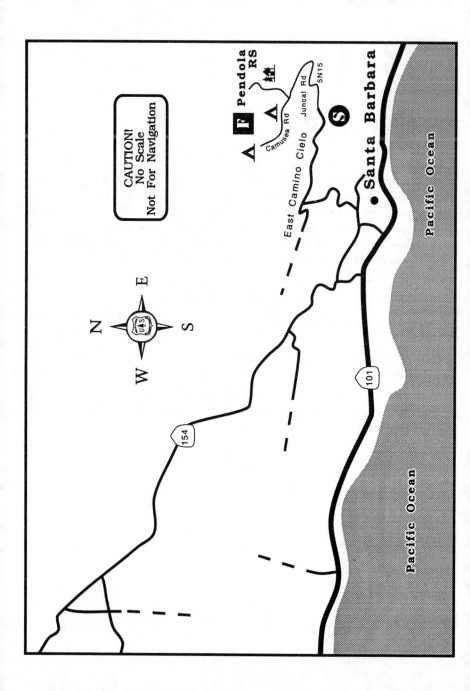

Area 1
CB-1

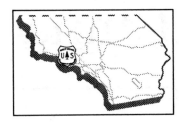

CAMUESA ROAD

DESCRIPTION: Santa Barbara (K12) is a nice clean place. Even the dirt roads are clean and nice. That's not to say you won't need a car wash after you get back, but you won't have rivers of mud flowing out of your driveway. Your objective is to get headed north on Gibraltar Road. Try using Mission off the freeway, to a right at Mountain Drive which virtually turns into Gibraltar Road. Follow this to a right (east) on East Camino Cielo. (Remember West Camino Cielo on the **Refugio Pass** trail?) East Camino Cielo takes you directly to the dirt, first Juncal then **Camuesa Road** (5N15). About 8 miles into this, you reach a "Y" at the Pendola Ranger Station. The road to the right (5N16) dead ends in 3 miles and left (still 5N15) 5 miles. Home is backwards.

MAPS: ACSC Santa Barbara County (J13, H13/14). DeLorme p89 (A7), p76 (D1). Los Padres National Forest (L19). USGS 34119 and 34120.

MILES: Dead-end. 33 miles including both dead-ends and back to paved East Camino Cielo.

AUTHORITY: Los Padres National Forest, Santa Barbara District, Los Prietos, Star Route, Santa Barbara, CA 93105 (805) 967-3481.

REMARKS: There is a picnic area out the right dead-end (Agua Caliente Road (5N16) that makes a nice break from downtown Santa Barbara. No nearby trails, but consider taking Camino Cielo westward and do **Refugio Pass** backwards.

China Lake

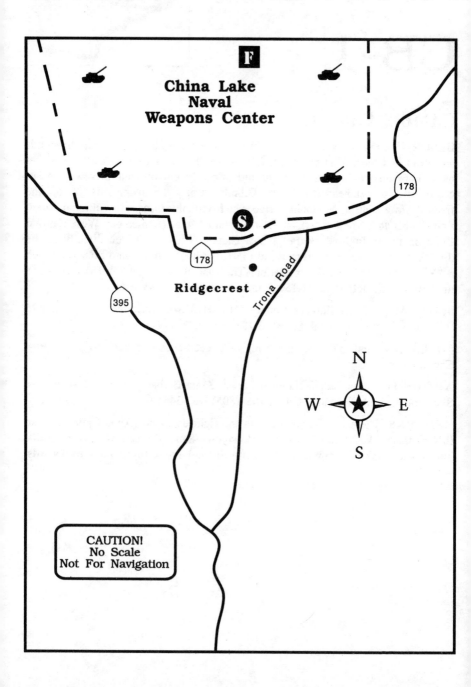

Area 3
CB-7

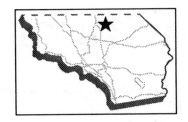

CHINA LAKE

DESCRIPTION: Indian rock art at its best, and guided at that! Contact the Maturango Museum (below) and make arrangements for the tour of the China Lake Naval Weapons Center. Passenger cars allowed, but I felt more in style in my 4X. Beside, I got to use my CB on the base by acting as the sweep. What is Indian rock art? 100 to 6500 year old pictures chipped into the patina (desert varnish on the rocks) of which we know next to nothing about the exact meaning. Other highlights include geology, historic info, hunting blinds, rock circles, rock shelters, flaking sites and bed rock mortars. The LA Times had an article (March 3, 1986) by Julie D. Taylor entitled, "Ancient Rock Art Stirs Imagination". Be patient with the Navy's occasional rescheduling of tours. It took me 6 months to finally get in. If you're a skier, you know home is south on 395. If you're not, it's still the same direction.

MAPS: ACSC San Bernardino County (B1). ACSC Kern County (B21). DeLorme p52 (C2). Desert Access Guide #4 (D5). USGS 35117.

MILES: Dead-end. 85 miles from the Weapon Center entrance, round trip.

AUTHORITY: Tour arrangements made through the Maturango Museum, 100 East Las Flores, P. O. Box 1776, Ridgecrest, CA 93555 (619) 375-6900.

REMARKS: Make a weekend out of it by staying over night. Get info from the Chamber of Commerce, 301 S. China Lake Blvd., P. O. Box 771, Ridgecrest, CA 93555-0771 (619) 375-8331. Nearby trails are **Barnett Opal Mine, Last Chance Canyon** and **Burro Schmidt's Tunnel**.

Cinder Cone

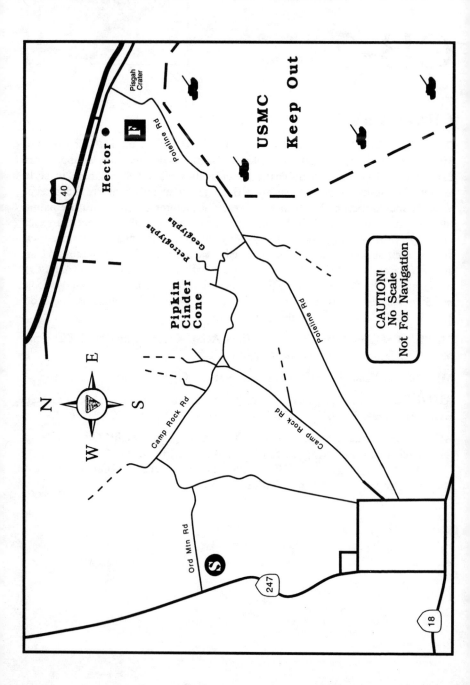

Area 6
CB-17

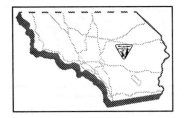

CINDER CONE

DESCRIPTION: This is one of five trails that help you learn Lucerne Valley. It crosses from west to east. Like **Camp Rock Road**, off I-15, head east on HWY 18 to HWY 247 north (left). Follow paved HWY 247 15 plus miles to unsigned, graded dirt, Ord Mountain Road for a right (east). In 10 to 11 miles you meet **Camp Rock Road** for a right (southeast). When Camp Rock makes its sharp right, go straight, you may be confused, but be confident the main road leads to the Pipkin **Cinder Cone** (F5) where lava is still mined. In this section, as you drive through an inconspicuous area with dark rock on your left, look for petroglyphs within 100 feet of the road. The road and directions are rough for the next 4 miles. East for about 1 ½ miles takes you to the rougher, 3 mile run that goes southeast between two good sized buttes and out to a poleline road. If you're lucky enough to get lost where the road dead-ends at some pipes (both ends of the canyon), take the hike into this rock art laden area. Lost near the fences? They enclose geoglyphs (vague, giant rock symbols on the ground). Left on the better poleline road leads you out to old HWY 66. Go left to Hector and I-40 west to home.

MAPS: ACSC San Bernardino County (F4, E6). DeLorme p82 (C1), p83 (B5/6). USGS 34116, Desert Access Guide #11 (A4, F/G3).

MILES: Loop. 44 miles from paved HWY 247 to ol' HWY 66, but plan on more.

AUTHORITY: San Bernardino County, private and BLM, California Desert Information Center, 831 Barstow Road, Barstow, CA 92311 (619) 256-8313.

REMARKS: Stoddard Well Road, Box Canyon, Camp Rock Road and **Dry Lake Loop** are the other 4 trails in Lucerne Valley. Go well prepared for extra time and miles in the area from the **Cinder Cone** to the Poleline Road. Use the many microwave towers for orientation. Do not enter the Twentynine Palms Marine Corps Base property to the east of the pole line road throughout the last part of your journey.

Clark Grade

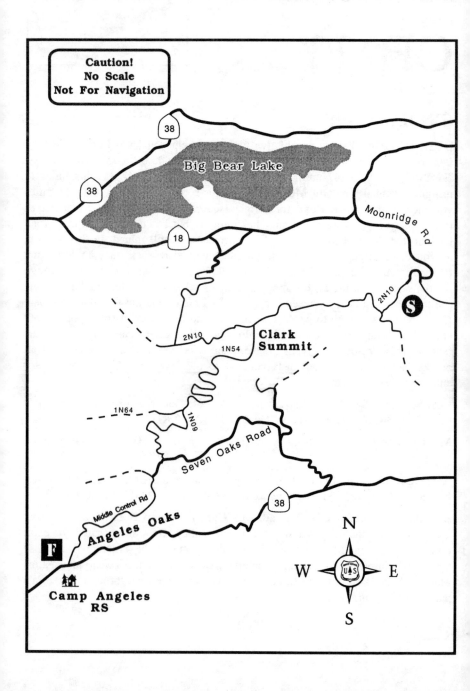

**Caution!
No Scale
Not For Navigation**

38

Big Bear Lake

38

Moonridge Rd

18

2N10

2N10

S

1N54

Clark
Summit

1N64

1N09

Seven Oaks Road

Middle Control Rd

38

Angeles Oaks

F

N

W ⊕ E

S

Camp Angeles
RS

Area 5
CB-14

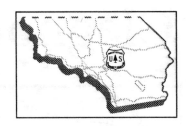

CLARK GRADE

DESCRIPTION: Moderate roads and some decision making let you practice navigating close to home. When you get to the summit, hike more or less south, southwest to the rock outcropping that will give you a spectacular view of the trails you will be going down. Wind your way around the south shore of Big Bear Lake on HWY 18 and make a right on Moonridge Road. At the end of the golf course and at the zoo, make a right (west) on Country Club. With a little attention, you should flow right into the Skyline Ridge Road (2N10). Stay on this to a left (south) on 1N54 at **Clark Grade**. If you goof, 2N10 takes you back down to Big Bear and HWY 18. Pass up the right on 1N64. 1N54 will take you down to an intersection with 1N09 for a left. Then a right on the main road will take you out to HWY 38 at Angeles Oaks. Home is down and out HWY 38, through Redlands to I-10.

MAPS: San Bernardino National Forest, San Bernardino Meridian, (H3, G4). ACSC LA and Vicinity, all trails not shown, summit at (F17). DeLorme p96 (C2, C1), they call Radford both Radford and Sugarloaf. Sidekick (Big Bear). Desert Access Guide #14 start at (B4), finish not shown on Desert Access Guides. USGS 34116 and 34117.

MILES: Loop. 19 miles from Country Club to HWY 38 at Angeles Oaks.

AUTHORITY: San Bernardino National Forest, Big Bear District, P. O. Box 290, Fawnskin, CA 92333 (909) 866-3437. San Gorgonio Ranger District, 34701 Mill Creek Road, Mentone, CA.

REMARKS: Allow time to explore several routes. If a downhill trail starts getting wet, stop. One trail leads into a quagmire. This is not the correct route. Nearby is **Wildhorse Meadow** or on the other side of the lake are **Holcomb Valley**, **Holcomb Creek** and very rough **Crab Flats**. 2N10 and 1N54 are closed during the winter due to snow and the entire area is extra treacherous during this season.

Cleghorn Mtn

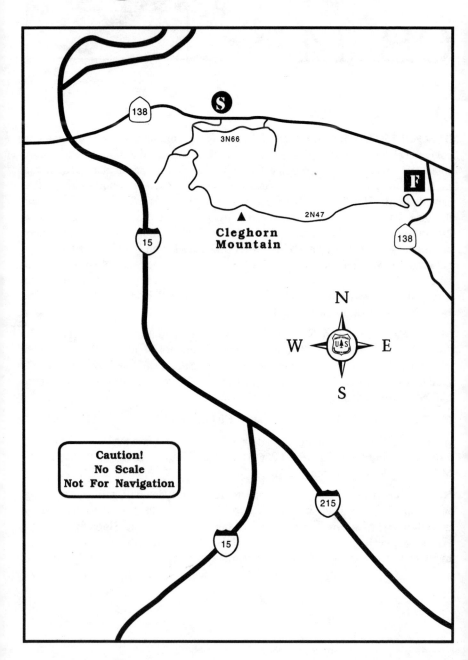

Area 5
CB-14

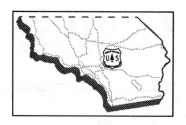

CLEGHORN MOUNTAIN

DESCRIPTION: Just like **Cajon Mountain**, go toward Vegas on I-15 and then east on HWY 138. When you are real close to the railroad tracks again, start looking for your turn to the right. Road designation is 3N22 and is just beyond the real Cajon Pass. Follow this road up toward **Cleghorn Mountain**. At the first major intersection you go right (actually straight). This is 2N47. This leads you past the mountain and out to HWY 138. Continue on down 138 for about 2 miles and you're staged for **Cajon Mountain**. Home is north (left), transitioning to west on 138 and I-5 south.

MAPS: San Bernardino National Forest, San Bernardino Meridian, (C2, D2). ACSC LA and Vicinity, no trail shown, peak at (E13). DeLorme p95 (B4, B5). USGS 34117.

MILES: Loop. 13 miles, from paved 138 to 138.

AUTHORITY: San Bernardino National Forest, Cajon District Ranger, Star Route Box 100, Fontana, CA 92335 (909) 887-2576.

REMARKS: Although described as 3 trails, use this one along with **Cajon Mountain** and **Sugarpine Mountain** to fill a very long day. **Pilot Rock** is also nearby.

Coachella Canal

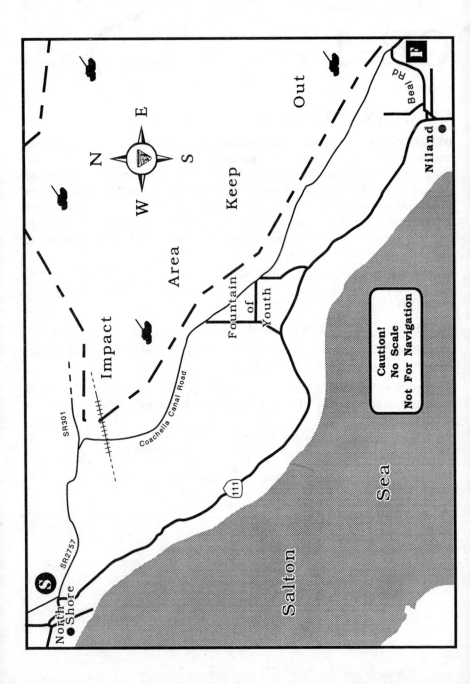

Area 10 CB-39

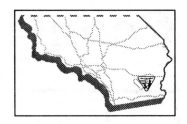

COACHELLA CANAL

DESCRIPTION: Just to plug the gap between **Sand Hills** and either **Red Canyon** or **Bradshaw Trail**, I've included **Coachella Canal**. This also gives you a quick way off the canal road for those other trails. So like either one, go out I-10, pass up Palm Springs, and in Indio take HWY 111 southeast. This time pass up Mecca and go to North Shore (A2). Now, it really doesn't matter, but use Bay Drive northeast (left) to Club View left to Windlass left to Compass right to 72nd right to the canal road. Once into North Shore, you want to head mostly east until you hit the canal road. Sometimes I look for a tan church. The wash behind the church intersects the canal road at a siphon (canal gate). At the canal road (BLM SR2757), turn right (southeast) and in 7 or 8 miles you will pass the Bradshaw Trail (BLM SR301). Continue on over or under the RR tracks and hard as it will be, pass up the pavement at the Fountain of Youth Spa. Roughly 14 miles more of canal dirt road takes you to another paved section where you make a right (southwest) on Beal Road. Beal Road takes you out to HWY 111 in Niland and home is north or right.

MAPS: ACSC Imperial County (A2, C6). Desert Access Guide #18, start shown at (A6), finish shown on #20 (F3/4). DeLorme p108 (D2), p117 (B6). USGS 33115.

MILES: Loop. 34 miles from 72nd Street to Beal Road.

AUTHORITY: BLM El Centro Resource Area Office, 1661 S. Fourth St., El Centro, CA 92243. (619) 352-5842. BLM Palm Springs Resource Area Office, 63-500 Garnet Ave., P.O. Box 2000, North Palm Springs, CA 92258-2000 (619) 251-0812.

REMARKS: There is a large sign at the entrance to North Shore. Don't let my confusing directions make you think it's hard to get to the canal road. From the RR track crossing on, to your left (northeast), is an active gunnery range. Keep out. **Bradshaw Trail, Sand Hills, Painted Canyon** and **Red Canyon** are nearby.

Coon Hollow

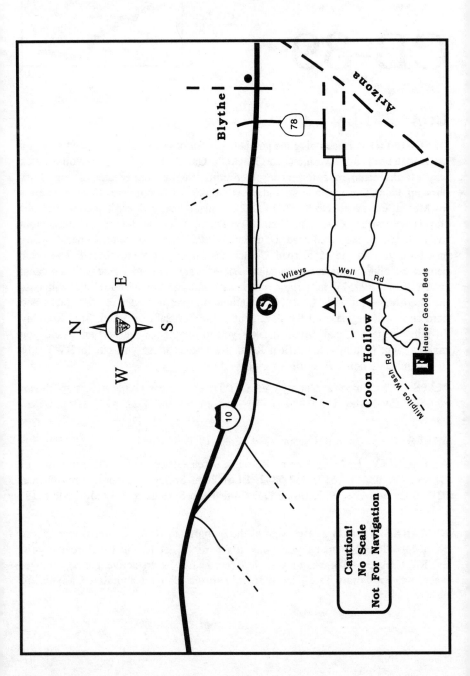

Blythe

Arizona

78

Wileys Well Rd

Coon Hollow

Hauser Geode Beds

Milpitos Wash Rd

F

N
E
S
W

10

Caution!
No Scale
Not For Navigation

Area 10 CB-39

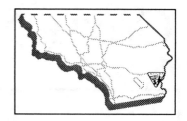

COON HOLLOW

DESCRIPTION: If you want to collect some of those round, hollow rocks with the crystals inside, this is the place. The Hauser Geode Beds (B/C10) is both legal to dig and continues to roll them out. Pretend you're going to **Wiley's Well** by driving east on I-10, almost to Blythe, for a right (south) on Wiley's Well Road. Pass up the well and go south another three miles to the **Coon Hollow** campground. After you make camp, continue south again to Milpitos Wash Road. Go right (west) and in 4½ miles turn left (south) on an unnamed road. Low, low will get you through a couple of steep, up and down dips at the diggin's. The beds lie about 4½ miles south in some small hills. This area is tough to find. Wait around for passer-bys to help or lead you out there. Since this trail is a dead-end, do a 180 to get home.

MAPS: ACSC Imperial County (A10, B/C9/10). DeLorme p110 (D3), p118 (A2/3), Desert Access Guide #21 (B1, A2). USGS 33114 and 33115.

MILES: Dead-end. 42 miles from I-10 to I-10.

AUTHORITY: BLM El Centro Resource Area Office, 1661 South Fourth St., El Centro, CA 92243 (619) 352-5842.

REMARKS: This area is popular with rockhounds. Before attempting to find the beds on your own, stop in a few camps and ask for help. Not impossible to find, but challenging. **Wiley's Well, Bradshaw Trail, Corn Springs** and **Graham Pass** are nearby.

Corn Springs

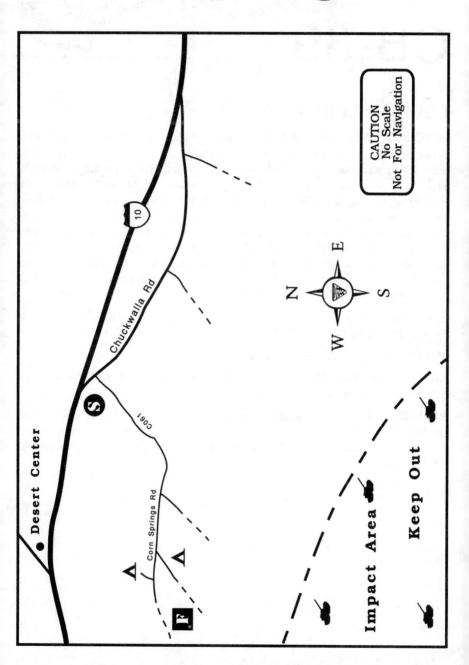

Area 10
CB-39

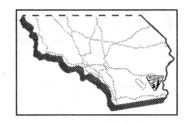

CORN SPRINGS

DESCRIPTION: This is actually an oasis located in a deep canyon. 60 native palms, 10,000 year old petroglyphs, 14 primitive camp sites, vault toilets, picnic tables, grills, water and you wonder what's out in the desert. Like so may other trails, head toward Palm Springs on I-10, continue over the Chiriaco Summit and pass Desert Center to Chuckwalla Road south. Within ¾ mile, make a right (southwest) on Corn Springs Road (BLM C061). 7 miles later you're in the campground. 5 miles later, you're on rough road. My recommended way out is the way in. It is, however, possible to get clear through to Red Cloud Mine Road, but not recommended for the inexperienced. Use I-10 to get home regardless of your dirt route.

MAPS: ACSC Riverside County (E22, E/F20). DeLorme p110 (C1), p109 (C6). Desert Access Guide #18 (G/H4/5, G5). USGS 33115.

MILES: Dead-end. 26 miles round trip back to Chuckwalla Road.

AUTHORITY: BLM Palm Springs-South Coast Resource Area, 63-500 Garnet Ave, P.O. Box 2000, N. Palm Springs, CA 92258-2000, (619) 251-0812.

REMARKS: Painted Canyon, Red Canyon and **Bradshaw Trail** are nearby. Best to avoid the heat of late spring through late fall. Carry much water under any circumstance.

Covington Flat

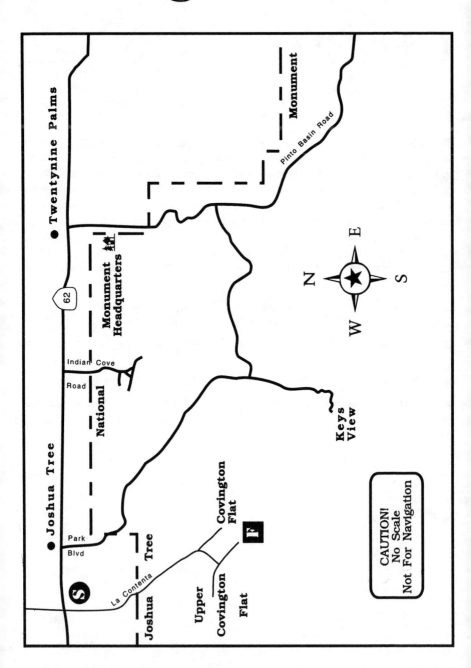

Area 8
CB-33

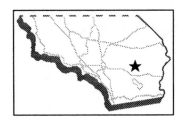

COVINGTON FLAT

DESCRIPTION: I like to poke my nose into every corner of an area. This is a way to look at the little used, northwest corner of Joshua Tree National Monument. Use I-10 east toward Palm Springs, but pass up HWY 111 and take HWY 62 north. Past Yucca Valley, in Paradise Valley look for your next right on La Contenta Road. If you blink, it's called Yucca Mesa on the other side. South takes you right into the Covington Flat Picnic area at the end of the road. Back 1/2 mile you could have turned right (southwest) again into the Upper Covington Flat area. Since further south is a Wilderness Area, get back home the way you came in.

MAPS: ACSC Riverside County (B13). DeLorme p97 (D5/6). Joshua Tree National Monument brochure, no coordiantes. Desert Access Guide #14 (F5/6, F/G6). USGS 34116.

MILES: Dead-end. 20 miles round trip to the upper flats and back to HWY 62.

AUTHORITY: Joshua Tree National Monument, 74485 National Monument Drive, Twentynine Palms, CA 92277 (619) 367-7511.

REMARKS: Although there are many roads in the vicinity, remember the Monument is a Wilderness Area which limits vehicular travel. Nearby trails are **Desert Queen**, **Squaw Tank** and **Gold Park**. Don't cheat yourself out of the beauty of the springtime desert bloom. Go in mid to late spring.

Coyote Canyon

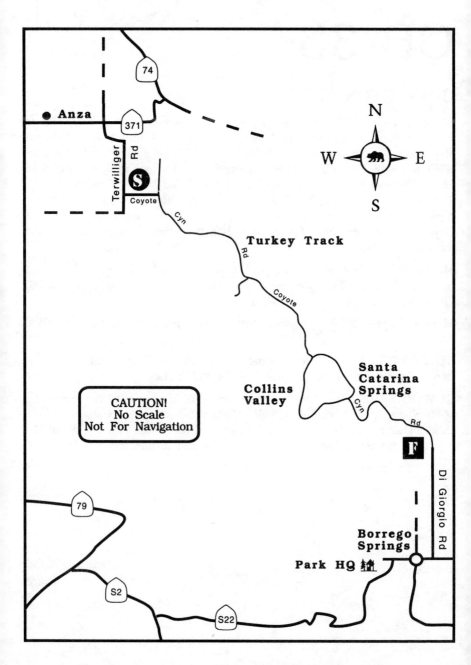

Area 9
CB-36

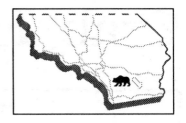

COYOTE CANYON

DESCRIPTION: A 4-WHEELER magazine **Coyote Canyon** trip got lost trying to find the start of the dirt road! With that, they gave it a 3 for difficulty (10 being worst). It's much worse. If you don't like steep, rocky grades that you may have to come back up, don't do this one! Take I-15 south to HWY 79 east (freeway sign says south) in Temecula/Rancho California. Use 79 to HWY 371 left (northeast). In Anza take Kirby Road right (south), through the two 90 degree turns. It's now Terwilliger Road. Replenish supplies and say hello to Terry Grant at Kamp Anza. As you continue further down Terwilliger Road, look for 6 orange reflectors on a telephone pole to your left (east) (A10). Go left. This is Coyote Canyon Road which you follow to the dead-end for a right and you're on your way. When you see a great expanse of canyon ahead, stop and check it out on foot for ¾ mile. You may not want to drive any further. This is the infamous Turkey Track Grade. Follow the periodic signs to Borrego. There, home can either be up (west) on HWY S22 back to 79 and I-15 or S22 east to HWY 86 and I-10.

MAPS: ACSC San Diego County (A10, C12). Anza-Borrego Desert State Park map (A1/2, C3/4). Highly recommended is Lindsay's *The Anza-Borrego Desert Region* (ISBN 911824-67-7) book and map (trip 2, backwards). DeLorme p114 (A4), p115 (B5), Sidekick (Coyote Canyon). Desert Access Guide #19 (A1, C3). USGS 33116.

MILES: Loop. 25 very tough miles from Terwilliger Road to DiGiorgio Road in Borrego Springs.

AUTHORITY: Anza-Borrego Desert State Park, P. O. Box 428, Borrego Springs, CA 92004 (619) 767-5311.

REMARKS: Check with the ABDSP first and at least get the Park map. This is a very ecologically sensitive area which is closed from June 16 through September 15 each year. **Rockhouse Canyon, Vista Del Mal Pais** and **Fonts Point** are close by.

Ty Prettyman

Crab Flats

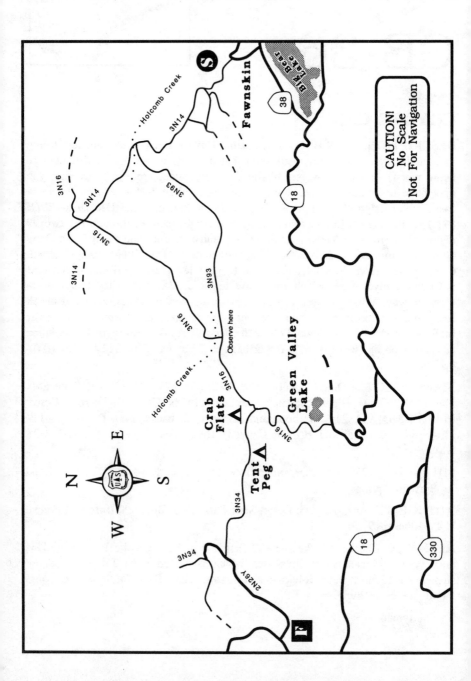

Area 5 CB-14

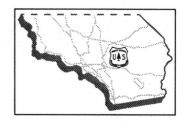

CRAB FLATS

DESCRIPTION: If you have ever wondered what the real 4-wheelers do, this is it. This is tough. This is rocky. This is not for the beginner. This is for the experienced in the direction described. It is for the well equipped veteran in the opposite direction. Enough said? At the north side of Big Bear Lake is Fawnskin. Starting out paved, take 3N14 north until you cross **Holcomb Creek**. Turn left (southwest) virtually in the creek. This is tough 3N93. Follow it for about 5 miles until 3N16. If you want to see tough before doing it, bypass 3N93 and take 3N14 to a left on 3N16. Just after you make the hairpin at the Holcomb Creek crossing, walk through the 100 yards of rocks in the southeast corner of this intersection. (Yes mother, that's the trail!) Follow 3N16 to 3N34 right to **Crab Flats** and Tent Peg Campgrounds. The really tough stuff starts at Dishpan Springs and continues until you get out at the rocky stream crossing near Fisherman's Camp. Yes, it's actually possible to cross the stream here and no it hasn't gotten worse since I wrote this Guide. Shortly after the stream crossing, you come to 2N26Y for a left. This soon turns to pavement and will take you out through Cedar Glen and Lake Arrowhead. Much deserved home is down the hill via HWY 18.

MAPS: San Bernardino National Forest, San Bernardino Meridian, (G2/3, E/F2/3). ACSC LA and Vicinity, no trail shown, Crab Flats at (E16). DeLorme p96 (B1), p95 (B6). Sidekick (Lake Arrowhead & Big Bear). USGS 34116 and 34117.

MILES Loop. 15 miles from start of paved 3N14 to 2N26Y (Hook Creek Road).

AUTHORITY: San Bernardino National Forest, Arrowhead District, P. O. Box 7, RimForest, CA 92378 (909) 337-2444. Also, Big Bear District, P. O. Box 290, Fawnskin, CA 92333 (909) 866-3437.

REMARKS: I'll say it again - rough, rough, rough in spots. Best avoided in the winter and after heavy rains. Creek crossings become impossible. Chains advisable under all conditions. **Holcomb Creek**, **Holcomb Valley** and **Butler Peak** are nearby. See them for a way to check out some of the rough before doing it.

Chuck Thompson

Culp Valley

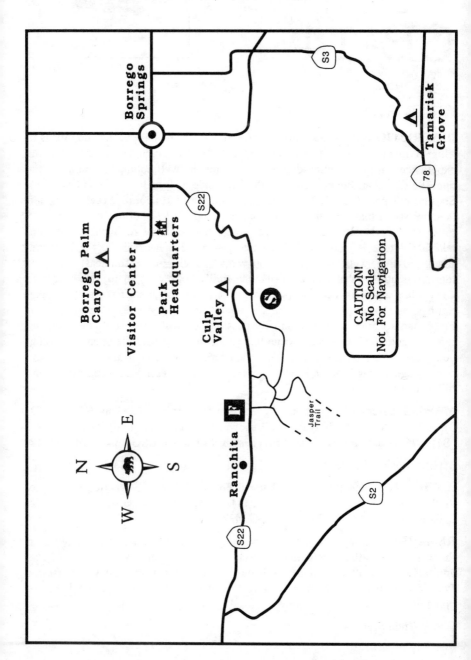

Area 9
CB-36

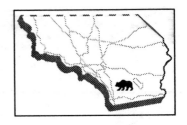

CULP VALLEY

DESCRIPTION: As you head into Borrego Springs via HWY S22, you pass Ranchita (D11). 4 miles east you'll find the campground sign to **Culp Valley**. In another 1¼ miles, near mile post 10.5, you could easily pass the Culp Calley dirt road off to your right (southwest). Use this road. In less than a mile, there's another road to the left to a picnic area at the old Palori homesite. A little shy of 4 rough miles up through the high chaparral brings you to a cross road. Right (north) goes back to S22. Left here leads down the rougher Jasper Trail and straight leads on with this trail description. In ½ mile you'll intersect a familiar, double road if you did **Grapevine Canyon**. Right here gets you back to S22 and another right leads back to home, if it's at Culp Valley campground.

MAPS: ACSC San Diego County (D12, D11). Anza-Borrego Desert State Park map (D3, D2/3). Highly recommended is Lindsay's *The Anza-Borrego Desert Region* (ISBN 911824-67-7) book and map (portion of trip 1A). DeLorme p115 (C5, C4) and their roads are not accurate. Desert Access Guide #19 (B4). USGS 33116.

MILES: Loop. 5 miles from HWY S22 to same.

AUTHORITY: Anza-Borrego Desert State Park, P. O. Box 428, Borrego Springs, CA 92004 (619) 767-5311.

REMARKS: First stop should be the visitor center where you can get the Park map. **Culp Valley** altitude is cooler in the hot season. Remember, look, but don't take anything from the Park. **Grapevine Canyon** is nice to work in conjunction with this one.

Cut Across Trail

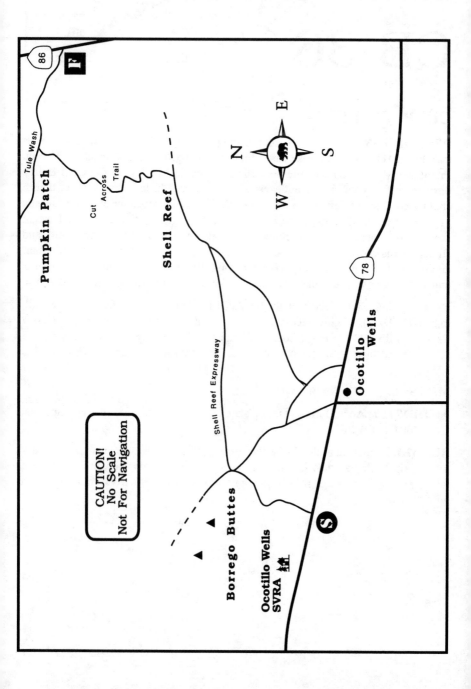

Area 9
CB-36

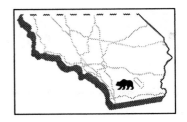

CUT ACROSS TRAIL

DESCRIPTION: Another no mapper just like **Poleline Road**. But it may be easier to find, not drive to, the **Pumpkin Patch** via the **Cut Across Trail**. After you get to Borrego Springs (C12) via its many approaches, go south on Borrego Springs Road (HWY S3) to a left (east) on HWY 78 to the Ocotillo Wells State Vehicular Recreation Area. In the confusion of taking Main Street north (left) to Quarry Road right (northeast), have confidence you will find Shell Reef Expressway off toward the northeast (all signed). Cross San Felipe Wash and go to the reef. It's the scarred up hill with the dark top about 5 or 6 miles out. At the northeast end is a faint trace of the trail. Cross you fingers and follow this for about 3 miles until you come to Tule Wash. Left (west) will take you to the 20 foot high hills and the **Pumpkin Patch**. Right (east) in Tule Wash will take you out to HWY 86. Right on HWY 86 gets you over to HWY 78 for a right (west) back to the start at Ocotillo Wells. Left leads to Indio, I-10 and home for most.

MAPS: Now the bad news. No map, not even Lindsay's *The Anza-Borrego Desert Region* (ISBN 911824-67-7) book and map, shows this trail. Also beware ACSC San Diego County (D14) Cut Across Trail is not the one I'm talking about. DeLorme p116 (C1) shows Shell Reef, Pumpkin Patch and Tule Wash. Ocotillo Wells SVRA map shows Shell Reef Expressway and Shell Reef, but no roads beyond. Desert Access Guide #20 (A4). USGS 33116.

MILES: Loop. 18 miles from HWY 78 to HWY 86, but allow 25 or so.

AUTHORITY: BLM El Centro Resource Area Office, 1661 S. Fourth St., El Centro, CA 92243 (619) 352-5842. Ocotillo Wells State Vehicular Recreation Area, P. O. Box 360, Borrego Springs, CA 92004 (619) 767-5391.

REMARKS: At all costs, avoid this area, paved and dirt, during flash floods and hot weather. This moderately rough one is for the well prepared. Allow time to explore and discover. **Pumpkin Patch, San Felipe Wash** and **Poleline Road** are nearby.

Mike Smith

Cypress Mtn

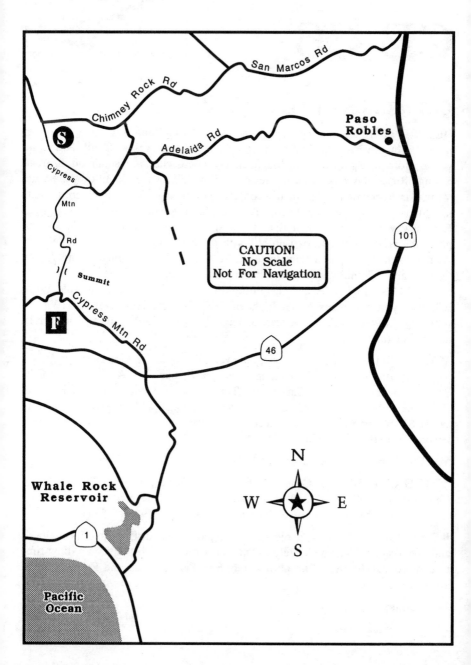

Area 1
CB-1

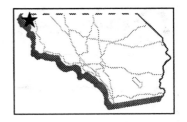

CYPRESS MOUNTAIN

DESCRIPTION: This is the most northerly trail I describe. Go north on HWY 101 to the San Marcos Road turnoff, 8 miles out of Paso Robles. Go west (left) until you reach Chimney Rock Road, more or less straight. At the fire station 9 miles down the road, make another left (south) on Cypress Mountain Road. In the area of the abandoned Klau mine, you will pass paved Adelaida Road. Just after the summit, a whole 2,210 feet, you reach paved Cypress Mountain Road. This leads to HWY 46. Right for a nice drive back down the coast (HWY 1) or left back to HWY 101.

MAPS: ACSC San Luis Obispo County (C4, D4). DeLorme p45 (C4, D5). USGS 35120.

MILES: Loop. 14 miles from Chimney Rock Road to HWY 46.

AUTHORITY: San Luis Obispo County (public road).

REMARKS: Nearby **Santa Rita Creek** is a natural. Combine this with a water skiing trip to Lake Nacimiento, a trip to the Hearst Castle or a wine tasting tour around Paso Robles and Templeton. Do the dirt before the wine tour.

Del Sur Ridge

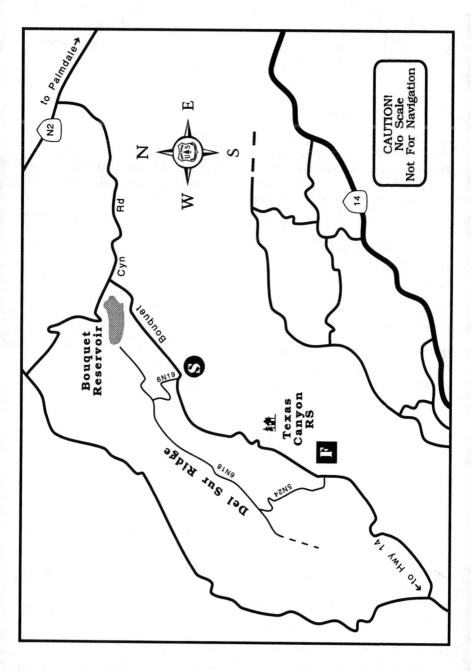

Area 2
CB-4

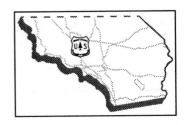

DEL SUR RIDGE

DESCRIPTION: Nearby where you start and finish this one, there are no less than 8 campgrounds. Nothing exotic, but nice for the weekend and leisurely trail exploration. Just like **Green Valley**, from HWY 14 in Palmdale take a left (west) on N2 (F3). At Bouquet Canyon Road (E3) turn south (left) for 10 miles to 6N19 for a right (north). At the intersection with 6N18 go left. Right leads to a locked gate near Bouquet Reservoir. Look, but don't touch the gate. If you miss your next left (south) on 5N24, in about a mile you will encounter another locked gate at some private property. 5N24 takes you back to paved Bouquet Canyon Road. Go right for home via HWY 14 or I-5.

MAPS: Angeles National Forest, San Bernardino Meridian (D3, D4). ACSC LA and Vicinity (C5, D5). DeLorme p78 (D3), p92 (A2). USGS 34118.

MILES: Loop. 11 miles paved Bouquet Canyon to Bouquet Canyon.

AUTHORITY: Angeles National Forest, Saugus District, 27757 Bouquet Canyon Road, Saugus, CA 91350 (805) 252-9710.

REMARKS: Another Spring trip for a weekend of camping and flowers. **Tule Ridge**, **Sierra Pelona**, **Green Valley**, **Liebre Mountain** and **Warm Springs** are all reasonably close.

Desert Queen

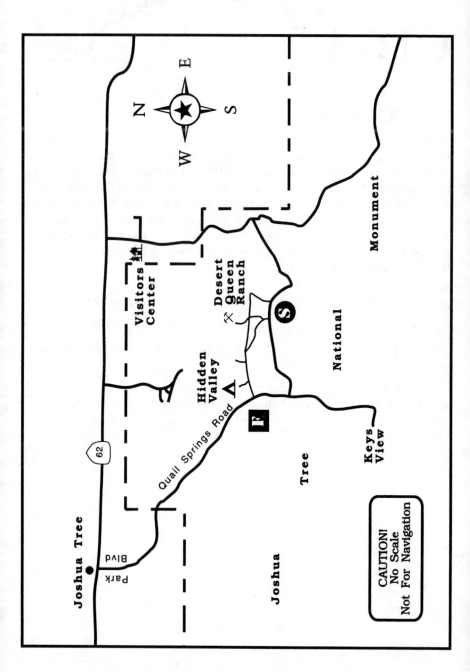

Area 8
CB-33

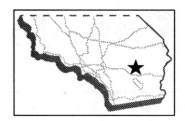

DESERT QUEEN

DESCRIPTION: First call the number below and make reservations to see the Desert Queen Ranch (actually the mine too). Next go out I-10 east toward Palm Springs, but pass up HWY 111 and take HWY 62 north. In Joshua Tree (the City) go south (right) on Park Blvd. which turns into Quail Springs Road. Follow this past the Keys View turn off and across from the Squaw Tank trail is the dirt road to the ranch and mine. Go north to the locked gate and wait for the ranger who will escort you in for your tour of the ranch. When finished, go straight at the gate (not back the way you came in) and follow any of the several dirt road alternatives back to Quail Springs Road. Done the way I do it, you come out at the Hidden Valley Area.

MAPS: ACSC Riverside County (B15, B14). DeLorme p98 (D1), p97 (D7). Desert Access Guide #14 (I/J7). No coordinates on the Joshua Tree National Monument map. USGS 34116.

MILES: Loop. A whole 6 miles if you don't drive in circles coming out from the ranch.

AUTHORITY: Joshua Tree National Monument, 74485 National Monument Drive, Twentynine Palms, CA 92277 (619) 367-7511.

REMARKS: Take this one in mid to late spring and in a good year you can't help but fall in love with the desert wildflowers. **Covington Flat**, **Squaw Tank** and **Gold Park** are all nearby trails. The Ranch is open only on weekends during the Fall, Winter, and Spring.

Diablo Dropoff

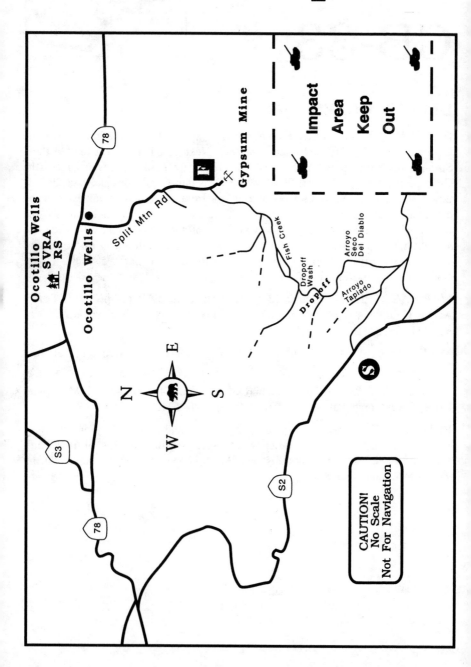

Impact Area Keep Out

Gypsum Mine

78

Ocotillo Wells SVRA RS

Ocotillo Wells

Split Mtn Rd

Fish Creek

Dropoff Wash

Dropoff

Arroyo Seco Del Diablo

Arroyo Taplado

S

N E S W

S3

S2

78

CAUTION! No Scale Not For Navigation

Area 9
CB-36

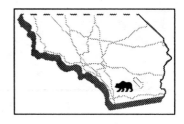

DIABLO DROPOFF

DESCRIPTION: This may distort your confidence about the ABDSP drop-offs. It is mild compared to **Pinyon Mountain,** but monstrous for the beginner! The soft sand is very forgiving going downhill and nearly impossible, in dry weather, going up hill. Contrary to **Pinyon Mountain,** however, you can turn around (before you go down) and go back if you don't like what you see. Like **Blair Valley,** it's easier to find your way from Julian, but I'll lead you from Borrego Springs (C12). South from the Christmas Circle on HWY S3 (Borrego Springs Road), for a right (west) on HWY 78, to a left (southeast) on HWY S2. A little shy of 28 miles (you just traveled a portion of the Great Southern Overland Stage Route; did you have to push at Foot & Walker Pass?) you come to a signed, dirt road, Vallecito Creek. Follow this left (southeast) for about 6 miles, past signed Arroyo Tapiado, to signed Arroyo Seco Del Diablo. Turn left (northwest) here. 6¼ miles out this arroyo you come to a 4 X 4 post (look hard) on you right that says Fish Creek crossover. In about 1 mile you come to the first and longest of 3 drop-offs on this route. Use all 3 to get into narrow, rough and rocky Dropoff Wash. In another mile you're out to Fish Creek for a right (northwest) and a left on paved Split Mountain Road in 9 or so miles. At HWY 78, go right to the Salton Sea (HWY 86) or left (west) back to Julian.

MAPS: ACSC San Diego County (G13/14, F15). Anza-Borrego Desert State Park map (G4/5, F6). Highly recommended is Lindsay's *The Anza-Borrego Desert Region* (ISBN 911824-67-7) book and map (part of trip 4D). DeLorme p123 (A7), p116 (D1) with Fish Creek crossover road not shown. Start on Desert Access Guide #19 (D7/8) and finish on #20 (A6). USGS 33116.

MILES: Loop. 24 miles from paved S2 to Split Mountain Road.

AUTHORITY: Anza-Borrego Desert State Park, P. O. Box 428, Borrego Springs, CA 92004 (619) 767-5311.

REMARKS: First stop should be the visitor center where you can get the Park map. This trail must be avoided during flash floods. It is dangerous! **San Felipe Wash, Blair Valley, Sandstone Canyon** and the dangerous **Pinyon Mountain** are nearby.

Dick Cumiskey

Dos Cabezas

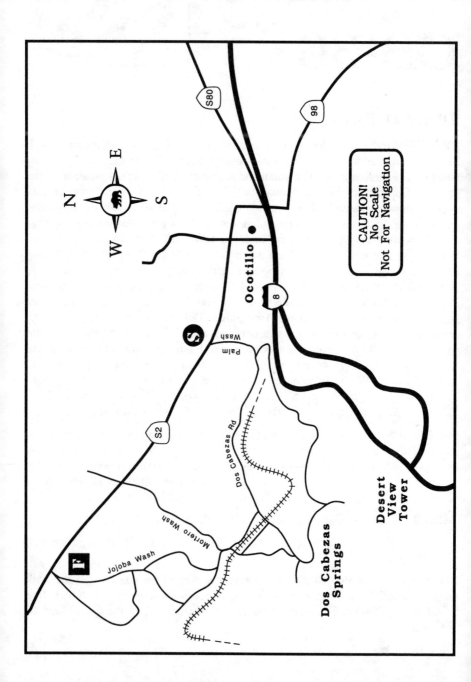

Area 9
CB-36

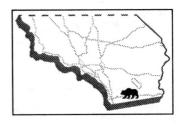

DOS CABEZAS

DESCRIPTION: I suppose two heads are better than one to see the Dos Cabezas at the springs. They look like 3 or 4 to me. Besides, it will take two heads to figure out my directions and the frequently, flash flood rearranged roads. Like **Painted Gorge**, I'll direct you from San Diego, but if you think it's quicker via El Centro, use it. Take I-8 east out of San Diego and as you descend the grade by the Desert View Tower, start anticipating Ocotillo. In Ocotillo, use HWY S2 northwest (left) for 3½ plus miles. Take Dos Cabezas Road (Palm Canyon Wash) left (south). At the tracks, turn right (northwest) and parallel them to the Dos Cabezas Station's water tower. Continue to stay to the north of the RR track and follow them for the next 2 or so miles. An early right (north) will take you down Mortero Wash, and 2 later turns will take you down Jojoba (pronounced like a laughing Santa Claus sheep) Wash to S2. No turn will take you to a dead-end further along the tracks. There are several record breaking, curved, wooden tressels that the RR buffs will enjoy in the area. S2 can take you right (southeast) back to I-8 or left (northwest) to Julian or Borrego Springs.

MAPS: ACSC San Diego County (J15, H14/15) doesn't show connection between RR tracks and Jojoba Wash. Anza-Borrego Desert State Park map (I6/7, H/I6). Highly recommended is Lindsay's *The Anza-Borrego Desert Region* (ISBN 911824-67-7) book and map (part of trip 4E). DeLorme p124 (B/C1, B1), no roads shown in Jojoba Wash on p123 (B7). Starts on Desert Access Guide #22 (A3/4) and ends on #19 (E9). USGS 32116.

MILES: Loop. 13 miles, with all the right moves, from S2 back to S2.

AUTHORITY: Anza-Borrego Desert State Park, P. O. Box 428, Borrego Springs, CA 92004 (619) 767-5311.

REMARKS: First stop should be the visitor center where you can get the Park map. Another area to avoid when ABC's Dr. George predicts flash floods. It is dangerous! **Painted Gorge, Yuha Wells** and **Diablo Dropoff** (beware) are nearby.

Dick Cumiskey

Dry Lake Loop

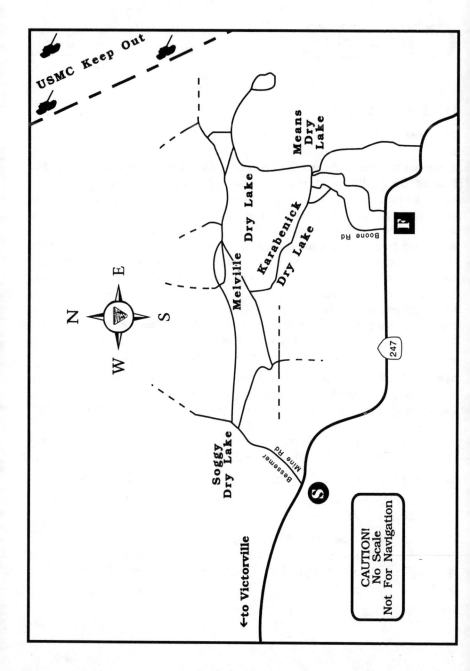

Area 6
CB-17

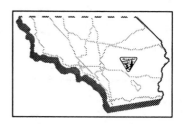

DRY LAKE LOOP

DESCRIPTION: The Lucerne Valley area takes some time to learn. That's why I have 5 trails in the area. This covers the southern section and is a good way to get dusty on a Sunday afternoon. Like **Camp Rock Road**, check out the Roy Rogers Dale Evans Museum in Victorville (F2), off I-15 before you head east on HWY 18. Be sure to check out the oldest living things on earth, the cresote clone rings claimed to be 12,000 to 14,000 years old. The fenced-off area is just to the south of Soggy Dry Lake. Use HWY 247 east to Bessemer Mine Road northeast. 3½ miles later, at the north end of Soggy Dry Lake take a right toward Melville Dry Lake. 4 more miles of dust should put you in another dry lake for a hard right (southwest) to Means Dry Lake. Right in the lake will lead you through the Karabenick Dry Lakes, but I recommend a wiggle straight out Boone Road to paved HWY 247. Go right for home via I-15 or left (east) via Yucca Valley and HWY 62 southeast to I-10 near the Palm Springs, HWY 111 turn off.

MAPS: ACSC San Bernardino County (G5). DeLorme p96 (A3), p97 (B4). Start on Desert Access Guide #14 (C/D2), through #11, with finish on #14 (E2/3). USGS 34116.

MILES: Loop. 21 miles around the loop from and back to HWY 247.

AUTHORITY: San Bernardino County, private and BLM, California Desert Information Center, 831 Barstow Road, Barstow, CA 92311 (619) 256-8313.

REMARKS: Stoddard Well Road, Cinder Cone, Camp Rock Road and **Box Canyon** are the other 4 trails in Lucerne Valley. Avoid this one in wet weather unless you want involuntary mud practice.

El Cariso

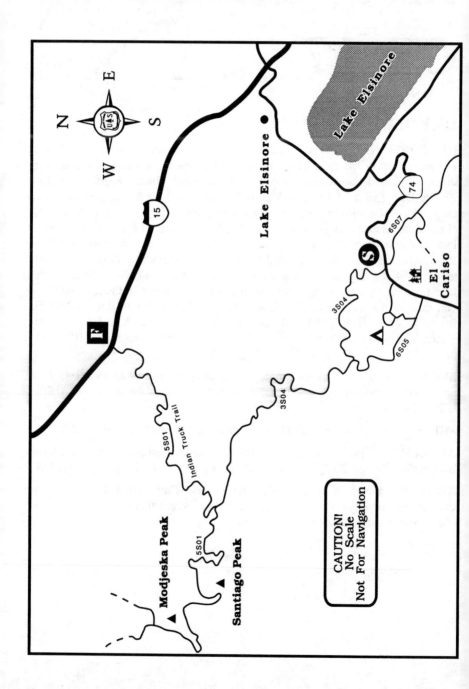

Lake Elsinore

N E W S

15

74

6S07

S

El Cariso

3S04

6S05

Lake Elsinore

3S04

5S01

Indian Truck Trail

5S01

Modjeska Peak

Santiago Peak

CAUTION!
No Scale
Not For Navigation

Area 7
CB-30

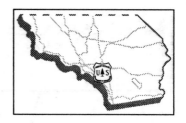

EL CARISO

DESCRIPTION: If you liked **Tenaja Truck Trail**, make a left (north) off HWY 74 and you're on your way. Remember, we got to HWY 74 by going south on I-5 to the Ortega Highway (HWY 74) in San Juan Capistrano for a left (east, B4/5). Some 30 odd miles out this sports car drivers delight is the El Cariso Ranger Station and campground where you should stop to get the latest info. Now this time go north on 3S04 almost to the Falcon group campground. You want to pick up the sharp right (north) that 3S04 makes and not continue on around the loop which leads back out to HWY 74 via 6S05. Some time after you make the sharp right, look for an intersection with 5S01. Left (west) or actually more or less straight takes you up to the old fire lookout station at the top of Saddleback Mountain. Right (due north) leads you down and out the Indian Truck Trail (5S01) to I-15 where I end this trail. Home is to your left (northwest) on I-15.

MAPS: Cleveland National Forest, Trabuco Ranger District (D3, D2/3). Although recently reprinted, this map has several incorrect gate symbols. ACSC Riverside County (E4) does not show 5S01, the Indian Truck Trail. DeLorme p105 (C4), p104 (C4). USGS 33117.

MILES: Loop. 11 miles from HWY 74 to I-15.

AUTHORITY: Cleveland National Forest, Trabuco District, 1147 E. 6th Street, Corona, CA 91720 (909) 736-1811.

REMARKS: Combine this with a trip to the San Juan Capistrano Mission when the swallows return. The Mission is right at the I-5/HWY 74 offramp. **Saddleback Mountain** and **Tenaja Truck Trail** are nearby.

Ian Wilson

Essex Road

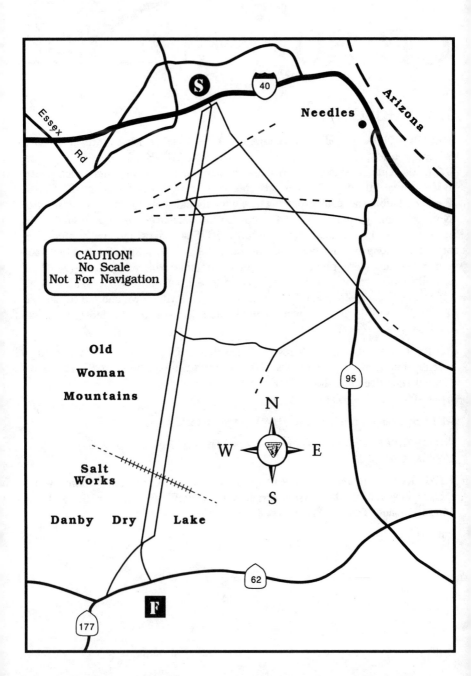

Area 6
CB-17

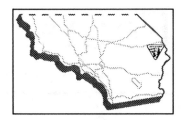

ESSEX ROAD

DESCRIPTION: I seemed to have a void in this area toward the end of writing the Guide, so Essex takes you from I-40 near Needles to HWY 62 via dirt. If you're an explorer, you won't pass up the many mines, springs and tough roads in the Old Woman Mountains to the west of this trip. It's best to get to Needles (E13), fuel up, then double back on I-40 to the freeway off ramp 19 miles west of town. Go south, south and more south on the unnamed, graded dirt road. It crosses the Danby Dry Lake, passes through the town of Iron Mountain and ultimately comes out on HWY 62 near the intersection of HWY 177. HWY 62 west (right) takes you back to I-10, north of Palm Springs for home.

MAPS: ACSC San Bernardino County (E12, H11). DeLorme p86 (B3), p100 (D1/2). Start on Desert Access Guide #13 (A6) through #12, and #16, finish on #15 (H/I6). USGS 34114 and 34115.

MILES: Loop. 57 miles from I-40 to HWY 62.

AUTHORITY: BLM Needles Resource Area, 101 West Spike's Road, P.O. Box 888, Needles, CA 92363 (619) 326-3896.

REMARKS: Just before you cross Danby Dry Lake, take a right to the several salt works and see how salt is evaporated. North of I-40 is **Mitchell Caverns.** This is not a hot weather trip.

Fonts Point

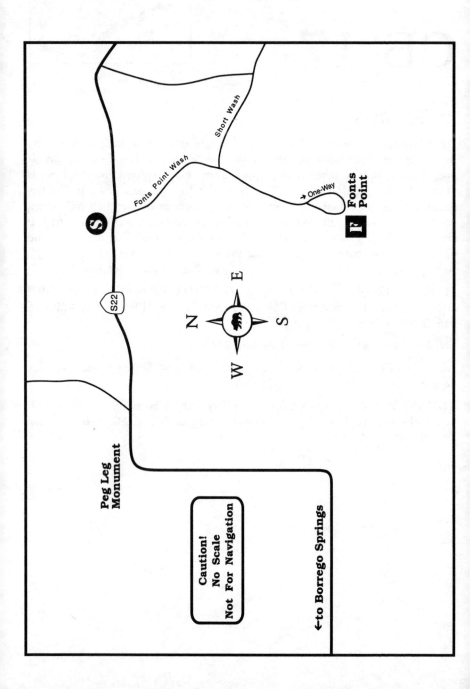

Area 9
CB-36

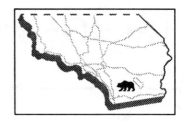

FONTS POINT

DESCRIPTION: This is the most spectacular badlands view in the Park. Nice chance to use 4WD because it's a little sandy at times. Father Font was the recording secretary on the Anza expedition. He thought the area was one step away from hell and the Indians the same from the human race. Just like **Rockhouse Canyon,** too many ways in to be specific, so get to Borrego Springs (C12). About 3½ miles east of Peg Leg Smith Monument (C13) on HWY S22 is well signed Fonts Wash. Go right (south), stay between the markers all the way to the left at the one-way "Y". At the parking area near the pipes, walk the 50 yards to the real Point. The last 25 steps take my breath away. Use the remainder of the one-way trail back to the wash and S22. On your way out, check out where Short Wash takes off to the right (east). You'll need to know where it is to do **Vista Del Mal Pais.**

MAPS: ACSC San Diego County (C14). Anza-Borrego Desert State Park map (C/D4/5). Highly recommended is Lindsay's *The Anza-Borrego Desert Region* (ISBN 911824-67-7) book and map (trip 3). DeLorme p115 (B6/7). Desert Access Guide #19 (D3). USGS 33116.

MILES: Dead-end. About 8 miles round trip from and back to S22.

AUTHORITY: Anza-Borrego Desert State Park, P. O. Box 428, Borrego Springs, CA 92004 (619) 767-5311.

REMARKS: First stop should be the visitor center where you can get the Park map. Remember, look, but don't take anything from the Park. **Coyote Canyon, Vista Del Mal Pais, Calcite Mine** and **Rockhouse Canyon** are nearby.

Mike Smith

Gold Park

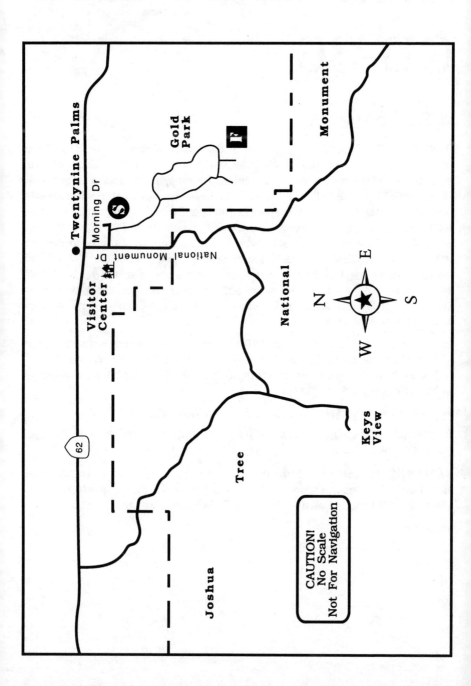

Area 8
CB-33

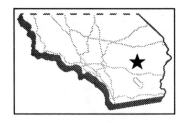

GOLD PARK

DESCRIPTION: No less than 9 mines in a 10 mile loop tell you gold mining is still alive and well in California. This is an area to respect the many keep out signs and try your best to stay on the public roads. I believe a couple of rough sections in the road remain that way to minimize the tourists. But you're not a tourist, you're a gold speculator! Just like **Desert Queen**, go east on I-10 toward Palm Springs, but pass up HWY 111 and take HWY 62 north. Now, pass up Joshua Tree and go into Twentynine Palms. At National Monument Drive turn right (south), then left (east) on Morning Drive. In ½ mile a dirt road will take off to your right (south). You take off here too. About 3½ miles you come to a "Y" in the road. Left or right takes you around a loop that you want to do, so it doesn't matter which way you go. The road's bad at first in both directions, but you finally end up in **Gold Park**. When you get back to this same intersection, you'll know which way is home.

MAPS: ACSC Riverside County (B15/16). DeLorme p98 (D1). Desert Access Guide #14 (J5/6) to finish on #15 (A7). USGS 33115, 33116, 34115 and 34116.

MILES: Dead-ending loop. 17 miles round trip with no mistakes which I can't do.

AUTHORITY: BLM, Palm Springs-South Coast Resource Area, 63-500 Garnet Ave, P.O. Box 2000, N. Palm Springs, CA. 92258-2000, (619) 251-0812.

REMARKS: **Covington Flat, Desert Queen, Squaw Tank** and **Old Dale Road** are all nearby trails. This area is typical of most mining, desert rat areas. Dusty, confusing and best avoided in the heat.

212

Grade Valley

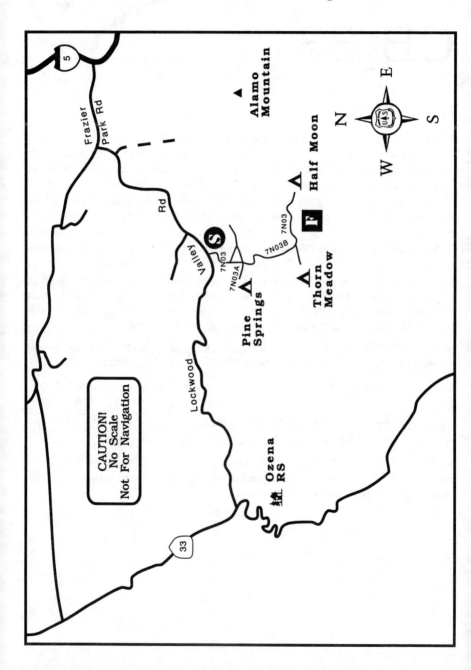

Area 1
CB-1

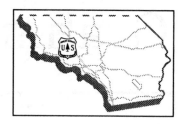

GRADE VALLEY

DESCRIPTION: Although I only describe five trails in the area, **Grade Valley** puts you right in the middle of 4X heaven. Use I-5 headed toward Bakersfield and just beyond Gorman take the Frazier Park turn off west. Make a left (southwest) on Lockwood Valley Road past Lockwood. At Mutau Flat Road (7N03) go left or actually the way the road bends, straight. Use 7N03 to a right at 7N03B. This leads to the Thorn Meadows Campground. Back 5 miles 7N03A leads to Pine Springs Campground. You can also explore Half Moon Campground on up 7N03. Regardless of where or when you decide to go home, it's always back north to paved Lockwood Valley Road and then east to I-5.

MAPS: ACSC Ventura County (D/E5, F5). DeLorme p77 (C5, D5). Mount Pinos Ranger District ORV Map (T7N, R21W to T6N, R21W), Los Padres National Forest Recreation Map (P18). USGS 34118 and 34119.

MILES: Dead-end. 18 miles in and out.

AUTHORITY: Los Padres National Forest, Mt. Pinos District, Chuchupate Ranger Station, Frazier Park, CA 93225 (805) 245-3731. Recorded message at (805) 245-3449.

REMARKS: **Quatal Canyon, Apache Canyon, Santa Barbara Canyon** and **Reyes Peak** are nearby. Be sure to get the ORV map so you stay on legal routes. This area is subject to winter closure.

Graham Pass

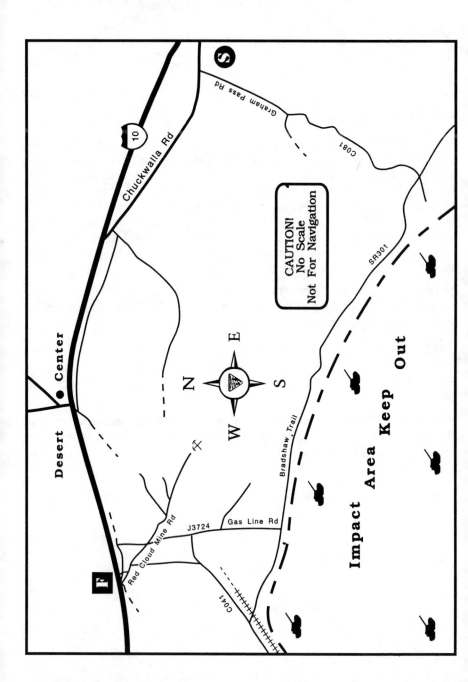

Area 10
CB-39

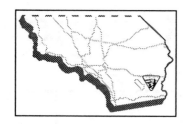

GRAHAM PASS

DESCRIPTION: This is just a disguised way to put you on more of the Bradshaw Trail. For me, it's more than a weekend if done all at once. Just like **Corn Springs**, head toward Palm Springs on I-10, continue over the Chiriaco Summit and pass Desert Center to Chuckwalla Road south. Wave at **Corn Springs** as you go by and continue on southeast to **Graham Pass** Road (BLM C081) for a right (south). 16 miles later you will make a right (west) on the Bradshaw Trail (BLM SR301). Pass up the Gas Line Road (BLM J3724) coming in on your right and some time later, just as you cross over the RR tracks, make a right (northeast) on BLM C041. Follow the RR tracks to I-10 at Red Cloud Mine Road. The setting sun tells you which way for home.

MAPS: ACSC Riverside County (F23, E/F19) the trail along the gunnery range is not shown. DeLorme p110 (D2), p109 (C5), Desert Access Guide #18, (J5, D5), portion of SR301 not shown. USGS 33115.

MILES: Loop. 51 miles from Chuckwalla Road to I-10.

AUTHORITY: BLM, Palm Springs-South Coast Resource Area, 63-500 Garnet Ave, P.O. Box 2000, N. Palm Springs, CA. 92258-2000, (619) 251-0812. El Centro Resource Area Office, 1661 South Fourth St., El Centro, CA 92243 (619) 352-5842.

REMARKS: Be aware the property to the south of the Bradshaw Trail is an active gunnery range. Keep out. **Bradshaw Trail, Corn Springs** and **Red Canyon** are nearby.

Grapevine Cyn

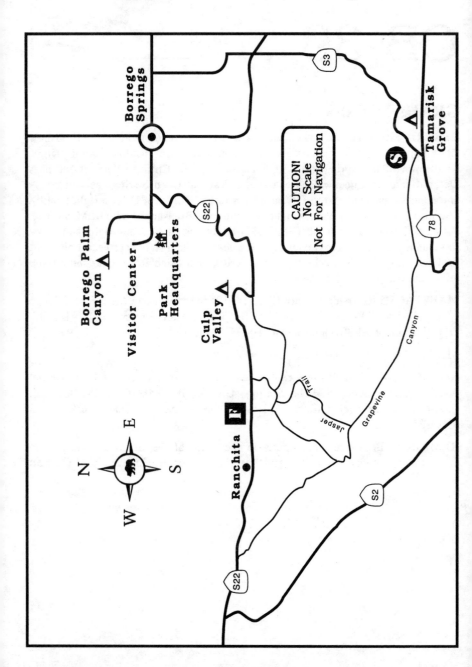

Area 9
CB-36

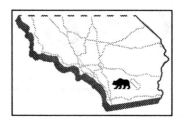

GRAPEVINE CANYON

DESCRIPTION: Whether you like birds, plants, Indian relics or scenic drives, this is a little known secret. Plan on a full day and use the Lindsay book for all the details. From Borrego Springs (C12), head south on HWY S3 to the Tamarisk Grove Campground. Turn right (west) in San Felipe Wash just west of the campgrounds. Take time to walk around each of the springs as you progress up the canyon. Wrong turns are of no consequence except for two. Most lead out to paved HWY 78 or S22. One to beware of is the rougher and more scenic Jasper Trail which cuts off to the right (north) about 8 to 9 miles from the start. In about another 2 miles is a right (northwest) which is the recommended way out to Ranchita. You should start climbing out of the canyon now. Straight leads up the rougher road to the Wilson ranch. You will know you're on the correct road because there are two good roads that run parallel to each other for the last mile or so. The paved road is S22. Right (east) goes down Montezuma Grade to Borrego Springs and left leads to HWY S2 and eventually HWY 78 or 79.

MAPS: ACSC San Diego County (E12, D11). Anza-Borrego Desert State Park map (E3, D2/3). Highly recommended is Lindsay's *The Anza-Borrego Desert Region* (ISBN 911824-67-7) book and map (trip 1B). DeLorme p115 (C/D5, C4). Desert Access Guide #19 (C5, A/B4). USGS 33116.

MILES: Loop. 13 miles from HWY S3 to HWY S22.

AUTHORITY: Anza-Borrego Desert State Park, P. O. Box 428, Borrego Springs, CA 92004 (619) 767-5311.

REMARKS: First stop should be the visitor center or Tamarisk Grove Campground where you can get the Park map. Late spring is best since early spring can put you in a very wet canyon. Remember, look, but don't take anything from the Park. **Culp Valley** is nice to work in conjunction with this one.

Mike Smith

Green Valley

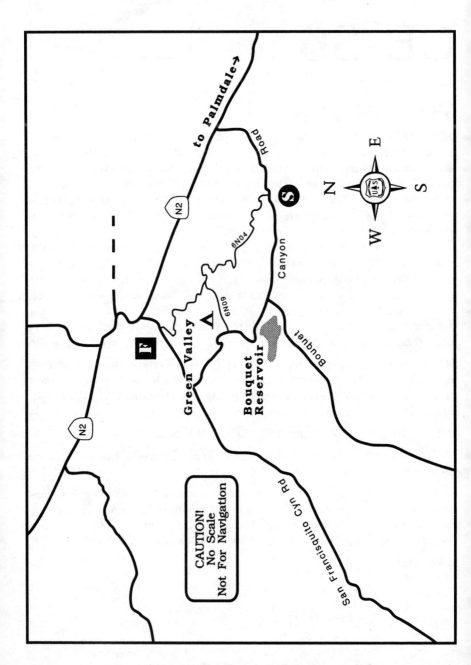

Area 2
CB-4

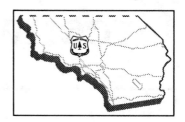

GREEN VALLEY

DESCRIPTION: Named after a campground that is actually a sidetrip, this trail is just more miles of introductory graded dirt road. Off HWY 14 in Palmdale, take a left (west) on N2 (F3). At Bouquet Canyon Road (E3) turn south (left) and in 3 miles turn right (northwest) on 6N04. About half way through this trip, 6N09 comes in from the southwest (left). This leads out to paved road or continue on 6N04 to paved San Francisquito Canyon Road which is my end for this trail. Continuing on across the road on 6N04 will intersect you with **Tule Ridge**. Do you really want to go home (south on San Franisquito Canyon Road to HWY 140 and eventually I-5) with all the other trails in the area to explore?

MAPS: Angeles National Forest, San Bernardino Meridian (E3, D2). ACSC LA and Vicinity (C6, B/C5). DeLorme p78 (D4, C/D3). USGS 34118.

MILES: Loop. 11 miles from paved Bouquet Canyon Road to San Francisquito Canyon Road.

AUTHORITY: Angeles National Forest, Saugus District, 27757 Bouquet Canyon Road, Saugus, CA 91350 (805) 252-9710.

REMARKS: Another Spring trip for the flowers. The California Poppy Reserve (15101 West Lancaster Road, Lancaster, CA 93536) is just a few miles north. **Tule Ridge, Sierra Pelona Lookout, Del Sur Ridge, Liebre Mountain** and **Warm Springs** are all reasonably close.

Greenwater Valley

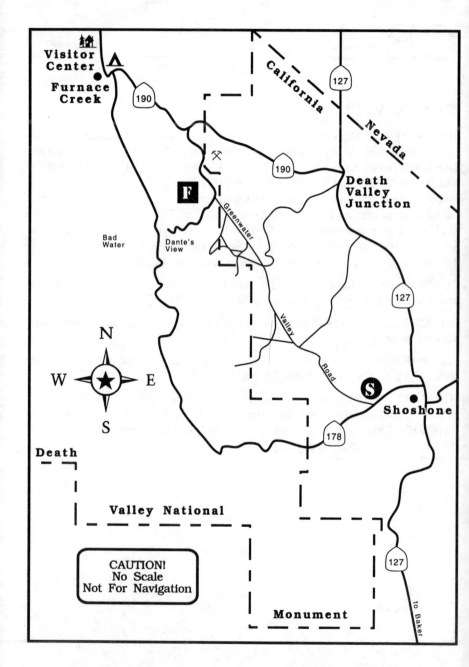

Visitor
Center
Furnace
Creek

190

California

Nevada

127

190

Death
Valley
Junction

Greenwater

F

Bad
Water

Dante's
View

Valley

Road

127

N
W ⭐ E
S

S

Shoshone

178

Death

127

Valley National

To Baker

CAUTION!
No Scale
Not For Navigation

Monument

Death Valley CB-7

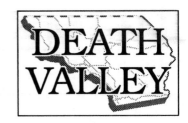

GREENWATER VALLEY

DESCRIPTION: This is one of two unpaved approaches to Death Valley that definitely puts a twist on getting there. It's lots of dirt, provides a panorama few take advantage of, and is relatively easy. Pretend it's a Vegas run, only at Baker, take a left (north) on HWY 127. 58 miles later in Shoshone (say show-show-knee at M14) use HWY 178 left (west) for just shy of 6 miles to the start of the dirt (M13). Usually unmarked, Greenwater Valley is your route for the next 28 miles to where you intersect the paved road (K11). To the left (southwest) takes you to a point 5,755 feet above Badwater (lowest point in USA, -280'), Dante's View (K10) - well worth the 12 mile round trip. To the right (north) puts you out to HWY 190 (J10/11) and another left (northwest) is the way to Furnace Creek (H/J9/10). Lots of decisions along the way. All lefts eventually dead end, except the Gold Valley site (M11). Two wrong rights take you back to HWY 127. Since I'm sure you're spending a night or two, home is probably the Furnace Creek Ranch or Inn. Consider dirt Harry Wade Road, just south of the Ashford Mill site (M/N11) for an exit twist.

MAPS: ACSC Death Valley (M13, K11). DeLorme, start p55 (A5/6) and finish p42 (B/C3) and they call the trail the Furnace Creek Wash Road. USGS 35116 and 36116.

MILES: Loop. 28 miles dirt from HWY 178 to Dante's View Road.

AUTHORITY: Death Valley National Monument, Furnace Creek, CA 92328 (619) 786-2331.

REMARKS: This is not a summer trip. Your first stop should be the Visitor Center in Furnace Creek. The nearby trail is **Titus Canyon**. Find Hugh Hepner (past president of the Death Valley 49er's Association) at the Furnace Creek Ranch for excellent 4WD tours.

Hi Mountain

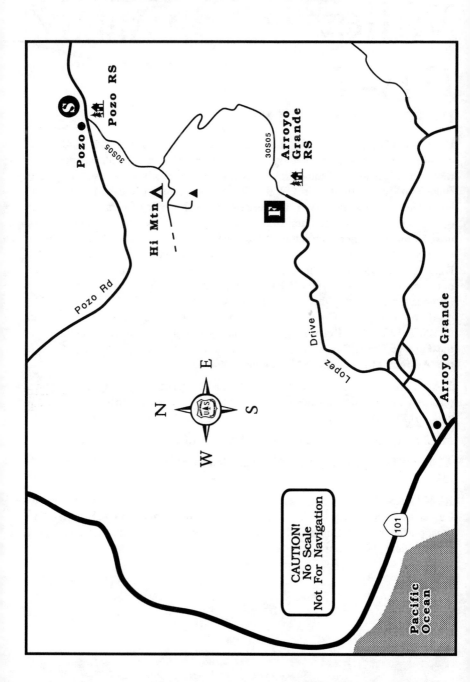

Area 1
CB-1

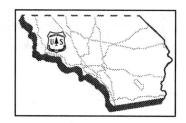

HI MOUNTAIN

DESCRIPTION: On your way out from **La Panza**, in Pozo, just make a left on 30S05. In case you forgot, Pozo is out in the middle of nowhere. Go north on HWY 101 to Santa Margarita for a right (east) on HWY 58 for 3 miles. At Pozo Road make another right (southeast) and start looking for Pozo and 30S05 for your right (south). Pozo Ranger Station is at this intersection. 4 miles in on the dirt go left to continue or take the side trip up to **Hi Mountain**. You know you're done when you pass the Arroyo Grande Ranger Station at the beginning of the paved road. Continue on down this highway, through Arroyo Grande to HWY 101 for your path home.

MAPS: ACSC San Luis Obispo County (F8, G8). DeLorme p60 (B1/2, C1/2). Forest Service Map, Los Padres National Forest (E10, E11). USGS 35120.

MILES: Loop. 16 miles from Pozo to start of pavement at Lopez Drive.

AUTHORITY: Los Padres National Forest, Santa Lucia District, 1616 Carlotti Dr., Santa Maria, CA 93454 (805) 925-9538.

REMARKS: There is a jeep trail to the east of the main route but not advised for the weak hearted. With creativity, you can actually get over to Stony Creek Campground or my **Agua Escondido** trail.

Holcomb Creek

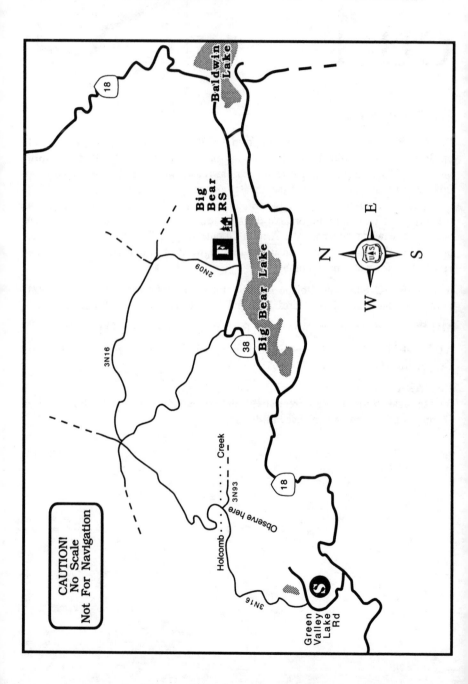

Area 5 CB-14

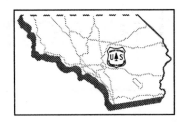

HOLCOMB CREEK

DESCRIPTION: When you want to add more miles to **Holcomb Valley** or just increase your familiarity with the area, try this. Off HWY 18 long before Big Bear Lake, make the hairpin left (west) on Green Valley Lake Road. Just before the lake, turn left (north) on 3N16. You stay on 3N16 all the way to 2N09 where you can make a right to complete this trip or continue straight to intersect **Holcomb Valley**. About 6 miles into 3N16, (refer to **Crab Flats**) check out the very rough 3N93 (F2/3). Your right on 2N09 takes you out to HWY 38 east of Fawnskin. Home is back down the hill, unless you are lucky enough to live up here.

MAPS: San Bernardino National Forest, San Bernardino Meridian, (F2/3, G2). ACSC LA and Vicinity (F16, E/F17). DeLorme p95 (C7), p96 (B1). Sidekick (Big Bear Lake) no coordinates. Start not shown on Desert Access Guides, finish on #14 (A4). USGS 34116 and 34117.

MILES: Loop. 23 miles from trail at Green Valley Lake Road to HWY 38 at Fawnskin.

AUTHORITY: San Bernardino National Forest, Arrowhead District, P. O. Box 7, Rim Forest, CA 92378 (909) 337-2444. Also, Big Bear District, P. O. Box 290, Fawnskin, CA 92333 (909) 866-3437.

REMARKS: Traffic on this popular road makes it dusty and slow. Other nearby trails, **Butler Peak**, **Holcomb Valley** and rough **Crab Flats**.

Holcomb Valley

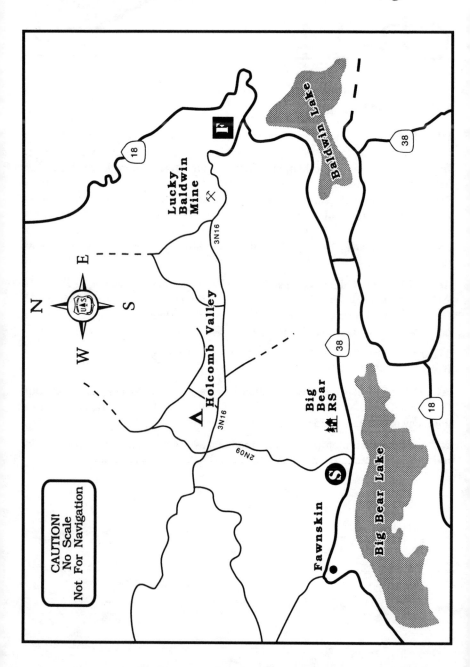

Area 5
CB-14

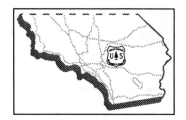

HOLCOMB VALLEY

DESCRIPITION: Wash the car and pack a picnic lunch before you leave. I see more passenger cars than 4Xs on this one. Stop in the Big Bear District Ranger Station and see if they still have a copy of the *Gold Fever Trail* handout. It helps you find Two Gun Bill's Saloon, Hangman's tree, Pigmy Cabin and more in this historic area. Signs along the way will help too. Use HWY 38 along the north shore of Big Bear Lake to Poligue Canyon Road (2N09) west of Fawnskin. Turn north here and look for your next turn, right, on 3N16. You follow this past the Lucky Baldwin Mine back down to HWY 38 again. From this side of the valley, home can be on down HWY 18 via the desert and I-15 or back along the lake and the way you came up.

MAPS: San Bernardino National Forest, San Bernardino Meridian, (G2/3, H2/3). ACSC LA and Vicinity (E17, E18). DeLorme p96 (B1, B2). Sidekick (Big Bear) no coordinates. Desert Access Guide #14 (A/B4, B/C3/4). USGS 34116.

MILES: Loop. 13 miles from paved HWY 38 and back to HWY 18.

AUTHORITY: San Bernardino National Forest, Big Bear District, P. O. Box 290, Fawnskin, CA 92333 (909) 866-3437.

REMARKS: Plan on a picnic in the woods for sure. This trail allows you to escape the summer heat and enjoy both the dirt and paved drives. Other nearby trails are **Holcomb Creek**, **Butler Peak** and beware, **Crab Flats**.

La Panza

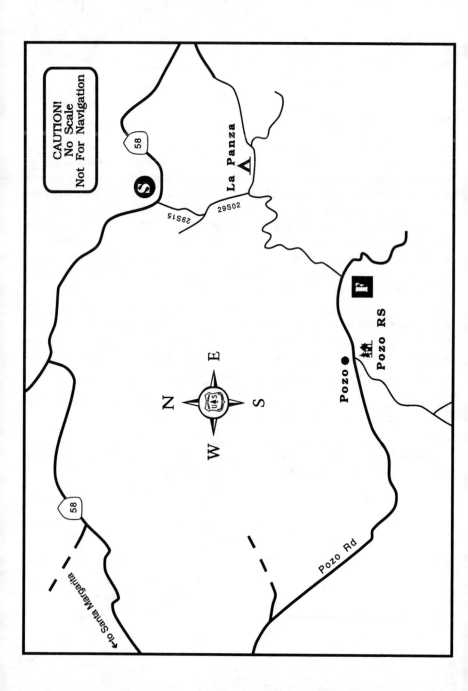

Area 1
CB-1

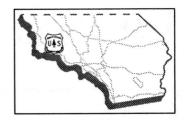

LA PANZA

DESCRIPTION: You choose. Midway between I-5 and HWY 101, approach via either the long (I-5) or slow (101) way. 20 miles east of Santa Margarita, use 29S15 which transitions to 29S02 south. You want to follow the signs toward La Panza Campground, but just before there, take a right (south) toward the Pozo Summit. Follow this to pavement at Pozo Road. You are now really out in the middle of nowhere. Continue on west toward Santa Margarita where you can pick up HWY 101 to somewhere.

MAPS: ACSC San Luis Obispo County (E9, F9). DeLorme p60 (A2, B2). Forest Service Map, Los Padres National Forest (F9, E/F10). USGS 35120.

MILES: Loop. 12 miles from HWY 58 to Pozo Road.

AUTHORITY: Los Padres National Forest, Santa Lucia District, 1616 Carlotti Dr., Santa Maria, CA 93454 (805) 925-9538.

REMARKS: The only nearby trails are **Agua Escondido** and **Hi Mountain**. But lots of trails along the main route will keep you guessing and occupied if it's miles you want. This is an all season route.

Laguna Hanson

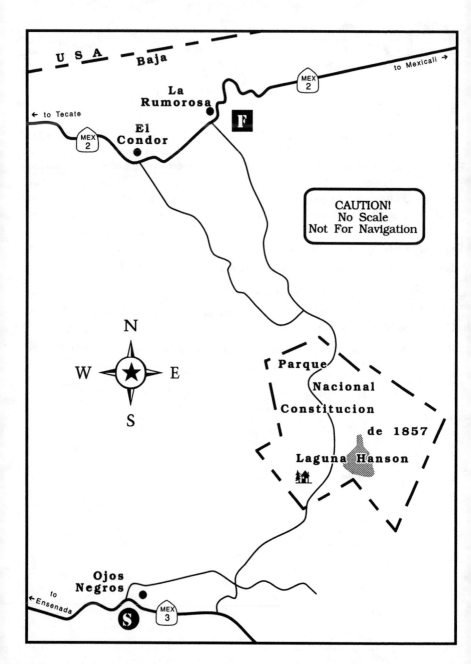

Baja
CB-36

LAGUNA HANSON

DESCRIPTION: The two Baja trails in this Guide are trail bait. Hopefully, they will show you an unexpected side of Baja and destroy the Baja bandido myth. Give Baja a chance! **Laguna Hanson** is a surprise. Pine forest and lake do not fit with the traditional desert-only view of our southern neighbor. The easiest way to get there the first time is to head east out of Ensenada (C2) to Ojos Negros (C3). Use the paved turnoff north to the first main dirt road in town. Confidently head right (east) and follow the well traveled, sometimes signed road to the *Parque Nacional* (C4). Allow plenty of time to work your way around all sides of the lake and be aware only rains fill the fragile body of water. I've seen it completely dry, flooded over the south, west and east side roads, and covered with snow. The area can be populated with Mexican campers or completely void of people. Camping seems to be acceptable about any place you light, and there are designated areas complete with outhouses and trashcans. Try a northerly exit knowing all easterly roads eventually dead end and most westerly roads lead to El Condor (B3/4). My exit goal is La Rumorosa (B4).

MAPS: ACSC Baja (C3, B4). The Baja Topographic Atlas Directory, start at pB22 (A/B1/2) and finish on pB7 (D3).

MILES: Loop. Considering the variety of routes, about 60 miles from MEX 3 to MEX 2.

AUTHORITY: No contact.

REMARKS: This is a year-round trip, with possibility of snow in the winter. Allow at least three days - one in, one out and a visitation day. Occasionally you may be approached by a non-uniformed ranger for camping fees. My philosophy is pay it and not argue over credentials. There are no facilities, gasoline or stores in the area. Take everything you need and remove your trash. Proof of citizenship is required for re-entry into the USA.

Last Chance Cyn

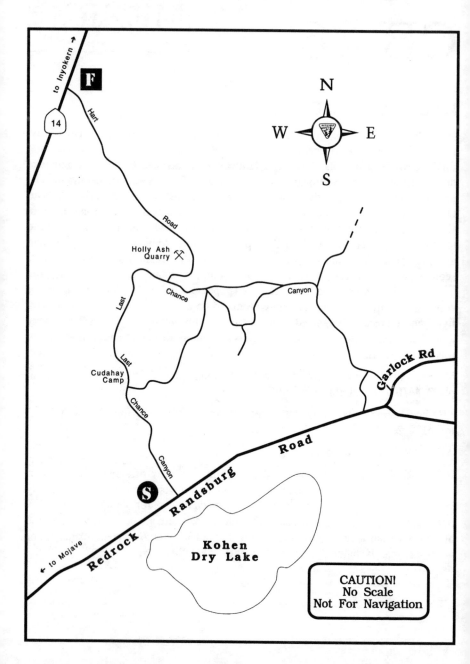

Area 2
CB-4

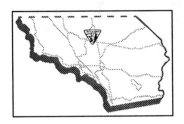

LAST CHANCE CANYON

DESCRIPTION: Last Chance Canyon bisects the El Paso Mountains on a north-south axis. Take Highway 14 from Mojave about 20 miles to Redrock-Randsburg Road and turn east for six miles. A tall, rusted metal pole marks the beginning of Last Chance Canyon Road, although the canyon begins in the El Pasos about one mile away. If you pass Saltdale Road, you've overshot by a quarter mile. Follow the dirt road north into the canyon as it twists and turns. The route alternates between roadbed and stream bottom. Erosion during heavy rains can influence the character and difficulty of this trail. Full size vehicles may have width problems on some turns. Follow the canyon for about four miles until it begins to open up near another dirt road coming in from the east (right). This is Pleasant Valley Road and connects with the upper part of Last Chance Canyon. Stay in the canyon bottom for another mile then look low in the cliffs to your left. The tunnel entrance near a shot up water tank was the powder storage room for the Old Dutch Cleanser mine at Cudahay Camp. Follow the canyon bottom another four miles to the Last Chance signpost and exit in whichever direction suits your mood and time requirements. The quickest way out is via Hart Road. The longest and roughest is via Goler Gulch.

MAPS: ACSC Kern County (D/E19, C/D18/19), BLM Desert Access Guide #7 (A/B2/3, A1). DeLorme p65 (A7). USGS 35117. Hilemans (#1, no coordinates). *Exploring the Ghost Town Desert* by Roberta Martin Starry (book, p37).

MILES: Loop. From paved road to Last Chance signpost, 7 miles; to Highway 14 by way of Hart Road, 13 miles.

AUTHORITY: Bureau of Land Management, 300 South Richmond Road, Ridgecrest CA 93555, (619) 375-7125.

REMARKS: The El Pasos have lots of trails and attractions to explore. Nearby trails are **Burro Schmidt's Tunnel**, **Barnett Opal Mine** and **Steam Well**. Camping is allowed on public lands, but a fire permit is required.

Roger Vargo

Liebre Mtn

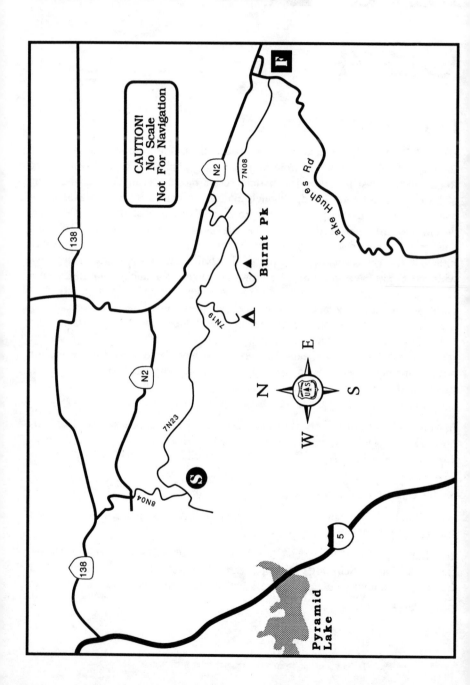

Area 2
CB-4

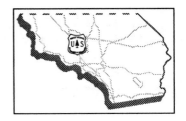

LIEBRE MOUNTAIN

DESCRIPTION: To keep from scaring you off, I didn't name this earthquake fault. HWY N2, just to the north of our route is the San Andreas earthquake fault. Take I-5 north toward Bakersfield. Then use HWY 138 east to N2 (B1) south for two miles to the gravel road (8N04). Three miles farther south brings you to your left (east) on 7N23. Pass up side roads 7N14 and 7N19 and follow 7N23 southeast to 7N08 (intersection at C2). 7N23 now leads out to HWY N2. An almost straight puts you on 7N08 which you follow to paved Lake Hughes Road. Left takes you back to N2 and right eventually leads back to I-5 and home. Several campgrounds make a nice close getaway and will give you the weekend to thoroughly explore several sideroads and features.

MAPS: Angeles National Forest, San Bernardino Meridian (B2, D2). ACSC LA and Vicinity (B3, B5). DeLorme p78 (C1, C3/4). USGS 34118.

MILES: Loop. 24 miles from 7N23 to paved Lake Hughes Road.

AUTHORITY: Angeles National Forest, Saugus District, 27757 Bouquet Canyon Road, Saugus, CA 91350 (805) 252-9710.

REMARKS: HWYs 138, N2 and the dirt road all yield spectacular fields of wild flowers in the Spring. Follow 138 clear across to I-15 near the Cajon Pass. Couple this with a bicycle ride along the California aqueduct for even more flowers. **Alamo Mountain**, **Warm Springs** and **Tule Ridge** are all reasonably close by.

Lockwood Creek

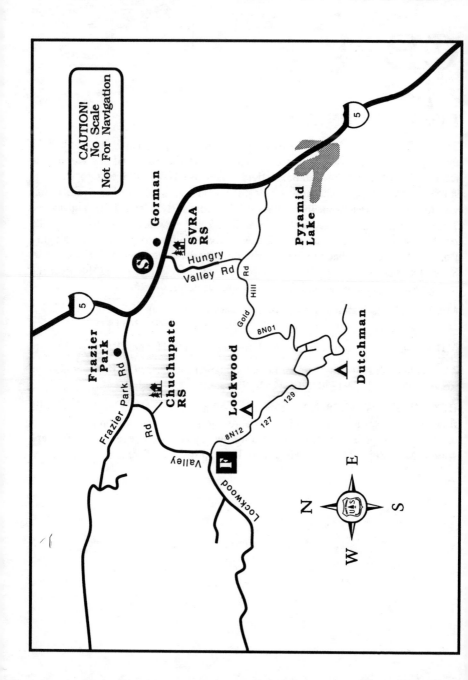

Area 1
CB-1

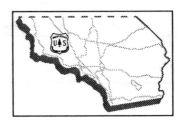

LOCKWOOD CREEK

DESCRIPTION: If you've thought about 90% of my trails have been too tame, lookout. The rocks can get you on this one. Near Gorman, off I-5, go west on the southerly frontage road to the Hungry Valley State Vehicular Recreation Area. Use (8N01), first called Hungry Valley Road, then Gold Hill Road up to Dutchman Flats campground. This transition is easy to miss. Look for the public bulletin board. Find the Miller Jeep Road (trail 129) on the east side of the campground. This leads down -really down! At the bottom head into the rocky, really rocky, Lockwood Creek Canyon (trail 127) to the northeast. Allow a couple of hours to follow and make your way through the next 3 miles. By the time you see passenger cars at the mouth of the creek, you're done, really done. No signs, just common sense will keep you on the most heavily traveled dirt road (8N12) to paved Lockwood Valley Road. Go right to another right at Frazier Mountain Park Road. This leads back to I-5 and home.

MAPS: Mount Pinos Ranger District ORV Map (T.8N, R.19W to T.8N, R.20W). Use the detail map in the lower right hand corner to get through the Vehicular Recreation Area. ACSC LA and Vicinity (B1), but all roads not shown. ACSC Ventura County, (D7, D/E6), Miller and Lockwood Roads not shown. DeLorme p77 (B6, B/C5). USGS 34118 and 34119.

MILES: Loop. 19 miles from the gate at Hungry Valley State Vehicular Recreation Area to paved Lockwood Valley Road.

AUTHORITY: Mt. Pinos Ranger District, Chuchupate Ranger Station, Frazier Park, CA 93225 (805) 245-3731. 24 hour recorded message (805) 245-3449. Also Hungry Valley State Vehicular Recreation Area, P. O. Box 1360, Lebec, CA 93243-1360 (805) 248-6447.

REMARKS: This one is rough. It is impossible for most stock vehicles to go up Miller Jeep Road. Frequent closures due to fire and rain. Snow makes it dangerous. Allow extra time. **Alamo Mountain, Quatal Canyon, Apache Canyon** and **Grade Valley** are nearby. **Liebre Mountain** and **Warm Springs** are across I-5, but close enough to call nearby. This area is subject to winter closure.

Los Coyotes

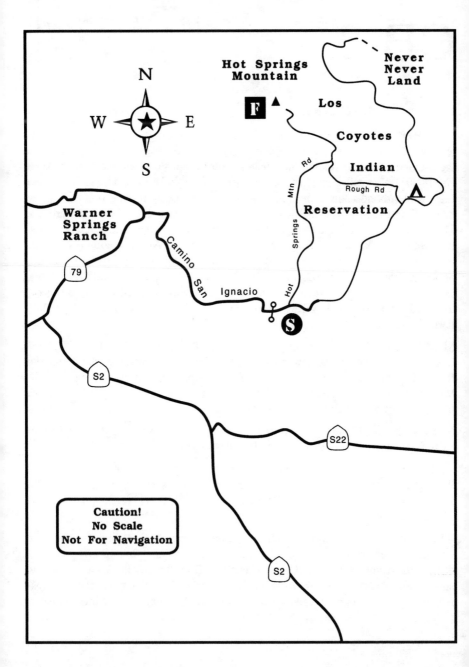

Hot Springs
Mountain

Never
Never
Land

Los

Coyotes

Indian

Reservation

Rough Rd

Warner
Springs
Ranch

Camino San

Ignacio

Mtn Rd

Hot Springs

79

S2

S22

S2

Caution!
No Scale
Not For Navigation

Area 9
CB-36

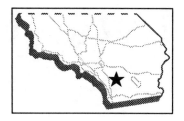

LOS COYOTES INDIAN RESERVATION

DESCRIPTION: I'll get you into the campgrounds, but beware from there on! This is the place where the High Desert Round Up is occasionally held. What that means is if you've heard of the infamous, rough Rubicon Trail you'll have a little perspective on some of the trail difficulty. There are sections around the Manzanita Loop, Ball Bearing Hill, Bobsled Run and others that make the Rubicon look like grandma's run to the store for a loaf of bread. Take HWY 15 south to Temecula/Rancho California. Use HWY 79 east (the freeway sign says south) all the way to Warner Springs Ranch. Just out of Warner Springs make a sharp left (east) on Camino San Ignacio. Follow the yellow line all the way to the entrance gate at the reservation. Get their map. Repeat, get their map and at least stay out of the upper right hand corner. This is never-never land for stock 4Xs. Other trails to avoid are the Jeep Squeeze, Left Turn Hill, Dangerous Road (name of and description!), Bronco Hill, an unnamed road near Rainbow Springs and unless you're a good hill climber, Dirty Shorts Hill (Marshmallow Hill). A trip to Hot Springs Mountain and back via Rough Road is fun. Go northeast out of camp and use Radiator Gulch. This leads to the waterfall. This is part of Dangerous Road. Home, if you followed my advice and your rig still rolls, is back the way you came.

MAPS: ACSC San Diego County (C10/11), but only Hot Springs Mountain Road shown. DeLorme p114/115 (B4) minimal roads shown. Desert Access Guide #19 (A3). USGS 33116.

MILES: Dead-end. Doing Hot Springs Mountain and Radiator Gulch totals 40 miles.

AUTHORITY: The "LOS COYOTES" Band of Mission Indians, Banning Taylor, Spokesman, P. O. Box 249, Los Tules Road, Warner Springs, CA 92086 (619) 782-3269.

REMARKS: Rough, rough, rough. That is my way of telling you to be cautious! Nearby, but not legal to drive to from the reservation is **Coyote Canyon**. Other nearby trails are **Thomas Mountain** and **Toro Peak**.

Ty Prettyman and Gene Markley

Lytle Creek

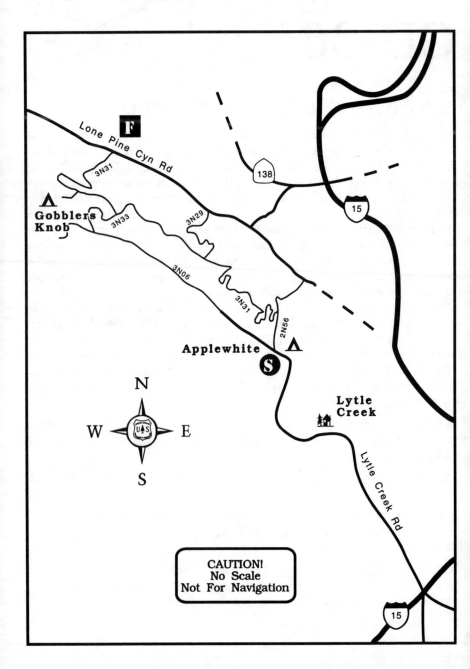

Lone Pine Cyn Rd

F

3N31

138

15

Gobblers Knob

3N33

3N29

3N06

3N31

2N56

Applewhite

S

Lytle Creek

N

W · E

S

Lytle Creek Rd

CAUTION!
No Scale
Not For Navigation

15

Area 4
CB-11

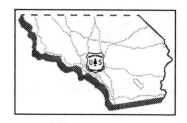

LYTLE CREEK

DESCRIPTION: Reasonable road, nearby home and if you're the first to Gobblers Knob (8 plus miles from the start), secluded camping. Off I-15 out of Fontana (C4), go north on Lytle Creek Road. Take the second unsigned, dirt right (north) on 2N56 just across from the Applewhite picnic area. In about a mile, a sign identifies your left (west). Turn up this, the Upper Lytle Creek Ridge. This is 3N31. The next 11½ or so miles offer several opportunities for indecision. They are actually chances to get back down to Lytle Creek Road or Lone Pine Canyon Road, which is where I end this trail. Left (northwest) on Lone Pine goes to Wrightwood and right (southeast) to Hwy 138 near **Mormon Rocks**. At HWY 138, make a right (west) to nearby I-15 and your southerly trip home.

MAPS: San Bernardino National Forest (B/C2/3, B2/3). ACSC LA and Vicinity (E/F13, E12). ACSC San Bernardino County (G1/2, G1). DeLorme p94 (B3/4, B3). USGS 34117.

MILES: Loop. 13 from Lytle Creek Road to paved Lone Pine Canyon Road.

AUTHORITY: San Bernardino National Forest, Cajon District Ranger, Star Route Box 100, Fontana, CA 92335 (909) 887-2576. This is the Lytle Creek Ranger Station you pass on the way up.

REMARKS: Beware, this is also used by dirt bikes and ATCs. Combine with **Mormon Rocks**.

Magic Mtn

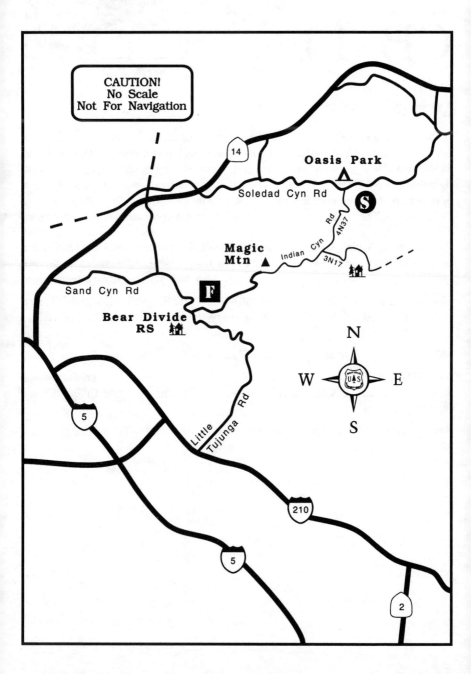

Area 4
CB-11

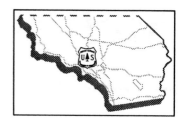

MAGIC MOUNTAIN

DESCRIPTION: No, this is not where you go for thrill rides and hot dogs. This is one of three local trips to hone your directional skills on maintained fire roads. Take HWY 14 toward Palmdale, but use the Agua Dulce (E4) turnoff south to Soledad Canyon Road east. Across from the private Oasis Park turn south on 4N37 (Indian Canyon Road). About 5½ miles into the road you reach an intersection with 3N17. Left leads to the North Fork Ranger Station and other trails listed below. Straight goes on out to pavement, via this description. About three miles is the spur road and locked gate to **Magic Mountain**. Pavement starts here. You come out on, now get this, Sand Canyon Road if you go right and Little Tujunga Road if you go left, which is a quicker way home.

MAPS: Angeles National Forest, San Bernardino Meridian (E4, D5). ACSC LA and Vicinity (D6, E5/6). DeLorme p93 (A4), p92 (B4). USGS 34117.

MILES: Loop. 15 miles including the 6½ miles of paved near the Bear Divide Ranger Station.

AUTHORITY: Angeles National Forest, Tujunga District, 12328 Gladstone Ave., San Fernando, CA 91342 (818) 362-1216.

REMARKS: You can spend a day combining this with **Messenger Flats** and **Pacifico Mountain**, both of which have campgrounds.

McPherson Peak

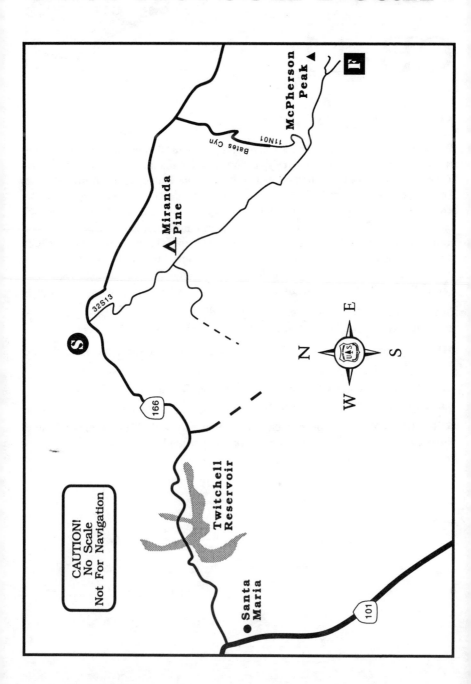

Area 1
CB-1

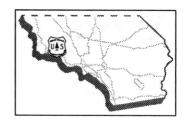

McPHERSON PEAK

DESCRIPTION: If ridge running is your bag, you might like this one. Go north on HWY 101 past Santa Maria (C3/4) to HWY 166 for a right (east). 25 or so miles of crossing the Twitchell Reservoir twice and winding along the Cuyama River brings you to your right (south) on Sierra Madre Road (32S13). 9 miles out you will pass the Miranda Pine Campgrounds (B8). 13 miles farther brings you to the Bates Canyon Road turnoff (11N01, gate locked at end during winter). Another 8 takes you to the peak and the dead-end. You know how to get home, follow your tracks back to paved HWY 166.

MAPS: ACSC Santa Barbara County (A7, D11). DeLorme p60 (D4), p75 (A6). Los Padres National Forest (H12, J15). USGS 34119, 34120, 35119, and 35120.

MILES: Dead-end. Can you believe I would send you out 30 miles from HWY 166 to just turn around and drive another 30 back?

AUTHORITY: Los Padres National Forest, Santa Lucia District, 1616 Carlotti Dr., Santa Maria, CA 93454 (805) 925-9538.

REMARKS: If you've got some hikers in the family, and want to have a reason for doing this one, consider this. Drop the hikers off at the peak and meet them at the Aliso Campground (D11) near New Cuyama. They will beat you down! Nothing really close by unless the gate at Miranda Pine Campground is open (closed during winter).

Gene Markley

Messenger Flats

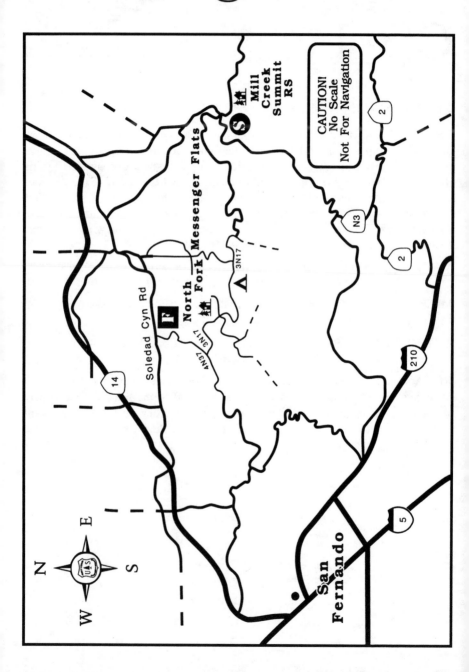

Area 4
CB-11

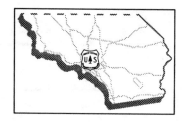

MESSENGER FLATS

DESCRIPTION: The Angeles National Forest has so many trails, I didn't know where to start. This means two things. One, lots of miles for you to explore. Two, lots of miles to practice navigational skills. Have fun. Off I-210 go north on HWY 2 (F6). Then use N3 (F5) to your left (northwest) all the way to the Mill Creek Summit (G4) where you pick up and stay on 3N17 all the way to the North Fork Saddle Ranger Station. Left gets you lost around Pappy Keef, right takes you across to nearby Perspiration Point and eventually the town of Acton, and straight on with the trail (3N17). At the intersection of 4N37, if you've done **Magic Mountain**, you're on familiar turf. A right leads out to paved Soledad Canyon Road. Soledad Canyon Road gets you headed back to HWY 14 and home.

MAPS: Angeles National Forest, San Bernardino Meridian (G4, E4). ACSC LA and Vicinity (D8, D6). DeLorme p93 (A6, A4). USGS 34118.

MILES: Loop. 19 miles from Mill Creek Summit to Soledad Canyon Road.

AUTHORITY: Angeles National Forest, Tujunga District, 12328 Gladstone Ave., San Fernando, CA 91342 (818) 362-1216.

REMARKS: This trail also coincides with **Magic Mountain** and **Pacifico Mountain**. Via the 3, you can virtually traverse most of the forest from west to east.

Ian Wilson

Mineral Hill

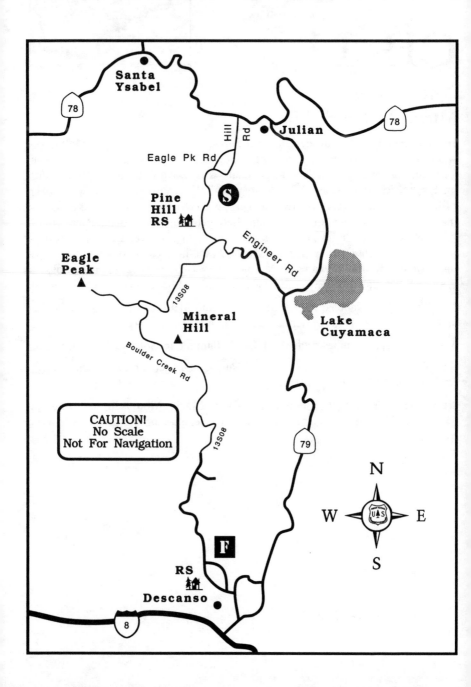

Area 9
CB-36

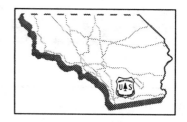

MINERAL HILL

DESCRIPTION: Several things make quaint Julian praiseworthy. The Julian Hotel, bed and breakfast inns, the Apple Festival, the bakery and more. Get there by going south on I-15 to HWY 78, in Escondido (E6), for a left (east). This joins HWY 79 and before long you're there, but you shouldn't be. Back about 1½ miles you need to go south on Pine Hill Road to Eagle Peak Road. In less than a mile, take a left on Boulder Creek Road (13S08). This is your route for the next 22 miles which ends in Descanso and back on HWY 79. 79 has an on ramp for I-8 and west to home. Do it backwards and end up in Julian for the night. That way you'll be closer to home for the next morning's drive.

MAPS: ACSC San Diego County (F10, H10). Cleveland National Forest, Descanso District (K8, K10). DeLorme p114 (D3), p122 (B4). USGS 32116 and 33116.

MILES: Loop. 22 miles from Eagle Peak Road to HWY 79.

AUTHORITY: Cleveland National Forest, Descanso Ranger District, 3348 Alpine Blvd., Alpine CA 92001 (619) 445-6235.

REMARKS: Nothing needs to be close to Julian, it's nice in itself. There are many roads and few signs that make one clean shot through the area nearly impossible. It's fair at any time to give up and retrace your route back to Julian. The only nearby trail is **Mount Laguna**.

Mitchell Caverns

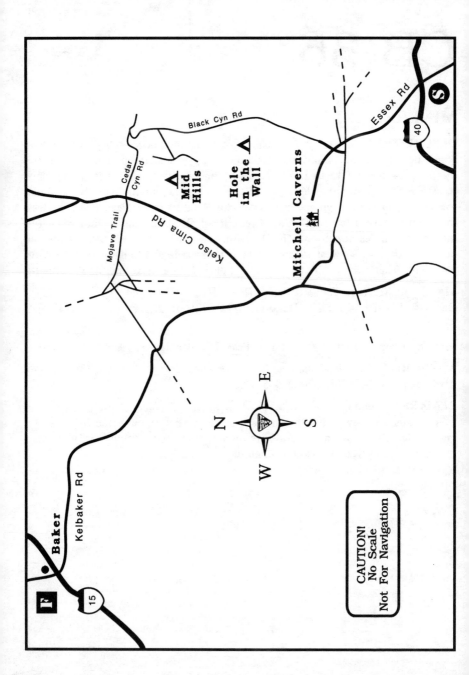

Area 3
CB-7

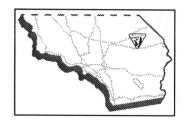

MITCHELL CAVERNS

DESCRIPTION: So you'd like to see Carlsbad Caverns in New Mexico, yet don't want to make the drive. Mitchell Caverns (E9/10) is a well kept secret that is not as big as Carlsbad, but does have some better stuff. Get to Barstow (E3) via I-15 and go east on I-40. Refueling at Barstow is a must. 84 plus miles out I-40 is Essex Road (E10) for your left (north) and in 15 miles you're at the caverns. Hang around or schedule in the impressive tour. Go back to the intersection of Black Canyon Road and make a tight left (north). Continue north to Hole-in-the-Wall or as I prefer, Mid Hills Campgrounds. Now I leave you hanging! This is your chance to explore. Trust there are enough good roads in the area to get you north and west to I-15 for the trip home. (Remember to check fuel.) This area may be my next guide - the East Mojave National Scenic Area. There are many trails. If you have *Mojave Road Guide* (ISBN 0-914224-13-1), you can follow it too. Generally, Black Canyon Road north, to Cedar Canyon Road west (left). Then use a 7 mile section of the Mojave Trail (slow going, 2 foot washboard), to an unnamed graded road southwest (left), to paved Kelbaker Road right (mostly west) out to I-15 and the town of Baker. Now, you really need gasoline! Home is south on I-15.

MAPS: ACSC San Bernardino County (E10, C7). Desert Access Guide #12 (G3), to #9 (A3), Baker not shown. DeLorme p85 (B7), p70 (B1). USGS 34115, 34116, 35115, and 35116.

MILES: Loop. 81 miles from I-40 to I-15, with no mistakes. Gasoline is critical on this trip.

AUTHORITY: BLM, California Desert Information Center, 831 Barstow Road, Barstow, CA 92311 (619) 256-8313.

REMARKS: Planning and preparation are critical for this trip. Best to avoid this in the heat of late spring, summer and early fall. Travel with others. **Afton Canyon** and **Zzyzx** are nearby the finish. *Mojave Road Guide* loaners are available at the Way Station in Barstow.

Mormon Rocks

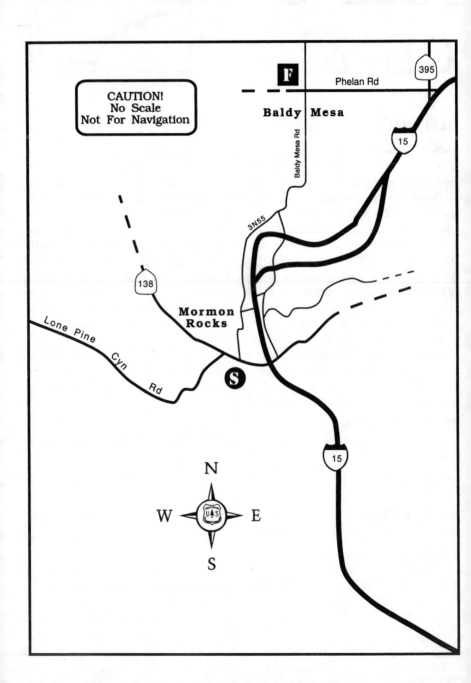

CAUTION!
No Scale
Not For Navigation

Baldy Mesa

Phelan Rd

Baldy Mesa Rd

3N55

138

Mormon
Rocks

Lone Pine Cyn Rd

S

F

395

15

15

N
W · E
S

Area 2
CB-4

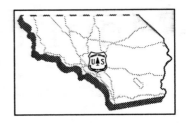

MORMON ROCKS

DESCRIPTION: The **Mormon Rocks** are those giant sandstone rocks you see to the west of the intersection of I-15 and HWY 138 on your way to Las Vegas. This trail is more just an area to explore than a specific route. Get to this intersection and go west on HWY 138 and just after you pass over the railroad tracks look for any one of several dirt roads off to your right (north). Try the scary ones along side the RR tracks in the narrow canyons, but respect the moving trains that pass very closely! There is also a road (3N55), ending up as Baldy Mesa Road, that leads to the top of the Cajon Pass. After you pass the first narrows, you will make a trip back to the 1940's. It's tough to find, but pick your way up the mountain to the mesa, then have lunch at the Summit Cafe on the east side of I-15. Home is down hill from here.

MAPS: San Bernardino National Forest, San Bernardino Meridian, (B/C2, B/C1). ACSC LA and Vicinity (E12). DeLorme p94 (B4). All these show the Ranger Station to the south of HWY 138 and don't show the actual Rocks which are to the north of 138. Desert Access Guide #10 (B/C8, B/C7). USGS 34117.

MILES: It's a loop if you go to the top of the Cajon Pass via Baldy Mesa Road. About 4 to 5 miles.

AUTHORITY: San Bernardino National Forest, Cajon Ranger District, Star Route Box 100, Fontana, CA 92335 (909) 887-2576.

REMARKS: Fun to combine with **Lytle Creek**. Use caution and common sense around the trains which go up and down the Cajon Pass frequently! Also understand the washes are off limits on Foreset Service Lands.

Mount Laguna

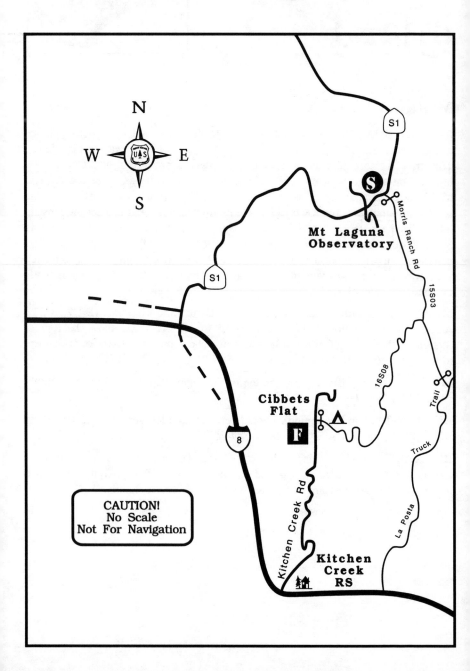

Area 9
CB-36

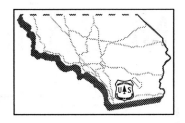

MOUNT LAGUNA

DESCRIPTION: Here's another observatory if the trip to Palomar (**Nate Harrison**) wasn't enough. But don't compare the roads. This one is moderate to worse the way I put you down to Cibbets Flat Campground. Just like you were going to Julian (E/F10), south on I-15 to HWY 78, in Escondido (E6), for a left (east) on HWY 78. In Julian, continue south on HWY 79 (E10). Before Lake Cuyamaca you want to go left (southeast) on HWY S1 (F11) to Morris Ranch Road (15S03). That's before the Mount Laguna Observatory by about a mile. Go south on this road for 3 1/2 miles to the right (southwest) down to Cibbets Flat Campground on 16S08. The road is rougher from here to pavement at the campground. That's Kitchen Creek Road which leads to I-8. Home is to your right or west.

MAPS: ACSC San Diego County (H12, H/J12). Cleveland National Forest, Descanso District (M9, M10). DeLorme p123 (B5) and they call Morris Ranch Road La Posta Truck Trail. Desert Access Guide #19 (B/C8, B/C9). USGS 32116.

MILES: Loop. 10 miles from HWY S1 to Kitchen Creek Road.

AUTHORITY: Cleveland National Forest, Descanso Ranger District, 3348 Alpine Blvd., Alpine, CA 92001 (619) 445-6235.

REMARKS: **Mineral Hill** is the only trail nearby. Gate on each end closed during winter.

Mulholland Drive

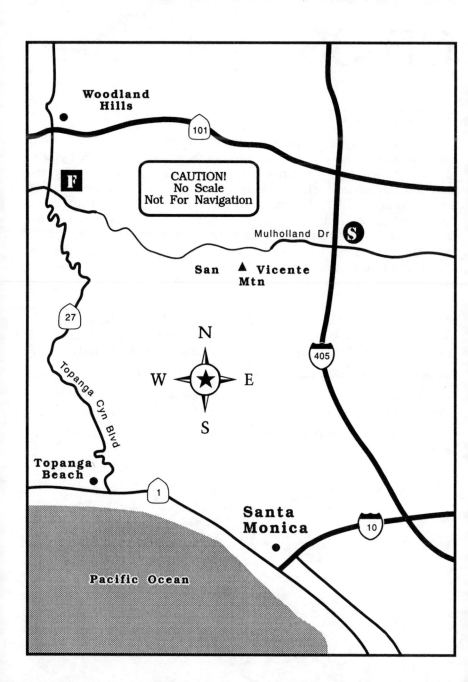

Area 1
CB-1

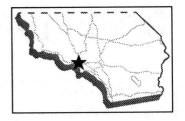

MULHOLLAND DRIVE

DESCRIPTION: All the noise you hear in the background is the ruckus from the old timers who say, "What, he includes Mulholland Drive in a dirt road book." They're right. Hardly an adventure, but maybe just what you want for your first time out. And so close to home too. There's even a Mulholland Drive ramp off I-405 just north of Sunset Blvd. It actually puts you on Rimerton first, but a couple of hundred yards north is Mulholland where you turn left (west). Paved for a while and then turns into dirt at Encino Hills Place. Half of the trail is through the Topanga State Park. You come out on HWY 27 or Topanga Canyon Blvd. North (right) goes to HWY 101 and left (south) to HWY 1 in Topanga Beach.

MAPS: ACSC LA and Vicinity (F5, F4). DeLorme p92 (D3, C2). USGS 34118.

MILES: Loop. 10 miles from I-405 to HWY 27.

AUTHORITY: LA County and Topanga State Park (310) 586-6543.

REMARKS: No nearby trails. Do this at night and look out for the parked cars. This is a lovers' lane of sorts. Nice views.

Old Dale Road

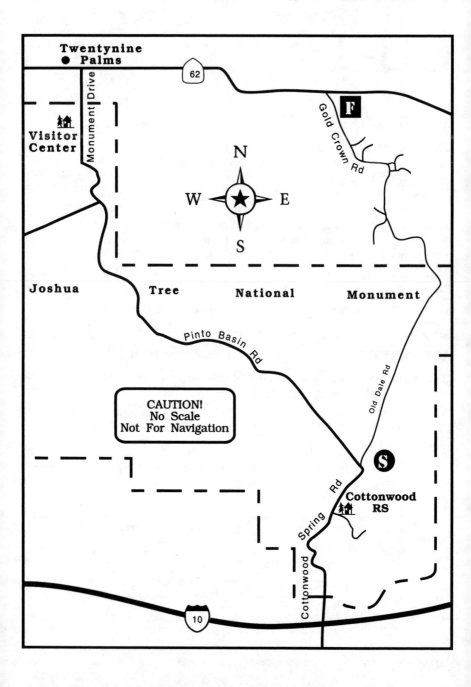

Area 8
CB-33

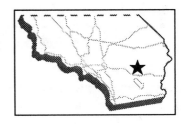

OLD DALE ROAD

DESCRIPTION: This trail takes you along a region where the Cahuilla and Serrano Indians lived. Regardless of the time of year, put yourself in their place, 500 years ago, as you cross the expansive Pinto Basin. As usual, for Joshua Tree National Monument, go east on I-10 toward Palm Springs, but pass up HWY 111 and take HWY 62 north and then east to Twentynine Palms. Go right (south) on National Monument Drive (Utah Trail to some). At the intersection of Pinto Basin Road, take it left (southeast) for 23 miles. You should now be at your next left turn (northeast) on Old Dale Road. Follow Old Dale Road out of the Monument, and continue on Gold Crown Road. Gold Crown eventually takes you back to HWY 62, east of Twentynine Palms.

MAPS: ACSC Riverside County (D17/18, B17). DeLorme p108 (B3/4), p98 (D3). Road names aren't correct in this area for DeLorme. Start on Desert Access Guide #18 (B/C3) with finish on #15 (B5/6). Joshua Tree National Monument Brochure with no coordinates. USGS 33115, 33116, 34115 and 34116.

MILES: Loop. 26 miles from Pinto Basin Road to HWY 62.

AUTHORITY: Joshua Tree National Monument, 74485 National Monument Drive, Twentynine Palms, CA 92277 (619) 367-7511.

REMARKS: Gold Crown Road near the finish of the trail is another mining road/area that may be a little confusing, but have faith, you'll make it. **Desert Queen**, **Squaw Tank**, **Pinkham Canyon** and **Gold Park** are all nearby trails.

Pacifico Mountain

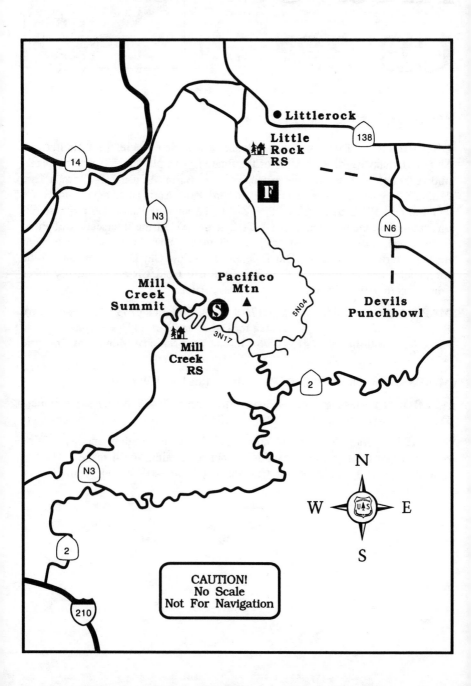

Area 4
CB-11

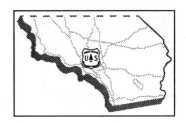

PACIFICO MOUNTAIN

DESCRIPTION: Starting at Mill Creek Summit, as several others, this is a long one on what I would hardly call dirt road. That means better than average. Off I-210 go north on HWY 2 (F6). Then use N3 to your left (north) all the way to the Mill Creek Summit where you go hard right (south) on good ol' 3N17. Take the short side trip up to **Pacifico Mountain** or continue on 3N17 to where you intersect gravel 5N04 for your left (northeast) turn. This leads out past the Little Rock Ranger Station and HWY 138 in the town of Littlerock.

MAPS: Angeles National Forest, San Bernardino Meridian (G4, G3). ACSC LA and Vicinity (D8, C/D8). DeLorme p93 (A6), p79 (D7). Sidekick (Little Rock), no coordinates. USGS 34117 and 34118.

MILES: Loop. 25 miles from Mill Creek Summit to HWY 138 in Littlerock.

AUTHORITY: Angeles National Forest, Tujunga District, 12328 Gladstone Ave., San Fernando, CA 91342 (818) 362-1216. Actually, the route is the border between the above and Valyermo District, 34146 Longview Road, Pearblossom, CA 93553 (805) 944-2187.

REMARKS: 9 campgrounds and many fishing holes along this trail make it worthwhile to explore if you're inclined. Also, don't miss the Devil's Punchbowl County Park off HWY 138 (J4). **Messenger Flats** also starts from the Mill Creek Summit. See **Valley Forge** too.

Painted Canyon

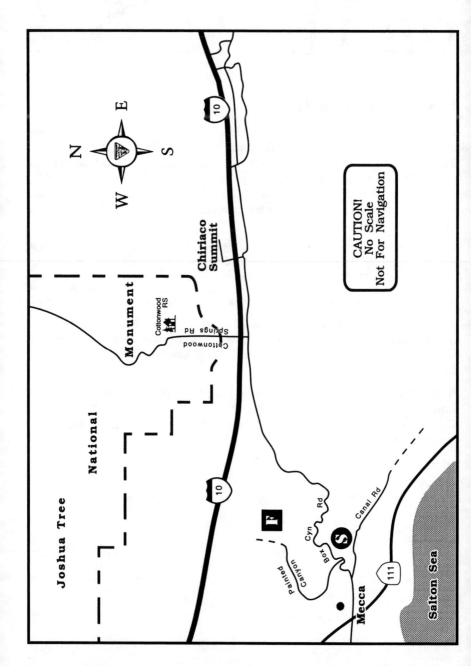

Area 10
CB-39

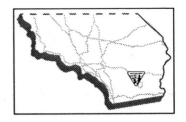

PAINTED CANYON

DESCRIPTION: Some time back, the LA Times (Magazine, April 20, 1986) wrote this up as some where between a rock and a hot place. Graded road and shortness make this trail a good side trip for your weekend in Palm Springs. So, go out I-10, but pass up PS. In Indio take HWY 111 southeast to Mecca (F15). Go left (east) on Box Canyon Road until you pass over the Coachella Canal and make a sharp bend in the road. Look for another left (northwest) on Painted Canyon Road (typically unsigned). This dirt road leads into **Painted Canyon**. 5 miles will take you through shades of Death Valley and to a dead end. The real **Painted Canyon** (F15/16) comes with a little hike further up the canyon. Reverse your travel to get back to paved Box Canyon Road and home.

MAPS: ACSC Riverside County (F15/16). Start on Desert Access Guide #17 (J7) and ends on #18 (A5). DeLorme p108 (D1, C1/2). Sidekick (Orocopia Mountains), no coordinates. USGS 33115 and 33116.

MILES: Dead-end. 10 miles to the dead-end and back to paved Box Canyon Road.

AUTHORITY: BLM, Palm Springs-South Coast Resource Area, 63-500 Garnet Ave, P.O. Box 2000, Palm Springs, CA 92258-2000, (619) 251-0812.

REMARKS: Use the referenced article to explore other features in the region, but be aware the Hidden Springs area is now closed to vehicles. **Bradshaw Road** and **Red Canyon** are nearby. Beware of **Red Canyon**.

Painted Gorge

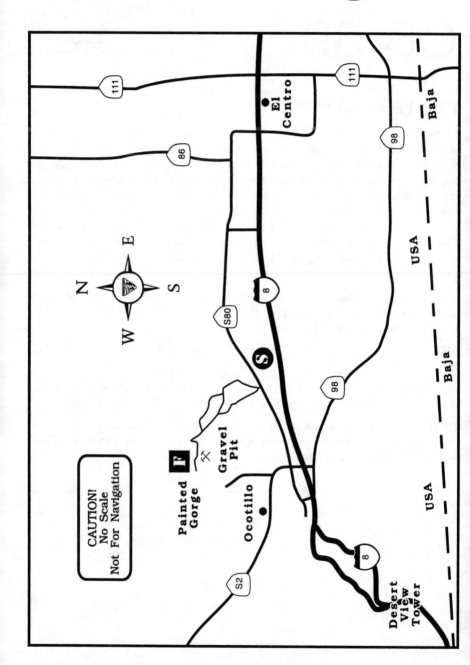

Area 9
CB-36

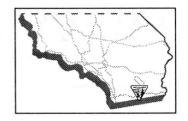

PAINTED GORGE

DESCRIPTION: This is a way to give you a taste of an area that's closed, without breaking the law. I'll direct you from San Diego, but if you think it's quicker via El Centro, use it. Take I-8 east out of San Diego and as you descend the grade by the Desert View Tower (H1), start anticipating Ocotillo. In Ocotillo, use HWY S80 northeast for about 4 miles to the Gravel Pit Road. This unmarked, but well traveled road should be obvious. Continuing north (left) will take you to worse road and eventually the **Painted Gorge**. Don't use the more northerly spurs. They are not quite as good as the one that passes the gravel pit. They are longer, but what the heck, like me, you may never be sure which one you're on anyway. Like all dead-end trails, the way out is the way in.

MAPS: ACSC Imperial County (G2). DeLorme p124 (B2). Desert Access Guide #22 (A/B2/3). USGS 32115 and 32116.

MILES: Dead-end. I turned around at 7 miles in, so it's a 14 mile round trip from HWY S80.

AUTHORITY: BLM El Centro Resource Area Office, 1661 S. Fourth St., El Centro, CA 92243 (619) 352-5842.

REMARKS: When ABC TV's Dr. George talks of summer flash floods, this is the area to avoid. **Yuha Well** is nearby.

Palen Pass

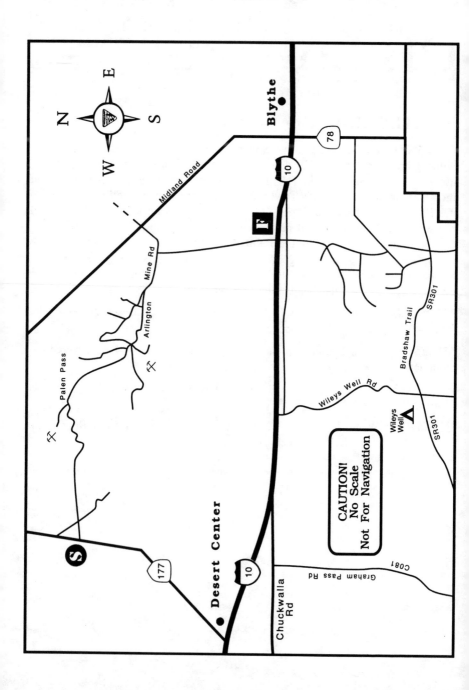

Area 8
CB-33

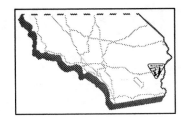

PALEN PASS

DESCRIPTION: Can you believe I give you a break about half way through this one with 3 miles of pavement. Palen is kind of like mountain climbing, you do it just because it's there! Go east on I-10 to Desert Center (E20) where you make a left (north) on HWY 177. In 17 miles (measure this one) you take an unmarked dirt road to your right (east). This leads to **Palen Pass**, down the other side and winds up in a group of mines called Arlington Mine Road. Follow this to pavement and before you cross the RR tracks, take a right (south) on the dirt road that parallels the tracks. This leads to paved road and then I-10 in Blythe. Spend the night feeding the mosquitos at the Colorado River then head for home on I-10.

MAPS: ACSC Riverside County (C22, E/F26). DeLorme p110 (A1), p111 (C5). Starts on Desert Access Guide #18 (G/H2) and ends on #16 (C10). USGS 33114 and 33115.

MILES: Loop. 38 miles from HWY 177 to paved Wells Road just before I-10.

AUTHORITY: BLM, Palm Springs-South Coast Resource Area, 63-500 Garnet Ave, P.O. Box 2000, N. Palm Springs, CA 92258-2000, (619) 251-0812.

REMARKS: **Palen Pass** is another one all by its lonesome unless you go south of I-10. **Wiley's Well**, **Coon Hollow**, **Corn Spring** and **Graham Pass** are a little farther than nearby.

Picacho Road

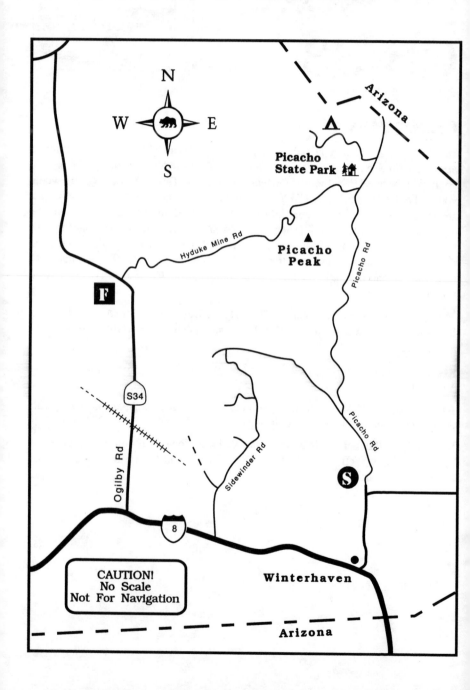

Area 10
CB-39

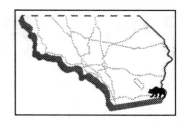

PICACHO ROAD

DESCRIPTION: If you have a boat, and don't mind too many miles of dirt road, try this one. It puts you right on the Colorado River without the crowds of Parker. I use an inflatable. Find your best way down to El Centro, on I-8 headed east toward Yuma. In Winterhaven, the 4th Street off ramp, with a wiggle or two, will put you right on HWY S24 which is **Picacho Road**. Eat dust for the next 17 miles into the State Recreation Area. Start back out the same way, but at Hyduke Mine Road make a right (west) to paved HWY S34. A left (south) takes you back to I-8 and home.

MAPS: ACSC Imperial County (H13, F11). DeLorme p127 (C6), p126 (A4), Hyduke Mine Road not identified. Desert Access Guide #21 (D/E8/9, B/C7). USGS 32114 and 33114.

MILES: Loop. 37 miles from paved S24 to paved S34.

AUTHORITY: Picacho State Recreation Area (619) 445-6477. BLM El Centro Resource Area Office, 1661 South Fourth St., El Centro, CA 92243 (619) 352-5842.

REMARKS: By the way, Picacho Peak is the plug-dome, volcanic outcropping in between your going and coming home routes. No trails really close by other than **Sand Hills** and don't do this pulling a boat.

Pilot Rock

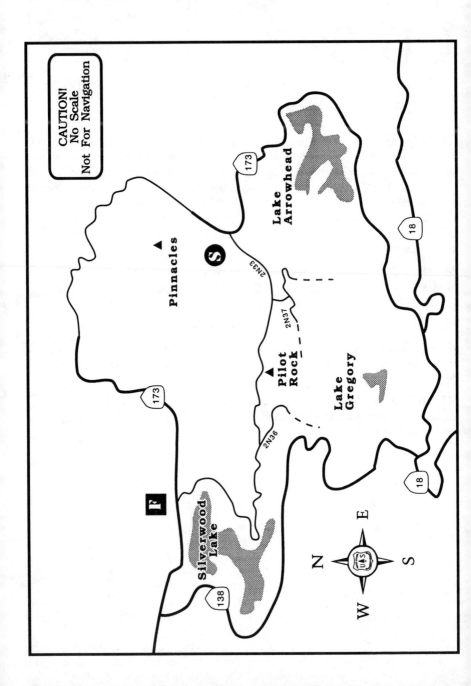

Area 5
CB-14

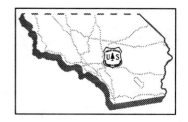

PILOT ROCK

DESCRIPTION: On this one I put you up the hill on the pavement and let you work your way back down on the dirt. As you get on the dirt, start to look for **Pilot Rock** and guess why they named it that. I think the Pinnacles are just as profound. Go north on I-15 to HWY 138 east to HWY 173 east. About the time the Pinnacles are behind you, start looking for your right (west) on 2N33. You will follow this and pass up two lefts on both 2N37 and 2N36. You come out on 173. Check this exit out on the way up. With so many other trails and the lake nearby, do you really want to go back 138 to I-15 for home?

MAPS: San Bernardino National Forest, San Bernardino Meridian, (E2/3, D2/3). ACSC LA and Vicinity, no trail shown, but Pilot Rock is shown at (E14/15). DeLorme p95 (B6, B5). Sidekick (Lake Arrowhead) but no coordianates shown. USGS 34117.

MILES: Loop. 9 miles from HWY 173 to 173.

AUTHORITY: San Bernardino National Forest, Arrowhead Ranger District, P. O. Box 7, Rimforest, CA 92378 (909) 337-2444.

REMARKS: The first turnoff is across from Rock Camp Fire Station and down the sewage treatment plant road. After the rains, the mud is bad. **Cleghorn Mountain**, **Sugarpine Mountain** and **Cajon Mountain** are all off HWY 138 and near Silverwood Lake.

Chuck Thompson

Pinkham Canyon

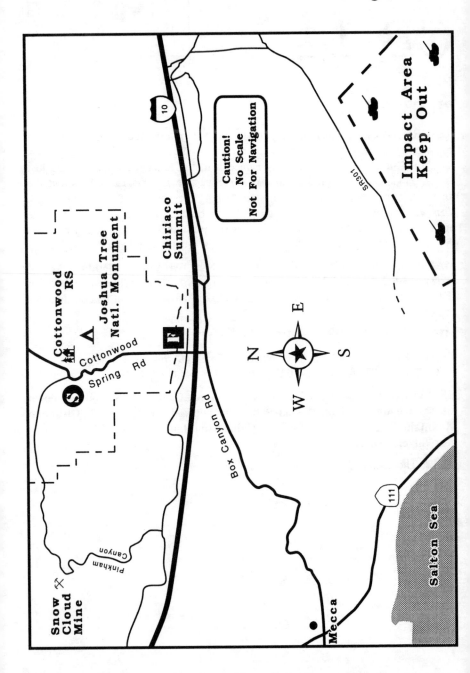

Caution!
No Scale
Not For Navigation

Impact Area
Keep Out

Cottonwood
RS

Joshua Tree
Natl. Monument

Cottonwood
Spring Rd

Chiriaco
Summit

SR301

N E
W S

Box Canyon Rd

111

Salton Sea

Snow
Cloud
Mine

Pinkham Canyon

Mecca

10

Area 8
CB-33

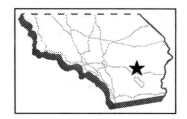

PINKHAM CANYON

DESCRIPTION: This one starts out easy, gets harder, then gets more obscure and by the time you can see I-10, you want to cut the fence to lessen your agony. Please don't cut the fence. Take the fast way to the southern end of Joshua Tree National Monument. Go east on I-10, past Indio and use Cottonwood Spring Road north just before the Chiriaco Summit. You will have to pay the fee to enter the Monument and in 6 miles west of the Visitor Center, you will go northwest toward the Snow Cloud Mine. Once past the mine the road degrades, but it is possible to get clear down **Pinkham Canyon**. When you see the interstate, you will have your choice of several parallel roads for your left (east) turn back to Cottonwood Spring Road. A right (south) at Cottonwood takes you back to I-10.

MAPS: ACSC Riverside County (D/E17, E16). DeLorme p108 (B/C3, C2). Sidekick (Orocopia) but no coordinates. Desert Access Guide #18 (B4, B5). USGS 33115 and 33116.

MILES: Loop. 28 miles from the Cottonwood Visitor Center to Cottonwood Spring Road near I-10.

AUTHORITY: Joshua Tree National Monument, 74485 National Monument Drive, Twentynine Palms, CA 92277 (619) 367-7511.

REMARKS: Don't be lulled into too much confidence by some of my other trails. This one is rocky and requires you know how to pick the indistinguishable road out of a featureless bed of rocks. **Squaw Tank** and **Old Dale Road** are nearby trails.

Pinyon Mountain

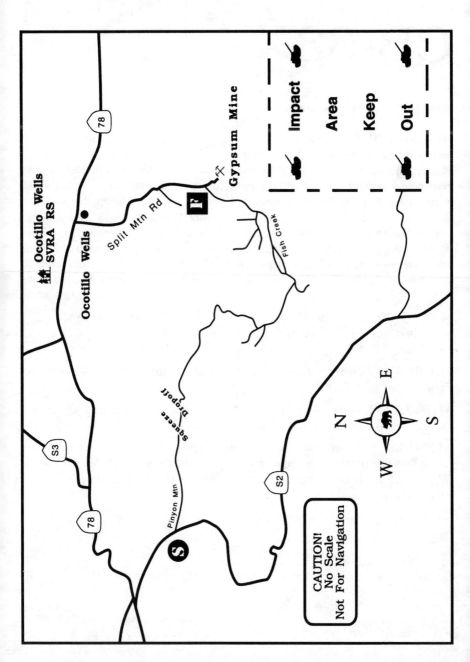

Area 9
CB-36

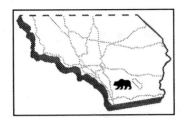

PINYON MOUNTAIN

DESCRIPTION: Visualize your 4X scraped on both sides, up side down and at the bottom of a narrow, rocky gorge. The Fat Man's Misery, a no full size vehicle narrow section, gives you the scrapes. Heart Attack Hill, where the rangers give you a 50/50 chance of rolling going down, puts you upside down at the bottom of the gorge. Other than that, it's a ball. Like **Blair Valley**, I'll lead you from Borrego Springs (C12), but it's easier to find your way directly there from Julian. Go south out of Borrego Springs on HWY S3, to right (west) on HWY 78, to left (southeast) on HWY S2. About 4½ miles down S2, at the Park boundary sign is your left (east) toward **Pinyon Mountain**. Many good, remote campsites in the next 7½ miles where you encounter the Squeeze. One mile later is the dropoff. No going back when down and no need to because the worst is behind you. You will know Split Rock when you pass it. Look for the bedrock mortars and obscure pictographs and petroglyphs in and around the rock. 17 miles through your journey, the road has calmed down (and you too, I hope), so continue generally east in Fish Creek. Check out signed, **Sandstone Canyon** along the way. North on paved Split Mountain Road leads to HWY 78 at Ocotillo Wells. Left (west) goes toward Julian and right to HWY 86 along the Salton Sea.

MAPS: ACSC San Diego County (E/F12, F15) road not shown through. Anza-Borrego Desert State Park map (E/F3/4, F6). Highly recommended is Lindsay's *The Anza-Borrego Desert Region* (ISBN 911824-67-7) book and map (trip 4A). DeLorme p115 (D5), p116 (D1). Start on Desert Access Guide #19 (B/C6) to finish on #20 (A6). USGS 32116 and 33116.

MILES: Loop. 31 miles from HWY S2 to HWY 78.

AUTHORITY: Anza-Borrego Desert State Park, P. O. Box 428, Borrego Springs, CA 92004, (619) 767-5311.

REMARKS: First stop should be the visitor center where you can get the Park map. Also inquire about the road conditions for the **Pinyon Mountain** trail. This area must be avoided during flash floods. It is dangerous! **Blair Valley, Sandstone Canyon** and **San Felipe Wash** are nearby.

Dick Cumiskey

Pioneer Town

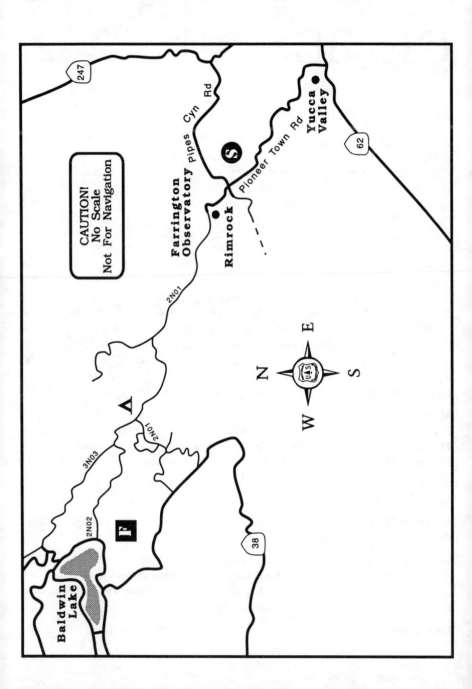

Area 5
CB-14

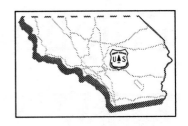

PIONEER TOWN

DESCRIPTION: Most trails I take you up the paved road and down on the dirt. I do the opposite on this one because I'd rather see you get lost at the beginning and close to what you've just been over rather than vice versa. Go toward Palm Springs on I-10, but turn north on HWY 62 just past the PS turnoff. Continue on to Yucca Valley and use Pioneer Town Road north (left). This is a funny intersection and is called the Yucca Trail at another point. Still on pavement, go about straight at the Rimrock/Pipes Canyon/Pioneer Town intersection. You are now on Rimrock. Follow this out to a left on Burns Canyon Road. Sign typically not there. Pavement then ends and in about 5 miles you need to make another unsigned left on the main road. For this one look for the Farrington Observatory (miniature observatory dome). Make your turn about ¼ mile before it. This is basically 2N02 which you follow to the east end of Baldwin Lake. On your way home, down the hill on HWY 38, HWY 18 or HWY 30, stop at the Big Bear District Ranger Station and get their map if you don't already have one.

MAPS: ACSC LA and Vicinity (F20, E18). ACSC San Bernardino County (H6, G4). DeLorme p97 (C4), p96 (B2). Sidekick (Big Bear) with no coordinates. Desert Access Guide #14 (F5/6, C3/4). USGS 34116.

MILES: Loop. 20 miles from end of pavement on Burns Canyon to east end of Baldwin Lake.

AUTHORITY: Start, public roads. End, San Bernardino National Forest, Big Bear District, P. O. Box 290, Fawnskin, CA 92333 (909) 866-3437.

REMARKS: Respect private property, but this is a perfect example where some owners have put up illegal, scary warning signs. Have chains if you try this in the winter or after rains. **Wildhorse Meadows** is a reasonably nearby trail.

Poleline Road

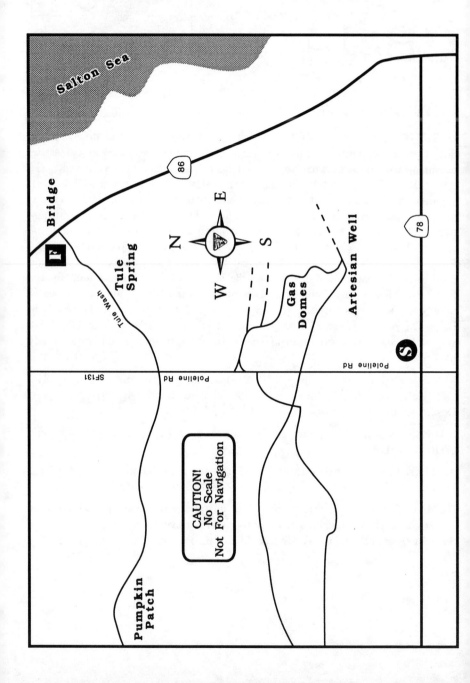

Area 9
CB-36

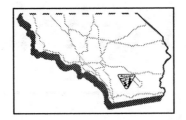

POLELINE ROAD

DESCRIPTION: The rattlesnakes even carry canteens in the summer and they avoid the area during the tropical storm season (July and August). From Ocotillo Wells, (that's 16 miles west of the Salton Sea on HWY 78) go east on HWY 78 for about 8 miles to marked **Poleline Road**. BLM designates this road SF131. Follow the poles north for about 3 miles. Look for a sign on right (Shell Reef Express Way) where a rugged road leads off to the east (right) to an artesian well (small pipe emits water every 90 seconds or so). Pass the well and veer left (northeast) along a large metal pipe. Follow what I call ATC wash for about a mile and start looking for some flat, white-covered hills to the northwest (left). Atop these hills are the Mud Pots (technically gas domes). Just past the second pot, follow the various choices northwest (keep to the north of the steep bluffs) back to **Poleline Road**. 1½ miles north is Tule Wash. Better than 3½ miles east in Tule brings you out at HWY 86 and a paved road to the north allows legal entry to 86. Left (north) to Indio and right to HWY 78. Good luck!

MAPS: Desert Access Guide #20 (A/B5, B3/4). Lindsay *The Anza-Borrego Desert Region* (ISBN 911824-67-7) book and map show the roads and Lindsay doesn't have coordinates. Mid right hand edge in the San Felipe Hills is the area (trip 1F). DeLorme p116 (C2) shows "4WD" road and "Flowing Well". USGS 33115 **and** 33116.

MILES: Loop. 13 miles from HWY 78 to HWY 86, but plan on 25.

AUTHORITY: BLM El Centro Resource Area Office, 1661 S. Fourth St., El Centro, CA 92243 (619) 352-5842. And soon to be Ocotillo Wells State Vehicular Recreation Area, P. O. Box 360, Borrego Springs, CA 92004 (619) 767-5391.

REMARKS: Avoid this area, paved and dirt, during flash floods and summer time hot weather makes the area more desirable during the spring. During and after winds the skimpy roads are impossible to find unless you have been there before. This one is for the well prepared. Allow time to explore and discover. **San Felipe Wash, Pumpkin Patch** and **Cut Across Trail** are nearby.

Pumpkin Patch

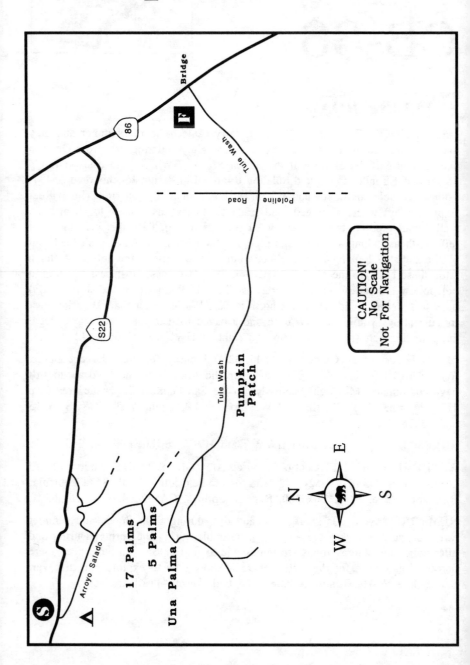

Area 9
CB-36

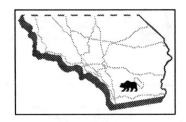

PUMPKIN PATCH

DESCRIPTION: It always amazes me how people find these places and now it's your turn. Within an area of 5 acres (walking required), is a collection of pumpkin shaped and sized concretions (actually, variously shaped, hard, giant, sand balls). Again, get to Borrego Springs (C12) any way. About 9 miles east of Peg Leg Smith Monument (C13), on HWY S22, is the Arroyo Salado primitive campgrounds on your right (south). Turn in and use the road through camp, past the **17 Palms** Oasis turnoff, and past 5 Palms. Don't stay in Arroyo Salado, which is easy to say and hard to do. Bypass the turn for Una Palma and get into Tule Wash. Now, as you're winding through these muddy washes, give the flash floods a thought. About 2 1/3 miles down (east) as Tule Wash widens out, will be some 20 foot high dirt hills (knobs) on the south (right). A right turn on the road, for 200 yards and you're in the heart of **Pumpkin Patch** (D15). Your way out is all the way down (east) in Tule Wash to bridge 58-14 and HWY 86. Left (north) takes you past S22 and eventually to I-10 in Indio and home.

MAPS: ACSC San Diego County (C15), Tule Wash to HWY 86 not shown. Start on Desert Access Guide #19 (E3) with the end on #20 (B3/4). Highly recommended is Lindsay's *The Anza-Borrego Desert Region* (ISBN 911824-67-7) book and map (trip 3B). DeLorme p116 (C1), no trail shown. USGS 33115 and 33116.

MILES: Loop. 17 miles from S22 to HWY 86 and if you do it right the first time, I'm jealous.

AUTHORITY: Ocotillo Wells State Vehicular Recreation Area, P. O. Box 360, Borrego Springs, CA 92004 (619) 767-5391.

REMARKS: First stop should be the visitor center where you can get the Park map. Remember, look, but don't take anything from the Park. **17 Palms, Vista Del Mal Pais, Cut Across Trail** and **Calcite Mine** are nearby.

Mike Smith

Quatal Canyon

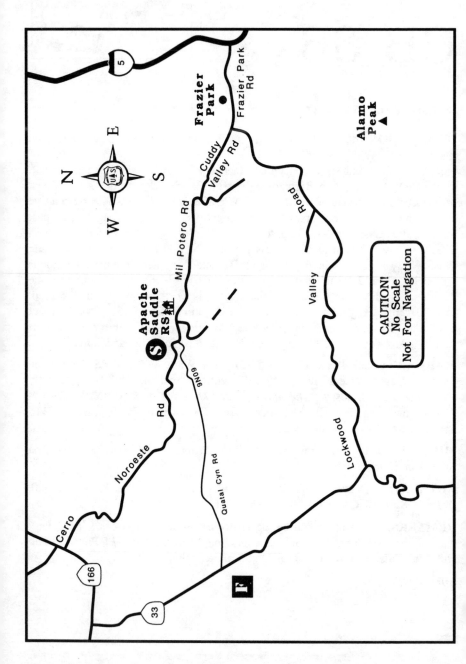

Area 1
CB-1

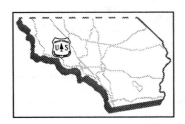

QUATAL CANYON

DESCRIPTION: Here's a shortcut that really works, ah provided it's not raining. It cuts 18 miles off your route from Frazier Park to HWY 33 south. But don't be fooled into believing you are in the desert by this beautiful canyon. Get on the I-5 headed toward Bakersfield and use the Frazier Park turn off west (C8), just beyond Gorman. In a mile, after you pass the Apache Saddle Fire Station, look for Quatal Canyon Road (9N09). Make a left (southwest) here. Nothing could be simpler. Follow this to paved HWY 33 just south of the town of Ventucopa. Right takes you to HWY 166. A left on HWY 33 takes you through Ojai, and eventually out to Ventura and HWY 101 for home. Actually, home is easier by retracing the dirt to pavement and I-5.

MAPS: ACSC Ventura County (C4, C1). DeLorme p76 (B4, B2). Mount Pinos Ranger District ORV Map (T9N, R22W to T9N, R25W). USGS 34118 and 34119.

MILES: Loop. 16 miles from Cerro Noroeste Road to HWY 33.

AUTHORITY: Los Padres National Forest, Mount Pinos District, Chuchupate Ranger Station, Frazier Park, CA 93225 (805) 245-3731. Recorded message at (805) 245-3449.

REMARKS: Nearby are **Apache Canyon, Grade Valley, Santa Barbara Canyon** and **Reyes Peak**. The main road is paralleled by 4WD sandy washes designated trail 106 on above Forest map. Give the sand a try, but don't get suckered into the motorcycle only trails that some of 106 turns into.

Brian Wolsky

Rainbow Basin

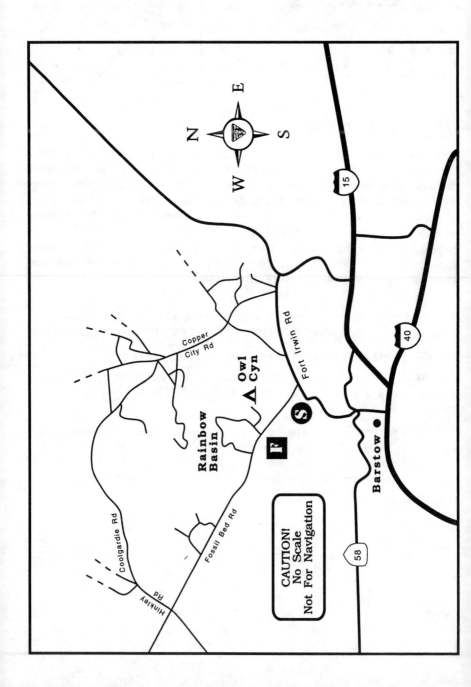

Area 3
CB-7

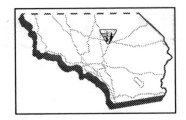

RAINBOW BASIN

DESCRIPTION: How about a drive around nothing and then find out it's really something? This is another one of those that'll get you there and then you're on your own to explore the canyons, mines, geological features and fossils. Besides, there are more roads out here than you can shake the proverbial stick at. And if I gave you directions, you'd be shaking the stick at me for getting you lost. Simply go north on I-15 to Barstow. Stop at the BLM Desert Way Station for the latest info and continue north on Barstow Road (D3). Pick your way 6 miles north of town for a left (northwest) when you hit Fossil Bed Road and before long you're at the Rainbow Basin National Natural Landmark. Owl Canyon Campground is a nice base, but frequently crowded. A big loop around the Landmark is made by going north on Copper City Road, left (northwest) on Coolgardie Road, left (south) on Hinkley Road and finally your last left (southeast) on Fossil Bed Road back to camp. From camp, retrace your steps back to I-15 and home.

MAPS: ACSC San Bernardino County (D3). DeLorme p67 (D7). Start on Desert Access Guide #10 (G1) through #8 and #11 to end on #7 (J6). USGS 34116, 34117, 35116, and 35117.

MILES: Loop. If you make the big loop around the Landmark, it's 24 miles.

AUTHORITY: BLM, California Desert Information Center, 831 Barstow Road, Barstow, CA 92311 (619) 256-8313.

REMARKS: Be sure to do a smaller 4 mile loop within the Landmark itself. The Way Station is identified off I-15 and is a must for any trip into the general area. No nearby trails. Be sure to travel only on routes that are marked as "Open".

Red Canyon

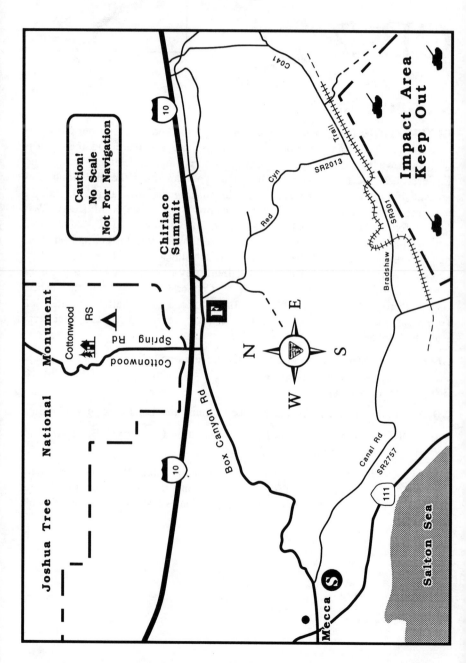

Area 10
CB-39

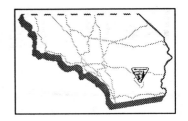

RED CANYON

DESCRIPTION: I'm glad I ran this one before I took the Santa Ana Register's reporter with me. Good place to practice triangulating. You retrace the first part of the **Bradshaw Trail** by going out I-10, pass up Palm Springs, and in Indio take HWY 111 southeast to Mecca. Go left (northeast) on Box Canyon Road and pick up the dirt road on the south side of the Coachella Canal for a right (southeast). The BLM calls this SR2757 (A6). In about 17 miles you should make a left (east) turn onto the Bradshaw Trail (C6). If the sign is up, the BLM calls this SR301. If you cross the RR tracks, you are about a mile too far. Several trails work. In about 8½ miles (D6), look for a miniature, Yosemite, El Capitan. This is **Red Canyon** or BLM SR2013. If you can climb the two tough hills to the ridge, you're mostly on your way. If the hills are too much, just do the **Bradshaw Trail**. Follow SR2013 out to the Chiriaco Summit on I-10. Do the best job you can. Heading north takes you out, but for me, it's different every time. At I-10, west takes you home.

MAPS: Desert Access Guide #18 (A6, C5). ACSC Riverside County (F15/16, E18) trail not shown in **Red Canyon**. DeLorme p108 (D1, C4). Sidekick (Orocopia) with no coordinates. USGS 33115.

MILES: Loop. 41 miles from Box Canyon Road to I-10.

AUTHORITY: BLM Palm Springs-South Coast Resource Area Office, 63-500 Garnet Ave, P.O. Box 2000, N. Palm Springs, CA 92258-2000 (619) 251-0812.

REMARKS: Don't go down into **Red Canyon**. I learned the hard way, without a winch, you're down for good. **Painted Canyon, Corn Springs** and **Bradshaw Trail** are nearby.

Red Pass

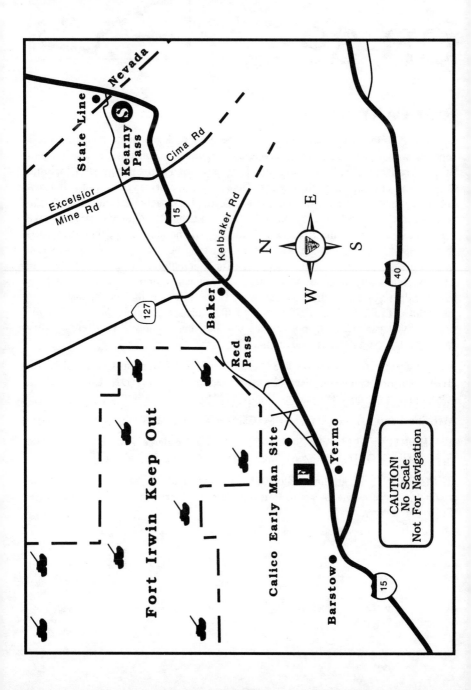

Area 3
CB-7

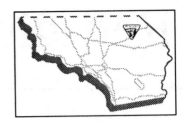

RED PASS

DESCRIPTION: I figured I had to have a real long trail for all you pole line runners. After you're traveling real light (no money) on your way back from Vegas, fuel up at State Line (B10). Go north, northwest out of town about 1 mile on the graded road. Turn left (southwest) on another road that heads toward Kearny Pass. You're on your way. This graded dirt road crosses Excelsior Mine Road, HWY 127 and finally ushers you to I-15 in Yermo about 15 miles east of Barstow. I know you haven't had enough, so be sure to stop at the Calico Early Man Site out Paradise Spring Road. Home is, well, you'd better spend the night in Barstow before heading south on I-15.

MAPS: ACSC San Bernardino County (B10, E4). DeLorme p57 (D6), p82 (A2) State Line not shown. Start on Desert Access Guide #6 (O/P6) through #8 and #9 to end at #11 (C1/2). USGS 34115, 34116, 35115 and 35116.

MILES: Loop. 91 miles from State Line to I-15 in Yermo.

AUTHORITY: Private and BLM, California Desert Information Center, 831 Barstow Road, Barstow, CA 92311 (619) 256-8313.

REMARKS: Planning and preparation are critical for this trip. Best to avoid this in the heat of late spring, summer and early fall. Travel with others. **Afton Canyon** and **Zzyzx** are along the way, on the other side of I-15.

Refugio Pass

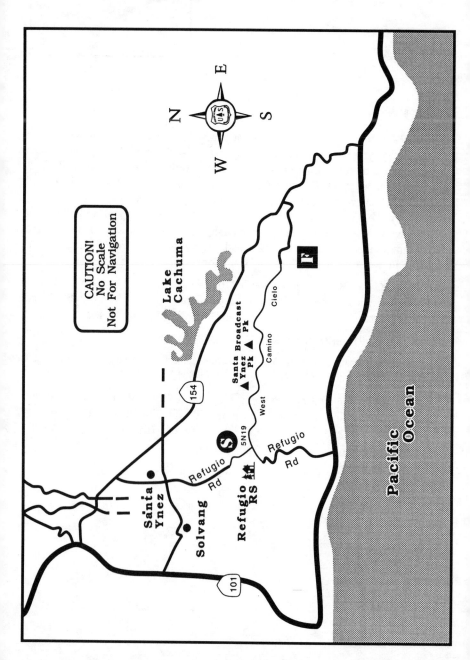

Area 1
CB-1

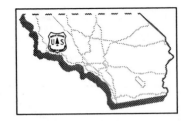

REFUGIO PASS

DESCRIPTION: You will feel like you're on an antenna farm about mid way through this one. Santa Ynez Peak and particularly Broadcast Peak (H9) hint at what's there. Let HWY 101 take you to your right (east) on HWY 246 (G6) toward Solvang. Pass it up and almost into downtown Santa Ynez (G7), turn right (south) on Refugio Road. In 7 miles the road turns to dirt which you want to stay on for about the next 14 miles. Near the Refugio Ranger Station (H8) you have a chance to bail out if you've had enough. (South on paved Refugio Road takes you right down to HWY 101.) Continuing on the dirt, now called West Camino Cielo or 5N19, leads you to 4 miles of pavement which intersects HWY 154 just above Goleta (K11). Home is via 101 just 6 miles south on 154.

MAPS: ACSC Santa Barbara County (H8, H10). DeLorme p74 (D4), p75 (D6). Los Padres National Forest (H18/19, J19). USGS 34119 and 34120.

MILES: Loop. 19 miles from where dirt starts on Refugio Road to pavement at HWY 154.

AUTHORITY: Los Padres National Forest, Santa Barbara District, Los Prietos, Star Route, Santa Barbara, CA 93105 (805) 967-3481.

REMARKS: The rough section east of the Refugio Ranger Station is not for all. Consider turning around and going back via paved Refugio Road if it's too bad for you. No nearby trails. Consider this one with a trip to the unique Danish village of Solvang to satisfy your sweet tooth. By the way, did you see any movie stars at the TV and radio stations?

Gene Markley

Reyes Peak

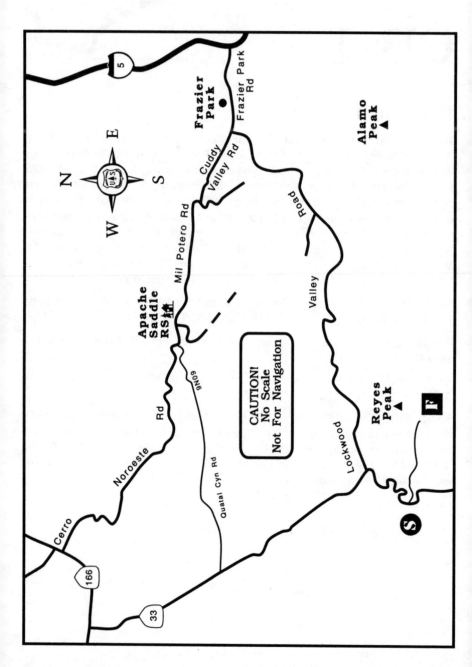

Area 1
CB-1

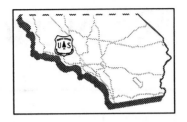

REYES PEAK

DESCRIPTION: Starting from the Pine Mountain Summit (5084') and climbing another 2500' to 7510', **Reyes Peak** offers an opportunity to check out your 4X at altitude, on good road. Just like **Apache Canyon**, get on I-5 headed toward Bakersfield and just beyond Gorman use the Frazier Park turn off west (C8). Follow Frazier Mountain Park, Mil Potrero, Cuddy and Cerro Noroeste Roads to HWY 166/33 or use the shortcut described in **Quatal Canyon**. When you hit HWY 33, go south (left) down the road 12 miles beyond Quatal Canyon Road. At the Pine Mountain Summit, go left (east) on 6N06 to **Reyes Peak**. Get back to 33 the same way you came in. Home is back either via Lockwood Valley Road northeast and I-5 or use 33 all the way to HWY 101.

MAPS: ACSC Ventura County (E/F2, F3). DeLorme p76 (C2, C3). Mount Pinos Ranger District ORV Map (T7N, R24W to T6N, R23W). USGS 34118 and 34119.

MILES: Dead-end. 14 miles round trip from HWY 33.

AUTHORITY: Los Padres National Forest, Mount Pinos District, Chuchupate Ranger Station, Frazier Park, CA 93225 (805) 245-3731. Recorded message at (805) 245-3449.

REMARKS: Since there is a gate, best to first check at the Ozena Ranger Station back where Lockwood Creek Road comes in from the east. This is actually a better way to get to the Pine Mountain Summit if you can find the turn off from Frazier Mountain Park Road to Lockwood Creek Road. **Quatal Canyon, Apache Canyon, Santa Barbara Canyon** and **Grade Valley** are nearby.

Brian Wolsky

Rockhouse Cyn

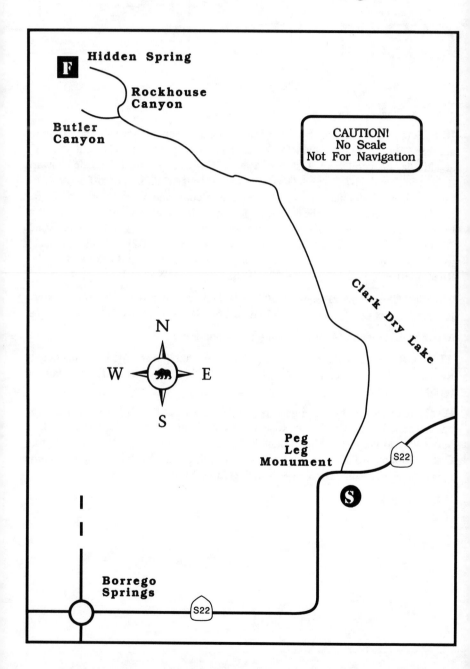

Hidden Spring

F

Rockhouse
Canyon

Butler
Canyon

CAUTION!
No Scale
Not For Navigation

Clark Dry Lake

N

W   E

S

Peg
Leg
Monument

S22

S

Borrego
Springs

S22

Area 9
CB-36

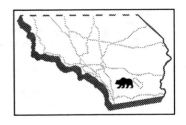

ROCKHOUSE CANYON

DESCRIPTION: If you want to check out the rocks before doing **Coyote Canyon**, then give this a try. However, this rough trail is not for the weak hearted. At Hidden Spring, if you hike up the ancient Indian trail to the top of Jackass Flats, you are rewarded with pottery shards and bedrock mortars. Too many ways in to be specific, so get to Borrego Springs (C12). About ¼ mile east of Peg Leg Smith Monument on HWY S22, go left on the unnamed dirt road toward Clark Dry Lake. Driving on the wet lake is a mistake. Pass up Butler Canyon and drive until you or your 4X can't take it any more. The trail is very rough and invisible at times. Under any circumstances, don't pass the no vehicles barrier ¼ mile before the spring. Like it or not, and keep it in mind on your way in, home is back the way you came.

MAPS: ACSC San Diego County (C13, B12). Anza-Borrego Desert State Park map (C4/5, B3/4). Highly recommended is Lindsay's *The Anza-Borrego Desert Region* (ISBN 911824-67-7) book and map (trip 3A). DeLorme p115 (B6, A5). Desert Access Guide #19 (C/D3, B/C1/2). USGS 33116.

MILES: Dead-end. 26 rocky miles in and out.

AUTHORITY: Anza-Borrego Desert State Park, P. O. Box 428, Borrego Springs, CA 92004 (619) 767-5311.

REMARKS: First stop should be the visitor center where you can get the Park map. Remember, look, but don't take anything from the Park. **Coyote Canyon, Vista Del Mal Pais** and **Fonts Point** are nearby.

Saddleback Mtn

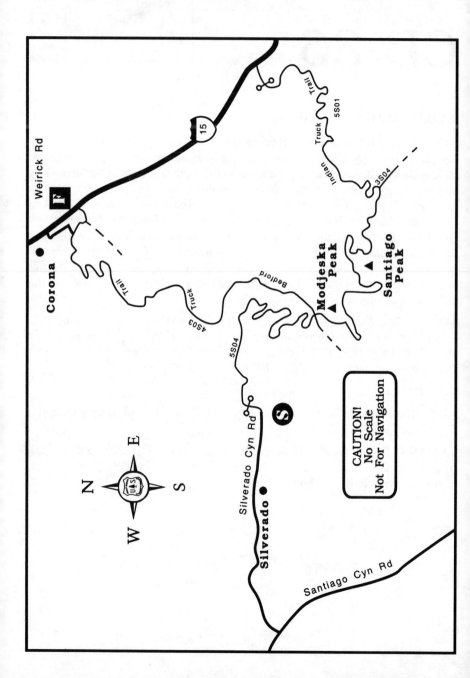

Area 7
CB-30

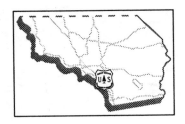

SADDLEBACK MOUNTAIN

DESCRIPTION: So you live in Orange County, don't like to get out of bed too early, want to be back home by about 2 pm and would like a spectacular view from Mount Wilson to the Coronado Islands off the coast of Mexico? This trail is made for you! **Saddleback Mountain**, more properly Santiago (the higher) and Modjeska Peaks, was used by the Forest Service as a fire lookout for years. Off HWY 55 in the town of Orange (D5) use Chapman Avenue east to Santiago Canyon Road right (southwest). Follow this to Silverado Canyon Road (E8) for a left. Go through the charming homes and town to the gate and dirt 5S04. At the major intersection some 7 miles up the trail, straight leads out the Bedford Truck Trail and comes out at the Weirick Road off ramp on I-15. This is the recommended route. The first right leads immediately to the locked, Harding Truck Trail gate. Use the second right for another 9 miles to the lookout. Choices down? Back the way you came. Down the recommended route or take the road a couple of hundred yards back down from the peak that may have confused you on the way up. This is the Indian Truck Trail (5S01). The next intersection down 5S01 is familiar to you (3S04) if you've done **El Cariso**. 3S04 leads out to HWY 74 and continuing on down 5S01 takes you out to I-15 and home.

MAPS: ACSC Orange County (E9, D10). Cleveland National Forest Map, Trabuco Ranger District (C2). DeLorme p104 (C3, B3/4). USGS 33117.

MILES: Loop. 38 miles from start of dirt, up to the peak and down Bedford to I-15.

AUTHORITY: Cleveland National Forest, Trabuco District, 1147 E. 6th Street, Corona, CA 91720 (909) 736-1811.

REMARKS: There is mucho traffico when this road is open, particularly after the first snow. **El Cariso** and **Tenaja Truck Trail** are nearby. The gate at Silverado is frequently closed, so call first.

San Felipe

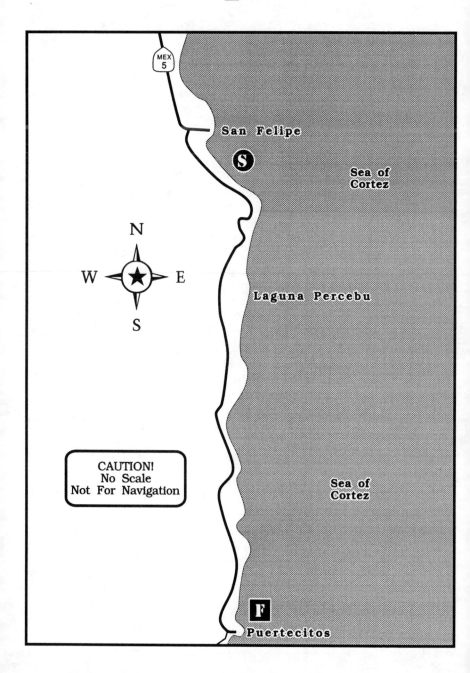

Baja
CB-36

SAN FELIPE

DESCRIPTION: The two Baja trails in this Guide are trail bait. Hopefully they will show you an unexpected side of Baja and destroy the Baja bandido myth. Give Baja a chance! **San Felipe** is just far enough south to escape border-town hype. I like the variety. Fishing, diving, boating, 4-Wheeling or a simple get-away avail the adventuresome. Cross the border at Mexicali (B5), head south 125 miles on MEX 5, follow the curve by the arch monument just outside San Felipe (E4/5) and you're there. When you see the beach, you can only go north on the one-way streets near the beach and through the main part of town. Your sand-trail journey starts about 1½ miles south of the fishing boat basin. Use the first dip that looks like a bridge for a left (east) onto the sand. If you're not prepared to lower your air pressure, and pump the tires back up again at the pavement, stay off the sand! Without a guide or someone who knows the way, plan on the crawl before you walk before you run approach. Become progressively familiar with the 45 mile route south, on the beach, to Puertecitos. Knowing when to skirt the rocks is mandatory. Knowing there are 25-foot tides is paramount! Knowing that temporary sand peninsulas become sand islands that get totally covered by the Sea of Cortez to become sandbars is strategic. Yank straps and hooks on all vehicles are necessary. Exit the beach about 4 miles north of Puertecitos. You may return from Puertecitos via the continually improving main road or re-run the beach.

MAPS: ACSC Baja (E/F4, F/G4). Sidekick, San Felipe, no coordinates, but describes the beach run. The Baja Topographic Atlas Directory, start at pB56 (B/C1) and finish on pB64 (E1).

MILES: Loop. 45 very cautious sandy miles from San Felipe to Puertecitos.

AUTHORITY: No contact.

REMARKS: This is not a casual first trip if you have no sand and tidal experience! Don't do this trip alone! Also, the day will come when it will be illegal to run up and down the beach. Moves are afoot to prohibit vehicles where I define beach entry. Use Mexico West and The Discover Baja Travel Club in the Products and Services Chapter for Mexico travel information.

San Felipe Wash

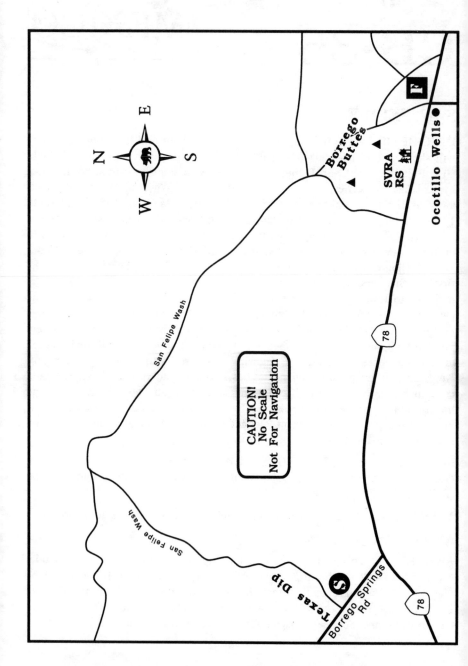

CAUTION!
No Scale
Not For Navigation

Area 9
CB-36

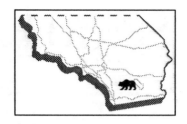

SAN FELIPE WASH

DESCRIPTION: Everything in Texas is big except the Texas Dip which is in California. That's where you start this one after you get to Borrego Springs (C12) via its many approaches. From Borrego Springs simply follow paved Borrego Springs Road (HWY S3) to the Texas Dip. The bottom is **San Felipe Wash** where you look for the road and a left (northeast). In 4½ miles you will intersect a big cross wash. You go right (southeast) here. If you miss this, you went to sleep for 5 minutes. This is still **San Felipe Wash** which you follow around both the west and east buttes of Borrego Mountain to your right. Now pay attention to traffic. You are in the ORV park. Look out all around you for it is an open area. **San Felipe Wash** is a 100 MPH road to the over enthusiastic. About the time you see flat lands to your right (south) you can make a right on any number of trails. If I gave you specifics, you'd just be frustrated trying to follow them out to HWY 78, which is where you will end up with any right. Right (west) on 78 leads back to Borrego Springs Road or further on, Julian. Left takes you out to the Salton Sea and HWY 86.

MAPS: ACSC San Diego County (D13/14, E14/15). Anza-Borrego Desert State Park map (F6, G7). Highly recommended is Lindsay's *The Anza-Borrego Desert Region* (ISBN 911824-67-7) book and map (portion of trip 1). DeLorme p115 (C6/7, C1). Desert Access Guide #19 (C/D4/5, E5). USGS 33116,

MILES: Loop. 11 miles from Borrego Springs Road to HWY 78 in Ocotillo Wells.

AUTHORITY: Anza-Borrego Desert State Park, P. O. Box 428, Borrego Springs, CA 92004 (619) 767-5311. Ocotillo Wells State Vehicular Recreation Area, P. O. Box 360, Borrego Springs, CA 92004 (619) 767-5391.

REMAKS: First stop should be the visitor center where you can get the Park map. The Texas Dip is a hot spot for the agave and other plants in the spring. Remember, be cautious in the ORV area. **Fonts Point** and **Vista Del Mal Pais** just look close. **Pumpkin Patch** is close, but difficult to find. **Cut Across Trail** is really close.

Sand Hills

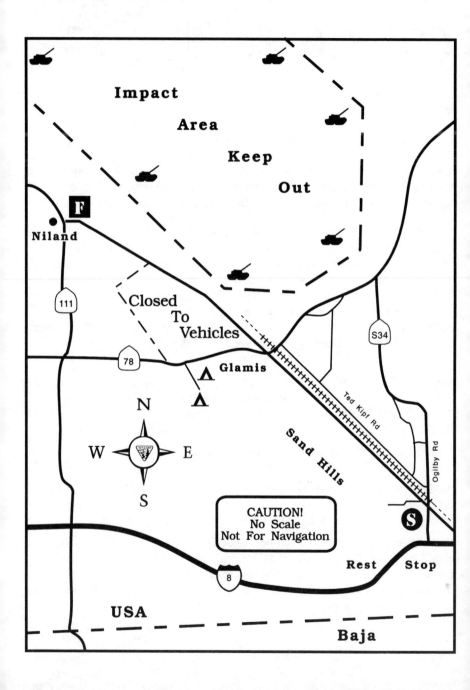

Impact

Area

Keep

Out

F

Niland

111

Closed
To
Vehicles

S34

78

Glamis

Ted Kipf Rd

N

W E

S

Sand Hills

Ogilby Rd

S

CAUTION!
No Scale
Not For Navigation

Rest Stop

8

USA

Baja

Area 10
CB-39

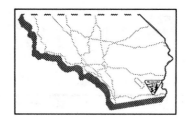

SAND HILLS

DESCRIPTION: No, I haven't gone crazy leading the unsuspecting into Glamis. However, this 50 mile run along the impressive and fragile sand dunes is near sand-rail heaven. Find your best way down to El Centro on I-8 headed east toward Yuma. Get a sample of the area at the roadside rest 16 miles west of Winterhaven. Continue on to Ogilby Road for a left (north) turn. At the RR tracks, for the next 18 miles, you have a choice of driving Ted Kipf Road to the north of the RR tracks or the poorer road to the south. Under any circumstances, make a left (northwest) turn near the tracks. When you get to HWY 78 (F9), plug your ears, make a left and if you didn't already know, you'll figure out why the first sentence. Anything that resembles a stock vehicle does not belong in this sand. It will stick you. But it's fun to watch, particularly at night at the base of Competition Hill. To continue, get back along side the RR tracks and go northwest for another 22 miles to Niland and pavement on HWY 111. Home is northwest on HWY 111 to I-10. You know the way from there.

MAPS: ACSC Imperial County (G11, C/D5). DeLorme p126 (B4), p117 (C5). Sidekick (Imperial Sand Dunes) no coordinates. Start on Desert Access Guide #21 (B/C8/9) through #22, finish on #2 (F3/4). USGS 32115 and 32114.

MILES: Loop. 50 miles from Ogilby Road to paved HWY 111.

AUTHORITY: BLM El Centro Resource Area Office, 1661 S. Fourth Ave., El Centro, CA 92243 (619) 352-5842.

REMARKS: Bradshaw Trail, Coachella Canal, and **Red Canyon** are nearby. This is another area to avoid in the heat of any season and particularly during flash floods.

Sandstone Cyn

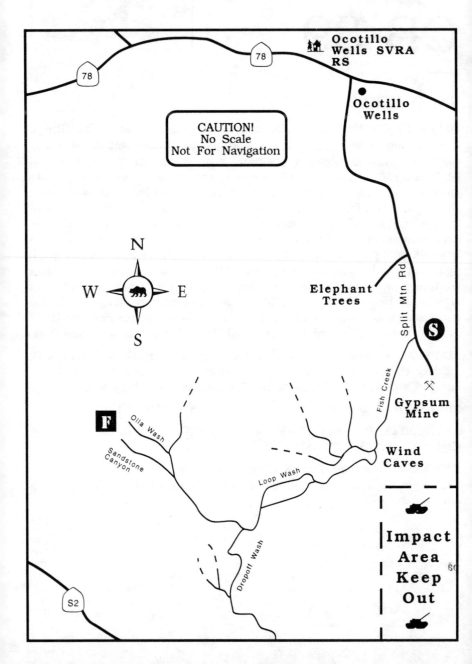

Ocotillo Wells SVRA RS

78

78

CAUTION!
No Scale
Not For Navigation

Ocotillo Wells

N

W E

S

Elephant Trees

Split Mtn Rd

S

Fish Creek

Gypsum Mine

F

Olla Wash

Sandstone Canyon

Loop Wash

Wind Caves

Dropoff Wash

S2

Impact Area Keep Out

Area 9
CB-36

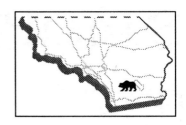

SANDSTONE CANYON

DESCRIPTION: This area is a geologist's dream come true. Anticlines, synclines, fanglomerates, wind caves, oyster shell reefs, and the most spectacular, narrow, vertically walled canyon in the Park. Use the motels in Borrego Springs (C12) as a base and from there, simply follow paved Borrego Springs Road (HWY S3) through the Texas Dip to HWY 78 left (east). In Ocotillo Wells go right (south) on Split Mountain Road to Fish Creek. Drive past the fanglomerates, anticline, wind caves (all worth checking out). Keep track of mileage and don't get suckered into Dropoff Wash (F/G14) some 9½ miles in. You'll know because it gets narrow and rocky real fast. Go 12½ miles from the start of dirt to the signed entrance to **Sandstone Canyon** (F14). It too dead-ends, but is usually passable for three miles. On your way back, the rougher Loop Wash can siphon you off to the left, but it leads back into Fish Creek. Good time to use a compass for I've driven in circles in this area. At paved Split Mountain Road go left (north) back to HWY 78 and left (west) again back to Borrego Springs.

MAPS: ACSC San Diego County (F15). Anza-Borrego Desert State Park map, Sandstone Canyon shown at (F/G5). Highly recommended is Lindsay's *The Anza-Borrego Desert Region* (ISBN 911824-67-7) book and map (part of trip 1D). DeLorme p116 (D1), p123 (A7). Desert Access Guide #19 (D6/7). USGS 32116 and 33116.

MILES: Dead-end. 29 miles from paved Split Mountain Road and back.

AUTHORITY: Anza-Borrego Desert State Park, P. O. Box 428, Borrego Springs, CA 92004 (619) 767-5311.

REMARKS: First stop should be the visitor center where you can get the Park map. This trail must be avoided during flash floods. It is dangerous! **San Felipe Wash** is the only thing nearby. Don't attempt what appears to be nearby **Diablo Dropoff** backwards. The dropoff is designated as one-way and up is tough, particularly in dry weather.

Dick Cumiskey

SantaBarbaraCyn

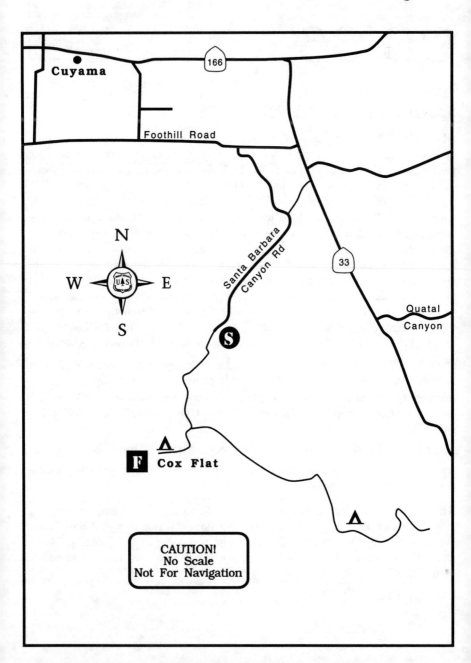

Area 1
CB-1

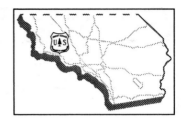

SANTA BARBARA CANYON

DESCRIPTION: If you want to see the good stuff, you have to backpack, but the dirt road cuts 5 miles off the walk. The hiking trails that lead west from road's end go through significant geological and archaeological areas. The Chumash Indians lived here. Their many pictographs and other remnants make the 10 mile walk rewarding for the ambitious, however remember that removing artifacts is illegal. In Ventura, take HWY 33 north to Foothill Road (D14) west (left). That's just before HWY 166. Follow Foothill to a left (south) on **Santa Barbara Canyon** Road. This eventually turns into your dirt road (9N11) out to Cox Flat and the locked gate beyond. The locked gate is where you can drop off the hikers. The gate to the east of the campground (8N15) may be unlocked and the road leads to Cuyama Peak where it dead ends. The way in is the way out too.

MAPS: ACSC Santa Barbara County (E14, E13). DeLorme p76 (B1). Los Padres National Forest (L16). USGS 34119.

MILES: Dead-end. 10 miles, round trip from end of Santa Barbara Canyon Road pavement.

AUTHORITY: Los Padres National Forest, Mount Pinos District, Chuchupate Ranger Station, Frazier Park, CA 93225 (805) 245-3731. Recorded message at (805) 245-3449.

REMARKS: This one is really out by itself unless you're a hiker. Remember **McPherson Peak**? From there you can hike (overnight) down to Cox Flat, but the cars will beat the hikers this time. Water available on the hike, but always plan on purifying it. This area is popular with horse people. **Quatal Canyon**, **Apache Canyon** and **Reyes Peak** are all nearby. Dry Canyon is subject to winter closure.

Santa Rita Creek

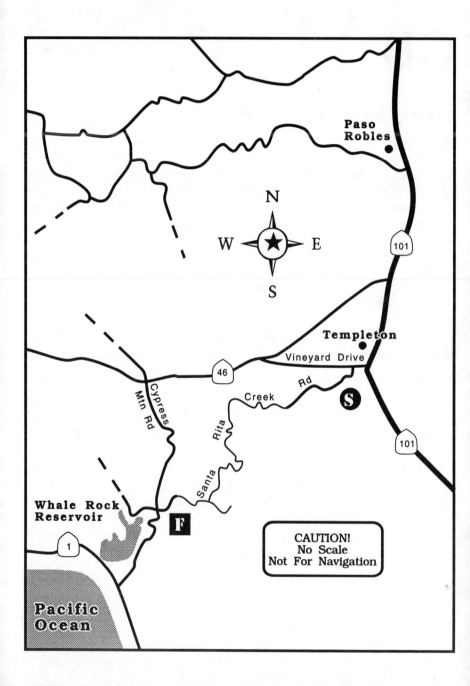

Paso Robles

Templeton

Vineyard Drive

101

101

46

Cypress

Mtn Rd

Creek

Rd

Santa

Rita

S

Whale Rock
Reservoir

1

F

CAUTION!
No Scale
Not For Navigation

Pacific
Ocean

Area 1
CB-1

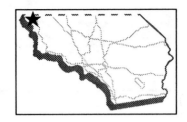

SANTA RITA CREEK

DESCRIPTION: Down the creek, up over the summit and across another creek. This well-maintained road lets you add more miles under your belt when you do **Cypress Mountain**. Use HWY 101 north to Templeton (D6) where you make a left (west) off HWY 101 for Vineyard Drive. Make the zig zag left (south) on Ridge Road and pick up your right (west) on Santa Rita Creek Road all the way to Cypress Mountain Road. For home, use HWY 1 left (south) to HWY 101 for a clear shot back to the barn.

MAPS: ACSC San Luis Obispo County (D6, E5). DeLorme p45 (D6), p59 (A5). USGS 35120.

MILES: Loop. About 16 miles including the pavement at both ends from HWY 101 to Cypress Mountain Road.

AUTHORITY: San Luis Obispo County (public road).

REMARKS: Nearby **Cypress Mountain Road** is a natural. There are also many side roads not shown on the ACSC map. Combine this with a water skiing trip to Lake Nacimiento, a trip to the Hearst Castle,or a wine tasting tour around Templeton and Paso Robles. Need I say again, do the dirt before the wine.

Sierra Pelona

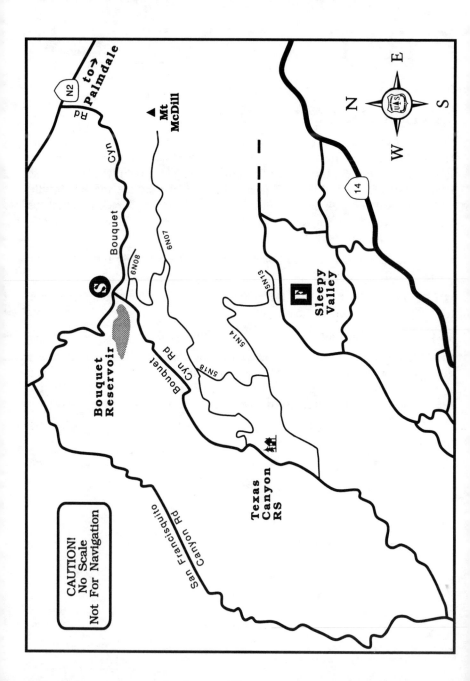

Area 2
CB-4

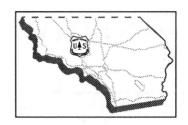

SIERRA PELONA

DESCRIPTION: There are no less than 4 different ways to start and finish this trail. You know what that means? Navigation practice. Again, all wrong turns lead to pavement or one locked gate. The approach is similar to **Green Valley**. Off HWY 14 in Palmdale take a left (west) on N2 (F3). At Bouquet Canyon Road (E3) turn south (left) and within a mile of the "Y" at the Bouquet Canyon Reservoir go east on 6N08. When you intersect 6N07, go southwest (right) to continue or left to Mount McDill's locked gate. The next obvious "Y" is 5N18 where you go left to continue or straight to pavement in four or five miles. Now comes 5N14 in either direction. Go left (east) on 5N14 to continue my trip or right to intersect Bouquet Canyon Road again. It's not over yet. 5N14 passes a right with 5N15 which is a very long trip to a locked gate. Stay on 5N14 until you reach a right with 5N13 and finally, pavement in Sleepy Valley. Whew! All the mained paved roads south, east and west lead out to HWY 14 and home.

MAPS: Angeles National Forest, San Bernardino Meridian (E3, D/E3/4). ACSC LA and Vicinity (C6). DeLorme p78 (D4). USGS 34118.

MILES: Loop. 18 miles from Bouquet Canyon Road to Sleepy Valley.

AUTHORITY: Angeles National Forest, Saugus District, 27757 Bouquet Canyon Road, Saugus, CA 91350 (805) 252-9710.

REMARKS: **Tule Ridge**, **Green Valley**, **Del Sur Ridge**, **Liebre Mountain** and **Warm Springs** are all reachable from here. If you're into rocks, Vasquez Rocks County Park offers some pretty interesting hiking.

Squaw Tank

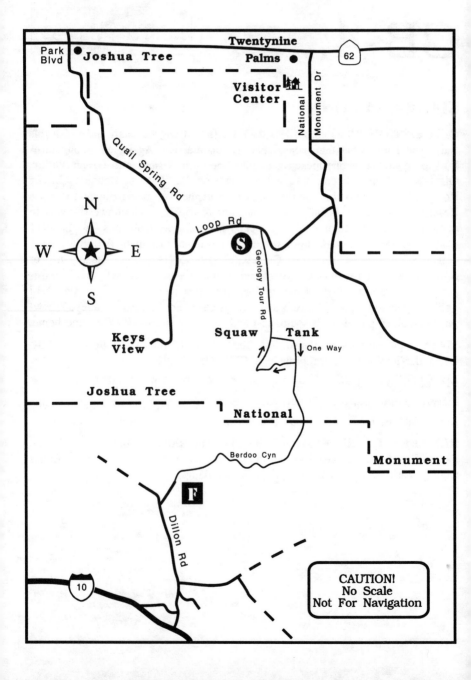

Area 8
CB-33

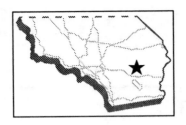

SQUAW TANK

DESCRIPTION: Tanks... desert... doesn't that mean General Patton? Most references to tanks in the desert refer to natural water storage areas. The Indians knew of these and would live around them. Just like **Desert Queen**, go east on I-10 toward Palm Springs, but pass up HWY 111 and take HWY 62 north. In Joshua Tree (the city) go south (right) on Park Blvd. which turns into Quail Springs Road. Follow this past the Keys View turn off to your right (south) at the Squaw Tank trail sign. Now don't cheat, pay your fee for the self guided geology tour booklet at the entrance. Take your time over the next 5 miles and learn a little about the area. You must get out of the car at Squaw Tank to find the bedrock mortars, petroglyphs and the tank. I recommend you go home the way you came in. However, here's an alternative for the well prepared. Continue on south in between points 12 and 13 on the tour. This takes you out Berdoo Canyon and eventually into Indio.

MAPS: ACSC Riverside County (B/C15, D14). DeLorme p98 (D1), p107 (B7). Starts and ends on Desert Access Guide #17 (J1, I3), with roads on #14. USGS 33116.

MILES: Loop. 26 miles, pavement to pavement.

AUTHORITY: Joshua Tree National Monument, 74485 National Monument Drive, Twentynine Palms, CA 92277 (619) 367-7511.

REMARKS: Don't go beyond the tanks in wet weather. The muddy dry lake bed, when wet, will swallow you up. Take this one in mid to late spring and in a good year you can't help but fall in love with the desert wildflowers. **Covington Flat**, **Desert Queen** and **Gold Park** are all nearby trails.

Steam Well

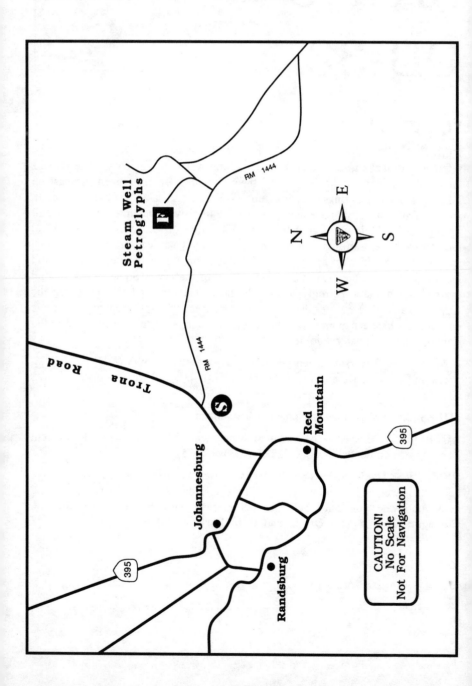

Area 2
CB-4

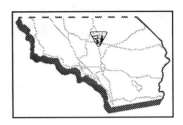

STEAM WELL

DESCRIPTION: They left their marks throughout the desert. Through the millennia, their meanings have been lost or muddled, but the images remain. The petroglyphs at Steam Well are a reminder of other people who have traversed the area when the world was a strange and mystic place. Take the Trona Road north (right) from HWY 395 about 1½ miles to a dirt road on the east (right) marked with a barrel and the words "Steam Well". The BLM calls this route RM 1444. Follow this road, staying on the most traveled path, another four miles to the silver propane tank marker and make a north (left) turn in the direction of Steam Well and soon another left turn at the BLM sign. Follow the road until it ends at a small canyon. Petroglyphs line the dark rocks on each side of the canyon, with more abundant glyphs on the left side. The BLM has placed interpretive signs in the area. Vandalism and theft are a threat to these ancient writings. Please take only photographs and leave only footprints. Home is the way you came in or try for Barstow via dirt, about 50 miles away.

MAPS: ACSC San Bernardino County (C1/2). BLM Desert Access Guide #7 (E2). Hileman's Randsburg #4 (no coordinates). DeLorme p66 (A/B3). USGS 35117.

MILES: Dead-end. 13 miles from HWY 395.

AUTHORITY: Bureau of Land Management, 300 South Richmond Road, Ridgecrest, CA 93555 (619) 375-7125.

REMARKS: There are lots of dirt roads in the area to explore, but collecting artifacts is not permitted. This can be part of an easy trip to Randsburg. Nearby trails are **Burro Schmidt's, Last Chance Canyon** and **Barnett Opal Mine**.

Roger Vargo

Stoddard Well Rd

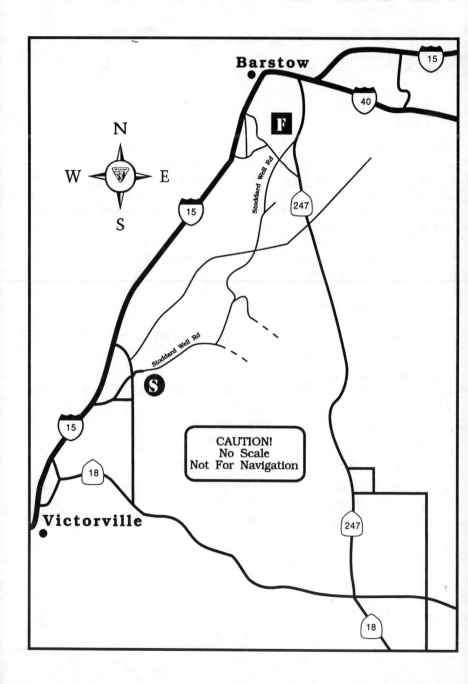

Area 6
CB-17

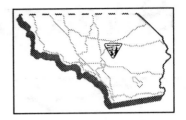

STODDARD WELL ROAD

DESCRIPTION: I give you five trails in this general area, but you could spend five months discovering its many secrets. **Stoddard Well Road** puts you through the west end of what most call Lucerne Valley. Simply go north on I-15 and use the **Stoddard Well Road** off ramp. This is more confusing than the road itself. The road goes north and east to intersect HWY 247 south of Barstow (E3). Take the above route north, then zig zag your southerly return with any of the many alternatives. Get to know the area a step at a time and gain confidence with your navigational abilities. Home is obviously south on I-15 from either end.

MAPS: ACSC San Bernardino County (F3, E3/4). DeLorme p81 (D5/6, B7). Desert Access Guide #10 (D/E5, G2/3). USGS 34116 and 34117.

MILES: Loop. 24 miles from the paved start at I-15 to the finish at HWY 247.

AUTHORITY: San Bernardino County, private and BLM, California Desert Information Center, 831 Barstow Road, Barstow, CA 92311 (619) 256-8313.

REMARKS: **Camp Rock Road**, **Box Canyon**, **Cinder Cone** and **Dry Lake Loop** are the other 4 trails in Lucerne Valley.

Sugarpine Mtn

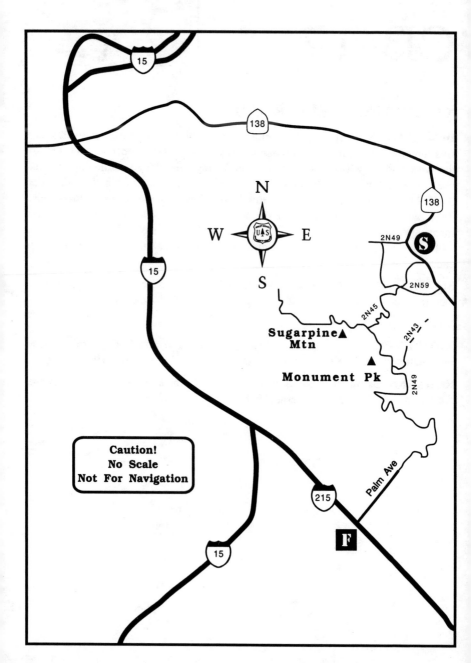

Area 5
CB-14

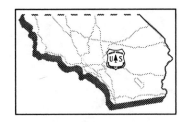

SUGARPINE MOUNTAIN

DESCRIPTION: Just like **Cajon Mountain**, go toward Vegas on I-15 and then east on HWY 138. About 1½ miles beyond where you came out on 2N47 on the **Cleghorn Mountain** trail, look for 2N49 for your right. Before you catch your breath, look for 2N59 for a left. At the confusing intersection with 2N45, take it right toward **Sugarpine Mountain**. When you intersect 2N49, go right for a ¾ mile trip to the peak or go left to continue. Pass up the left on 2N43 at Monument Peak and continue on down 2N49 to Palm Ave. in San Bernardino. Palm takes you out to I-215 and from there you should know home is south.

MAPS: San Bernardino National Forest, San Bernardino Meridian (C/D2/3, D3). ACSC LA and Vicinity, no trail shown, peak at (E13). DeLorme p95 (B4, B5). USGS 34117.

MILES: Loop. 15 miles from HWY 138 to Palm Ave.

AUTHORITY: San Bernardino National Forest, Arrowhead District, P. O. Box 7, Rim Forest, CA 92378 (909) 337-2444.

REMARKS: Although described as 3 trails, use this one along with **Cajon Mountain** and **Cleghorn Mountain** to fill a very long day.

TenajaTruckTrail

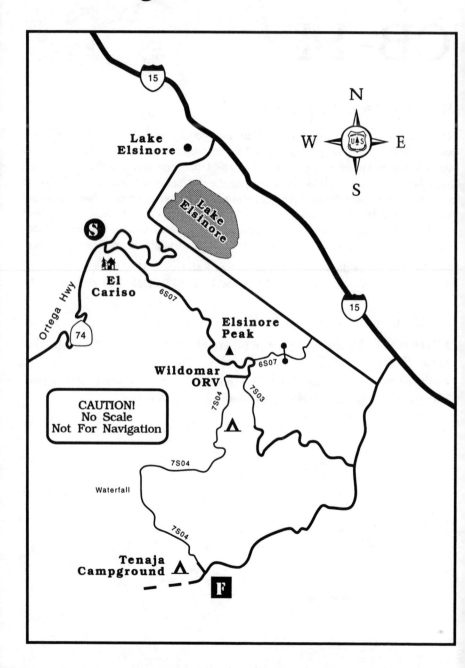

Area 9
CB-36

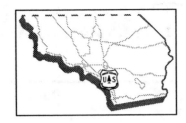

TENAJA TRUCK TRAIL

DESCRIPTION: You'll start high up on Ortega Highway, near the Coyote's old Elsinore Peak Trail. Take a moment to watch modern hang gliders and be prepared to finish looking at ancient Indian bedrock morteros. Consider this relatively easy trip south of Lake Elsinore a trip back through time. Go south on I-5 to the HWY 74 (B4/5) for a left (east). Almost 25 miles up this winding road watch for the El Cariso Fire and Ranger Station (D3/4) where you can get the latest road info. The next right puts you on paved 6S07 (D3/4) heading toward Elsinore Peak. Follow the blacktop to the end and your ears will let you know that you are on 7S04 (D/E4) at the Wildomar ORV Park. After about seven miles of dirt watch for the parking area about ¾ mile from a seasonal waterfall. If you've gotten this far you won't want to miss the tenaja and dozens of morteros at the Tenaja Campground. After exploring the campground (did you learn what a tenaja is?), a left turn onto Tenaja Road at the stop sign (D/E4/5) will soon put you onto Clinton Keith Road and I-15 for home.

MAPS: Cleveland National Forest, Trabuco Ranger District (D3/4, D/E4/5). ACSC Riverside County (E4/5, F4/5). DeLorme p105 (C4/5, D4/5). USGS 33117.

MILES: Loop. 22 miles from HWY 74 to Tenaja Road.

AUTHORITY: Cleveland National Forest, Trabuco District, 1147 E. 6th Street, Corona, CA 91720 (909) 736-1811.

REMARKS: Try this trail in the Spring to ensure water at the waterfall, but be wary of muddy roads if it has rained recently. It would also be a good idea to be able to visually (as opposed to physically) identify poison oak. **Saddleback Mountain** and **El Cariso** are nearby.

Don Carter

Thomas Mtn

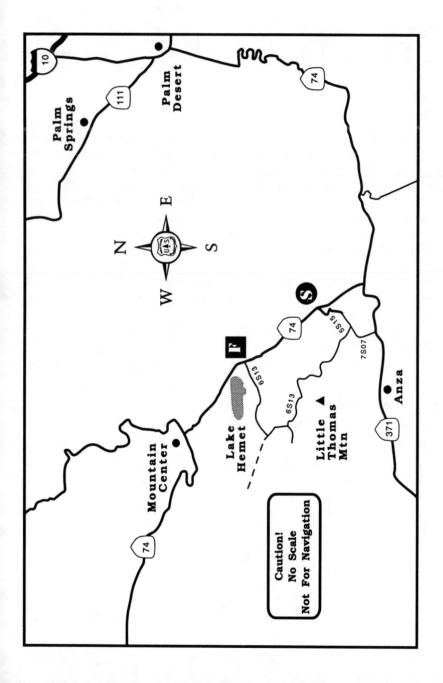

Area 7
CB-30

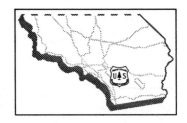

THOMAS MOUNTAIN

DESCRIPTION: Nothing spectacular, just a view the Palm Springs Tram would be jealous of. And such good roads too. This is one of those places you go to and in twenty years return and say, "I remember when ...". Head south on I-215 to the HWY 74 turn off for Hemet. Go through Hemet, Valle Vista and Mountain Center. After you pass Lake Hemet, start looking for the road you'll come out on, 6S13. In about 4½ miles you will see paved 5S15 for a right. Let the good road lead you northwest across the ridge, past the 3 campgrounds, by a side trip to Little Thomas Mountain, and down and out on 6S13, which you've already seen on the trip up. At the start, don't go straight from 5S15 to 7S07 which leads to a locked gate at the bottom. Same goes for your right (northeast) on 6S13. Home is a left (northwest) on HWY 74 or right to Palm Desert.

MAPS: ACSC Riverside County (F11, E10). San Bernardino Forest, San Jacinto and Santa Rosa Mountain Area (J/K7/8). DeLorme p106 (D4, C3). Desert Access Guide #17 (D5, B/C3/4). USGS 33116.

MILES: Loop. 18 miles paved HWY 74 to HWY 74.

AUTHORITY: Riverside County and San Bernardino National Forest, San Jacinto District, P. O. Box 518, Idyllwild, CA 92349 (909) 659-2117.

REMARKS: Nearby **Toro Peak** also makes a reasonable trip for the uninitiated. Combine this one with a trip to where the old meets the new in the town of Anza on either Anza Days (4th of July) or the Apple Festival in the fall. If you stop in Rudy's Cafe, you may be lucky enough to run into Red Skelton.

Titus Canyon

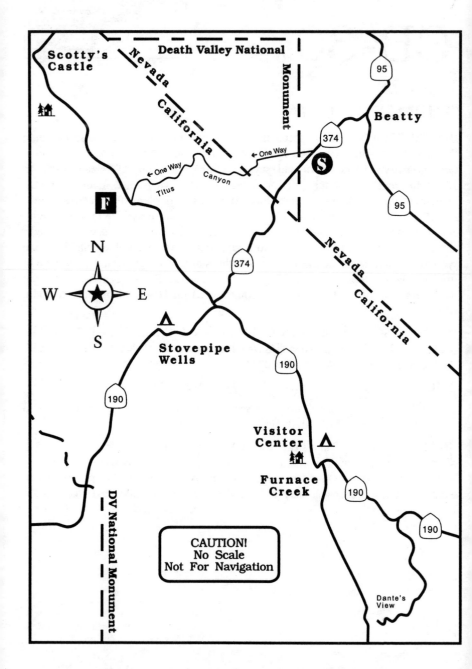

Death Valley CB-7

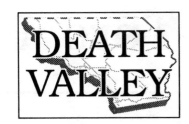

TITUS CANYON

DESCRIPTION: One-way **Titus Canyon** is another spectacular approach to Death Valley, and the Rhyolite (E9/10) ghost town at the start is an added bonus. Get to Beatty, Nevada (E10) any way you can. I use I-15 to Baker to HWY 127 north to HWY 95 northwest to Beatty. By the time this Guide goes to print, the tallest thermometer in the world will announce Baker long before you see the Mad Greek's and the Bun Boy. Go four miles southwest of Beatty on HWY 374 to the well marked turnoff for Rhyolite (E/F9/10). If you skip Rhyolite, go another mile plus to the road marked Titus Canyon (E/F9/10). 26 miles later you'll hit paved North Highway (F7) in Death Valley. You're missing the whole trip if you just drive it! Get some history on Leadfield, stop for the view of the Sierra and enjoy the grandeur of the canyon itself from mileage 17 on. Keep track of the exit as you do the last few miles before pavement. Notice how hard it is to find the mouth just a mile or two away. A right (northwest) leads to Scotty's Castle (D6) and left to Furnace Creek (H/J9/10). Home is probably in the valley for a few days, so relax and enjoy.

MAPS: ACSC Death Valley (E/F9/10, F7). DeLorme, start not shown on Southern DeLorme and finish on p29 (B6). USGS 35117.

MILES: Loop. 26 miles dirt from HWY 374 to North Highway.

AUTHORITY: Death Valley National Monument, Furnace Creek, CA 92328 (619) 786-2331.

REMARKS: This is not a summer trip. Your first stop should be the Visitor Center in Furnace Creek. The nearby trail is **Greenwater Valley**. Find Hugh Hepner (past president of the Death Valley 49er's Association) at the Furnace Creek Ranch for excellent 4WD tours.

Toro Peak

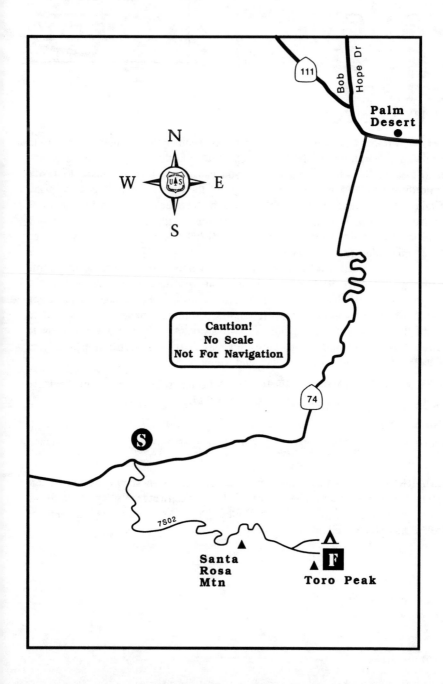

Area 9
CB-36

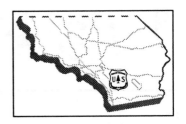

TORO PEAK

DESCRIPTION: If you plan to spend any time at all in the Anza-Borrego Desert State Park, particularly the northern end, this is almost as good as a flyover. From **Toro Peak** (½ mile hike to the real peak required) you can see **Coyote Canyon, Rockhouse Canyon, Font's Point** and the Borrego Buttes. What's more, you can also see the **Los Coyotes** Indian Reservation. Get to Palm Desert your best way. I use I-10 to Bob Hope Drive south and then pick up HWY 74 west (up the hill). In 19 plus miles, on your left (south) will be a big sign that is more visible out your rearview mirror than forward. This says Santa Rosa Mountain and is the Forest Service road 7S02. Take it to the top past several springs, undesignated campsites and a log cabin. When you park at the top, don't block the gate (road) to the top, which you will have to hike. Hang on to your hat at the windy top. Take your binoculars, map and compass to really figure out what's what. Home is a 180 and down the hill or on over the hill to Hemet.

MAPS: ACSC Riverside County (F11, F12). San Bernardino Forest, San Jacinto and Santa Rosa Mountain Area (K/L8, L8). DeLorme p107 (D4, D5). Desert Access Guide #17 (E/F6, F6/7). USGS 33116.

MILES: Dead-end. 24 miles round trip, HWY 74 and back.

AUTHORITY: San Bernardino National Forest, San Jacinto District, P. O. Box 518, Idyllwild, CA 92349 (909) 659-2117.

REMARKS: Nearby **Thomas Mountain** also makes a reasonable trip for the uninitiated. How about giving the Apple Festival in the little town of Anza, up the mountain and west on HWY 371, a try in the fall?

Tule Ridge

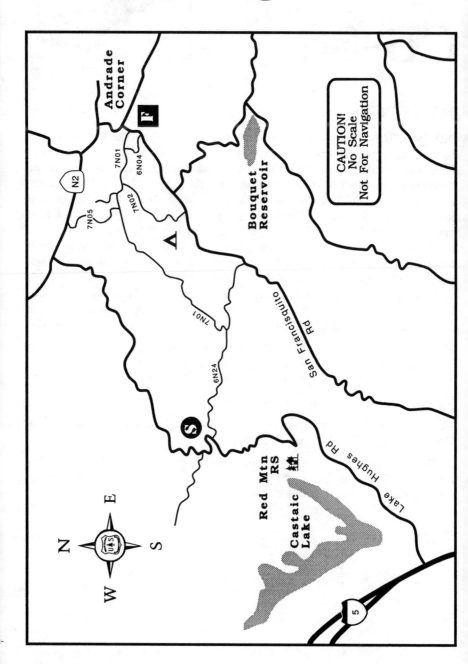

Area 2
CB-4

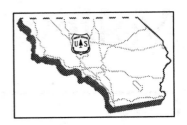

TULE RIDGE

DESCRIPTION: A rougher road and more of a navigational challenge than nearby trails, **Tule Ridge** will keep you guessing if you're on the right road. Fortunately, virtually all roading errors lead to dead ends or back to some paved road. Have fun! Just like nearby **Warm Springs**, take I-5 north to the Parker Road turnoff right (B/C4), to dead-end left (Castaic Road), to another right on Lake Hughes Road. Follow this road northeast to a right on 6N24. Five miles east, 7N01 intersects on the north. Decisions, decisions. Here, via 6N24, you are only three simple miles from pavement. But go for it, take 7N01 north. 7N01 all the way is my recommendation, but 7N02, 7N05 and 6N04 all lead back to civilization. 7N01 comes out near Andrade Corner.

MAPS: Angeles National Forest, San Bernardino Meridian (C3, D/E2). ACSC LA and Vicinity (C4, B5). DeLorme p78 (D2, C3/4), they call 6N24 Ruby Canyon. USGS 34118.

MILES: Loop. 18 miles from paved Lake Hughes Road to HWY N2.

AUTHORITY: Angeles National Forest, Saugus District, 27757 Bouquet Canyon Road, Saugus, CA 91350 (805) 252-9710.

REMARKS: Another Spring trip for the flowers. **Green Valley, Del Sur Ridge, Liebre Mountain** and **Warm Springs** are all reasonably close.

Valley Forge

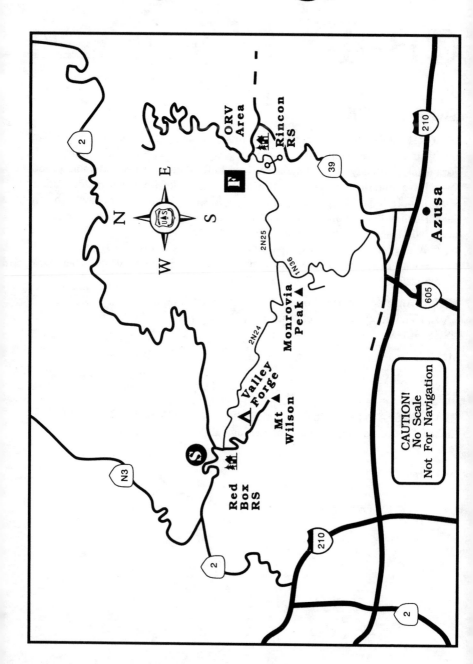

Area 4
CB-11

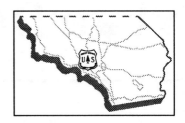

VALLEY FORGE

DESCRIPTION: Combine this ridge runner with a morning at Mount Wilson and then down and out in the Azusa area. In Flintridge (F6), take HWY 2 to the Red Box Ranger Station where you will go east (right) on 2N24. Follow this to a gentle left on 2N25 and out at the Rincon Ranger Station on HWY 39 if the gate is open. It's not open? Just look how well you will learn the road on the return trip or, use 1N36 just east of Monrovia Peak for an all dirt route down and out to I-210. Right on HWY 39 takes you to Azusa and left to a dead-end. Home? Gosh, you can probably see it from here.

MAPS: Angeles National Forest, San Bernardino Meridian (G5, J6). ACSC LA and Vicinity (E8, E9/10). DeLorme p93 (B6), p94 (C1). USGS 34117 and 34118.

MILES: Loop. 26 miles from HWY 2 to HWY 39.

AUTHORITY: Starts in Arroyo Seco District, Oak Grove Park, Flintridge, CA 91011 (818) 577-0050. Ends in Mt. Baldy Ranger District, 110 N. Wabash St., Glendora, CA 91740 (818) 335-1251.

REMARKS: As you exit, observe or play with the wild ones in the Azusa Canyon ORV area. For me, some of the folks using this area demonstrate how not to treat your 4X. **Pacifico Mountain** and **Messenger Flats** are nearby.

Vista Del Mal Pais

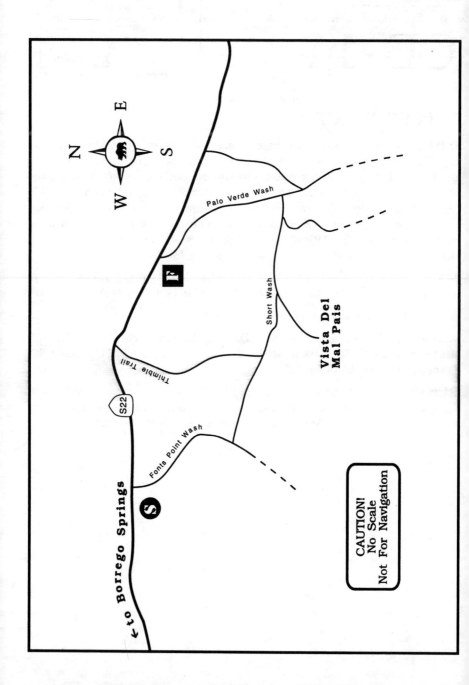

Palo Verde Wash

Short Wash

Vista Del Mal Pais

Trimble Trail

S22

Fonts Point Wash

to Borrego Springs

**CAUTION!
No Scale
Not For Navigation**

Area 9
CB-36

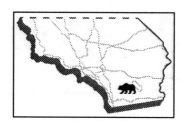

VISTA DEL MAL PAIS

DESCRIPTION: So you liked **Fonts Point** so much you want more, huh? The desert's not such a bad place after all! Repeating from other ABDSP trails, get to Borrego Springs (C12). About 3½ miles east of Peg Leg Smith Monument (C13), on HWY S22, is well signed Font's Wash. Go right (south) in the wash, obey the markers, and use Short Wash left (east) about 2 miles in. Look hard for the sharp right turn (south) out to the Vista. Another breath-taker. Within a mile are well hidden archaeological digs and pack rat nests that have been occupied for one million years. Will your house last that long? Retrace to Short Wash, go right (east) to rougher Palo Verde Wash where you make a left (north). This takes you back out to S22 and a left (west) back to Borrego Springs. Right leads to the Salton Sea and HWY 86.

MAPS: ACSC San Diego County (C14). Anza-Borrego Desert State Park map (C5). Highly recommended is Lindsay's *The Anza-Borrego Desert Region* (ISBN 911824-67-7) book and map (trip 3). DeLorme p115 (B7) **Vista Del Mal Pais** not shown. Desert Access Guide #19 (D3) and **Vista Del Mal Pais** not shown. USGS 33116.

MILES: Loop. About 10 from S22 back to S22.

AUTHORITY: Anza-Borrego Desert State Park, P. O. Box 428, Borrego Springs, CA 92004 (619) 767-5311.

REMARKS: First stop should be the visitor center where you can get the Park map. Remember, look, but don't take anything from the Park. **Coyote Canyon, Fonts Point, Calcite Mine, 17 Palms** and **Rockhouse Canyon** are nearby.

Wagon Flat

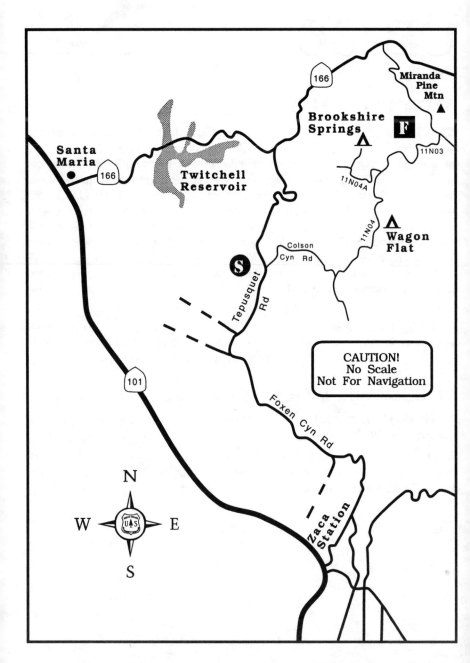

Area 1
CB-1

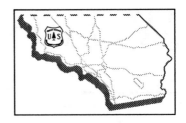

WAGON FLAT

DESCRIPTION: No less than 6 campgrounds along this trail make it worth checking out. The ACSC map only shows the main road and DeLorme shows many 4WD trails. Just one word of caution for the less-than-well-travelled roads, caution. About 16 miles after you turn inland (J6) on HWY 101 past Santa Barbara, start looking for your right on Zaca Station Road (F6/7). This runs into Foxen Canyon Road which you follow for the next 16 miles to another right (north) on Tepusquet Road (D5/6). About 4½ miles north is Colson Canyon Road for another right. Drive 'til your heart's content or at least to the locked gate at the end near Miranda Pine Mountain. The road changes names to La Brea Canyon Road (11N04) and Miranda Pine Road (11N03) at the end. Brookshire Springs (11N04A) offers a 10 mile side trip if desired, but be sure to close the cattle gate after you. Return to pavement via the same way you came in.

MAPS: ACSC Santa Barbara County (C/D6, B8). DeLorme p74 (A3), p61 (D4). Los Padres National Forest (F14, H13). USGS 34120 and 35120.

MILES: Dead-end. About 50 miles for the round trip to the end and back to Tepusquet Road.

AUTHORITY: Los Padres National Forest, Santa Lucia District, 1616 Carlotti Dr., Santa Maria, CA 93454 (805) 925-9538.

REMARKS: Many of the campsites do not have water, and trailers are not advised. Nothing really close unless the gate at the end is open. Then, you can cross over to the **McPherson Peak** (Sierra Madre Road, 32S13) trail. **Zaca Peak** is close the way the crow flys, but 35 miles the way you and I have to drive. The gate at Miranda Pine will be closed during wet weather.

Warm Springs

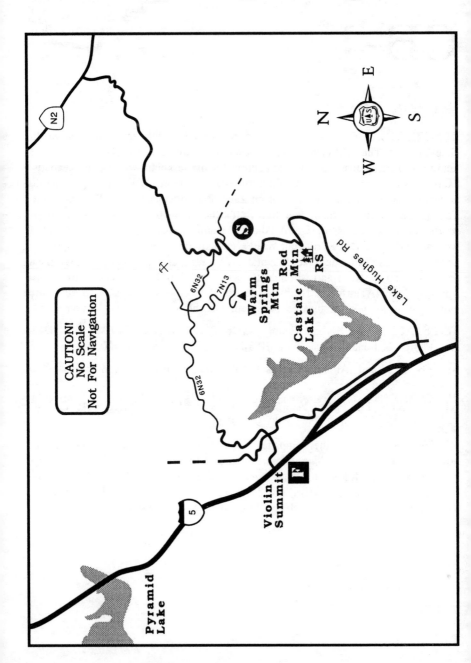

Area 2
CB-4

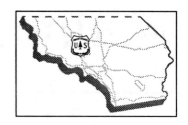

WARM SPRINGS

DESCRIPTION: A nice drive along an all graded canyon. Take the sidetrip up to Warm Springs Mountain Peak lookout, then out a different way, all on a Saturday afternoon. I-5 north to the Parker Road turnoff right, to dead-end left (Castaic Road, B/C4), to another right on Lake Hughes Road (and that's just to get off the freeway!). Follow this road northeast to a left on dirt 6N32. At the junction with 7N13, you have the option to go left to the lookout (C3), right to the dead-end Maxwell mine foot trail (C2) or continue straight on 6N32 back to I-5 near Violin Summit. Don't be confused by the right on 6N32C at Cienaga campground. The last bit of 6N32 is paved. Home is so close you probably know it's south on I-5.

MAPS: Angeles National Forest, San Bernardino Meridian (C3, B3). ACSC LA and Vicinity (C4, C3). DeLorme p78 (D2). USGS 34118.

MILES: Loop. 14 miles from Lake Hughes Road to I-5.

AUTHORITY: Angeles National Forest, Saugus District, 27757 Bouquet Canyon Road, Saugus CA 91350 (805) 252-9710.

REMARKS: The spring rains make the streams pretty exciting. **Alamo Mountain**, **Liebre Mountain** and **Tule Ridge** are all reasonably close by.

WildhorseMeadow

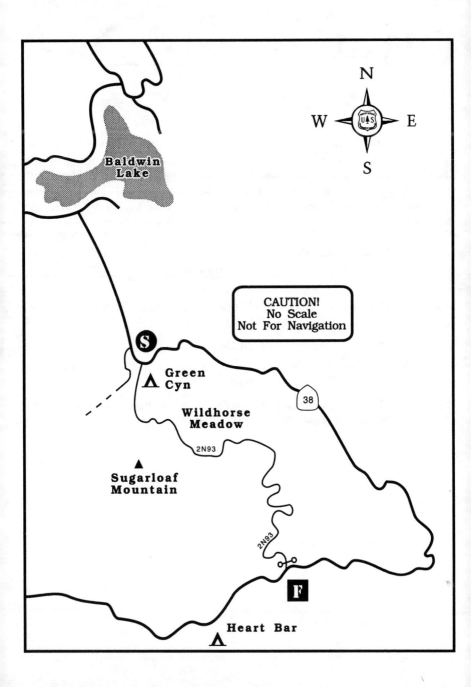

N
W E
S

Baldwin
Lake

CAUTION!
No Scale
Not For Navigation

S

Green
Cyn

Wildhorse
Meadow

38

2N93

Sugarloaf
Mountain

2N93

F

Heart Bar

Area 5
CB-14

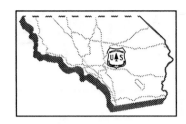

WILDHORSE MEADOW

DESCRIPTION: A place to start your hike to the top of Sugarloaf Mountain and otherwise a really sensitive meadow, the Wildhorse trail basically parallels HWY 38. I found the biggest mushroom of my life right in the road! Go toward Big Bear City (note City) via HWY 38 out of Redlands (E5). Look for your ending point about three or four miles past the Heart Bar Fire Station and Campground on your way up. About three miles before town, take a left on 2N93 (Wildhorse Meadow Road). This may say Green Canyon Campground which you pass by. Stay on 2N93 all the way back to HWY 38 where you will have to open and close the gate. HWY 38 leads down the hill to home, but you already know that.

MAPS: San Bernardino National Forest, San Bernardino Meridian (H2/3, H/J3). ACSC LA and Vicinity, trails not shown, Wildhorse Meadows at (F18). DeLorme p96 (C2), they call the whole trip Wildhorse Meadow Road. Desert Access Guide #14 (C4/5, C5). USGS 34116.

MILES: Loop. 13 miles HWY 38 to HWY 38.

AUTHORITY: San Bernardino National Forest, Big Bear District, P. O. Box 290, Fawnskin, CA 92333 (909) 866-3437, San Gorgonio Ranger District, 34701 Mill Creek Road, Mentone, CA 92359 (909) 794-1123.

REMARKS: At the lower end of the meadow is a foot trail that leads to Sugarloaf Mountain. Don't take your 4X up this, it is the hiking trail. The barrier has been torn down by someone choosing to reduce our privileges. Nearby is **Clark Grade** or on the other side of the lake are **Holcomb Valley** and **Creek**, and very rough **Crab Flats**. This area is subject to winter closure, but snow-fun when open.

Wiley's Well

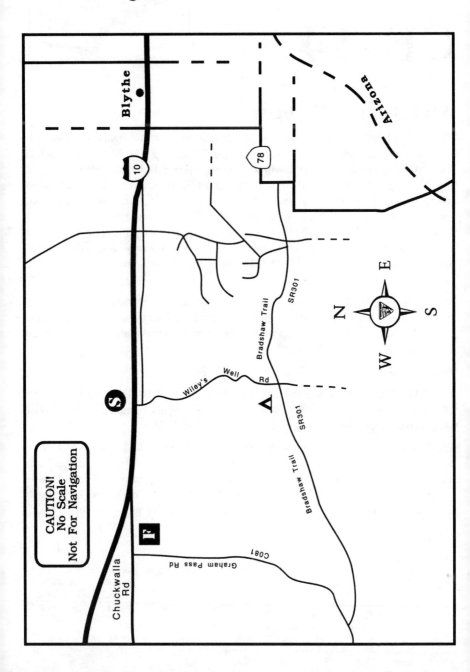

Area 10
CB-39

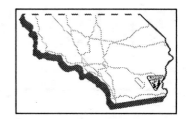

WILEY'S WELL

DESCRIPTION: This is one of the few trips I'll describe alternate routes in detail. Drive east, forever, on I-10, almost to Blythe, for a right (south) on Wiley's Well Road. There is a campground at **Wiley's Well**. The rock collectors and real desert rats love this place. Take a left (east) on the Bradshaw Trail (SR301) and in 11 miles you'll be on paved HWY 78 just south of Blythe (G26). The longer version goes west (right) on SR301 to Graham Pass Road (BLM C081) for another right (north). If you miss this right, you're in for a long one clear over to Salt Creek. See **Bradshaw Road** if you want to do this. Nevertheless, Graham Pass Road takes you to Chuckwalla Road where a left (west) will take you to I-10 (E22) in Hell (name of town, not religious place). Home is to your left (west).

MAPS: ACSC Riverside County (F24/25). DeLorme p110 (D3) end of short version on p119 (A5) and long version on p110 (D2). Start on Desert Access Guide #16 (B10) through #20 to end on #18 (J5). USGS 33114 and 33115.

MILES: Loop. Short version, 20 miles and the long version is 43 miles.

AUTHORITY: BLM Palm Springs-South Coast Resource Area Office, 63-500 Garnet Ave, P.O. Box 2000, N. Palm Springs, CA 92258-2000 (619) 251-0812.

REMARKS: Coon Hollow, Bradshaw Trail, Corn Springs and **Graham Pass** are nearby. Read about the nearby Hauser Geode Beds at **Coon Hollow**.

Yuha Well

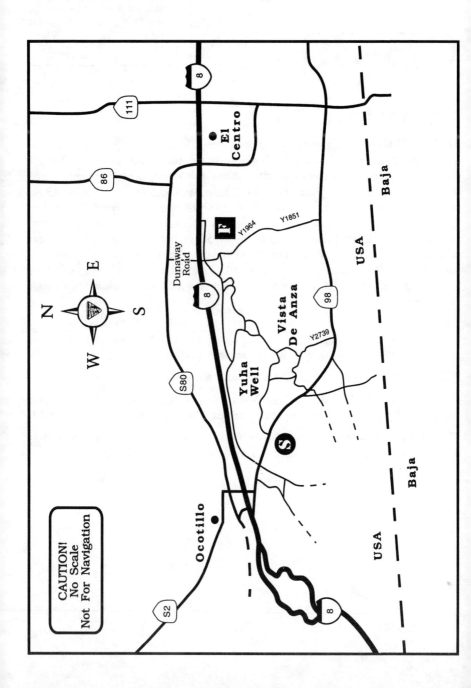

Area 9
CB-36

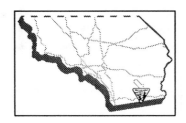

YUHA WELL

DESCRIPTION: More an area to randomly explore than a specific sight, this five by eight mile area is contained by pavement on three sides and private farms on the east. Explore until your heart's content, but leave some daylight for the return home. Just like **Painted Gorge**, take I-8 east out of San Diego and as you descend the grade by the Desert View Tower (H1), start anticipating Ocotillo. You will see an off ramp for HWY 98. Take it east. Just shy of five miles, take a dirt road off to your left. In another six plus miles you will be at **Yuha Well**. Spend some time just driving around. Look for the Vista De Anza Trail Monument and the giant geoglyphs (intaglios) in the area. The area is so flat in spots, if you travel with several friends in different directions, there's a chance you can keep them in sight for miles. Dirt roads lead back to either I-8 or HWY 98 for home.

MAPS: ACSC Imperial County (H2). DeLorme p124 (C2), all the roads and the well not shown. Desert Access Guide #22 (B4, B/C4). USGS 32115 and 32116.

MILES: I'll call it a loop if you enter as above and exit on Dunaway Road or the West Side Canal Road at I-8, 11 miles later.

AUTHORITY: BLM El Centro Resource Area Office, 1661 S. Fourth St., El Centro, CA 92243 (619) 352-5842.

REMARKS: There are several sections of poor road that may challenge some, but I don't see it as too hard. When ABC TV's Dr. George talks of summer flash floods and tropical storms coming up from the south, this is the area to avoid. **Painted Gorge** is nearby. Try to check out the fossil oyster shell beds and the Yuha intaglios.

Zaca Peak

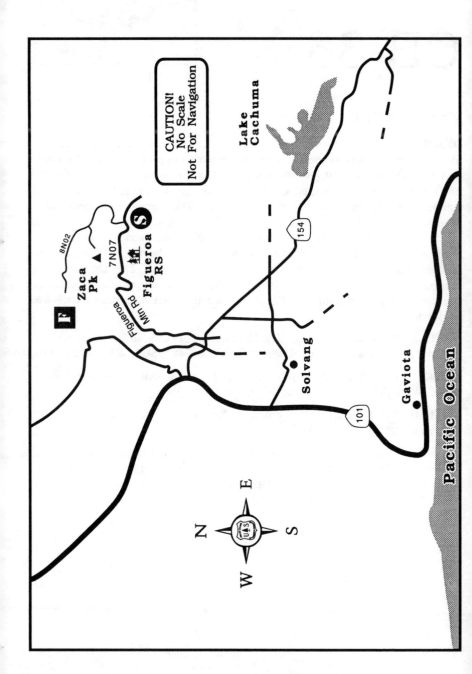

Area 1
CB-1

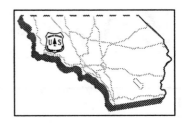

ZACA PEAK

DESCRIPTION: You would think a peak would give you a good, all around view. With the density of peaks in this area, you're lucky if you can see where you parked your car. Just like **Wagon Flats**, 16 miles after you turn inland (J6) on HWY 101 past Santa Barbara, start looking for your right on HWY 154 (F7). This time it's not Zaca Station Road. 154 takes you to Figueroa Mountain Road (7N07) for a left (north). About ½ mile after you pass the Figueroa Ranger Station, take a left (north) on Catway Road (8N02). The unnamed turn off ½ mile before the station is a little rougher. Eight miles out Catway, to your left, will be the rougher road (may be closed) to the peak. The ACSC shows the road ending in another three miles, but typical of this area, there is more for the adventuresome. Since this is a dead-end trail for the conservative, the way out is the way in, backwards.

MAPS: ACSC Santa Barbara County (F8/9, E8). DeLorme p75 (C4/5, B5). Los Padres National Forest (H16/17). USGS 34119 and 34120.

MILES: Dead-end. 24 miles to the end of road and back to Figueroa Mountain Road.

AUTHORITY: Los Padres National Forest, Santa Lucia District, 1616 Carlotti Dr., Santa Maria, CA 93454 (805) 925-9538.

REMARKS: Kind of a loner, **Wagon Flats** is the only, somewhat nearby trail. Combine this one with a trip to the unique Danish village of Solvang (G7) for some tremendous pastries. Gateway Road and Zaca Road are closed during the coldest months of winter.

Gene Markley

Zzyzx

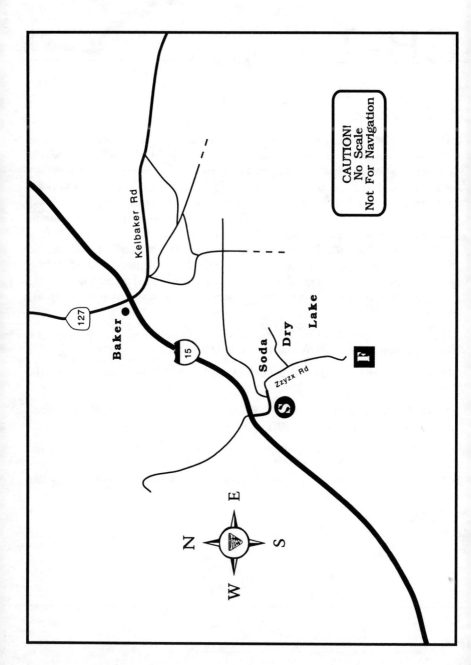

Area 3
CB-7

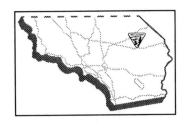

ZZYZX

DESCRIPTION: If there hadn't been something to write about in this area, I would have invented it. I love the name **Zzyzx** and I have the last word, or should I say Dr. Curtis Howe Springer did when he invented the name of his health spa back in the 1940's. You now belong to that very exclusive group of people who know what **Zzyzx** is about. I agree, so what! Soda Dry Lake is an environmentally sensitive area that should be respected. Stay off of it when it is wet. Go north on I-15 toward Las Vegas and use the Zzyzx Road exit which leads you south to the ranch. There is a self-guided tour at the ranch and BLM asks you park and camp outside the ranch proper. The gate is sometimes closed for special, private group tours. These tours may be arranged through California State University at San Bernardino. Since you're only four miles off the interstate, you'll probably eat your own dust on the way out to I-15 for your trip home south.

MAPS: ACSC San Bernardino County (D7). DeLorme p69 (C7), p70 (D7). Desert Access Guide #8 (J4/5, J5). USGS 35116.

MILES: Dead-end. 9 miles out to Soda Springs and back to I-15.

AUTHORITY: BLM, California Desert Information Center, 831 Barstow Road, Barstow, CA 92311 (619) 256-8313.

REMARKS: Don't drive on the lake when wet. It is disrespectful of our environment and dangerous. Nearby **Afton Canyon** is a great base camp. There are routes across the north end of the lake that connect with the Mojave Trail. See Casebier's book referenced in nearby **Afton Canyon** for details.

INDEX

352 INDEX

Odometer, Speedometer and Distance Formulas

Odometer Check Formula
$$C = \frac{O_2 - O_1}{M_2 - M_1}$$

Speedometer Check Formula
$$S = \frac{3600 \times (M_2 - M_1)}{T}$$

Distance to Horizon Formula
$$D = \sqrt{H} \times 1.317$$

Where:

   C = odometer Correction factor multiplier

   D = Distance to sea level horizon in statute miles*

   H = Height of observer's eye (<u>plus elevation</u> above sea level)

   M_2 = larger Milepost reading

   M_1 = smaller Milepost reading

   O_2 = final Odometer reading

   O_1 = initial Odometer reading

   S = actual Speed in miles-per-hour

   T = elapsed Time in seconds between mile posts

   1.317 is the statute mile multiplier

   3600 is seconds per hour (1 hour X 60 minutes X 60 seconds)

* For distance to objects <u>above sea level horizon</u>, assume the object elevation to be <u>another</u> height of eye, and add the two distances to horizon together ($D_1 + D_2$).

The Silver Coyote Program

ECOLOGICALLY
SENSITIVE
PROGRAM

The Silver Coyote Program is dedicated to ecologically compatible backcountry use. It features safe and responsible four-wheel-drive unpaved adventures and passive appreciation of Mother Nature. It has five parts:

4-WHEELING
NEWSLETTER

The *4-WHEELING* newsletter is the hub of the Silver Coyote Program. It announces Exploring Trips, college classes and tours, equipment seminars and other activities. It reports on past activities, new equipment and new vehicles. Driving tips, navigation techniques, backcountry people and the wonders of Mother Nature also make the headlines. It is published nine times per year from September through May.

EXPLORING
TRIPS

Exploring Trips are exciting treks into the backcountry. Some are weekend jaunts to nearby places or simply Sunday brunch at Lake Arrowhead. Others are vacations—true expedition quality experiences. Death Valley, the Baja Adventure, Whale Watching and the two week trip through Mexico's Copper Canyon are a few of the more adventuresome treks. Regardless of the destination, they all escape the crowds and chaos of workday life. They put you back in touch with Mother Nature!

CLASSES AND
TOURS

Classes and tours take on two perspectives — casual and professional. The Silver Coyote has conducted more than 300 classes at 26 colleges throughout Southern California. With over 4,000 participants, he is the recognized 4WD expert with the clean and easy set. He trains rangers, police departments, automotive personnel, and search and rescue people. There are lecture-only classes, hands-on seminars, or classes that include tours. The classes and tours are offered at many Southern California colleges. Harry Lewellyn is also available for company, club or private lectures, classes, seminars, tours and speaking engagements.

SILVER COYOTE
CARD

The Silver Coyote Card is like a club. It allows card holders to go on college tours without attending the lectures. The tour lecture is normally required for all tour drivers. Participate in any two classes, one of which is a tour and you automatically become a Silver Coyote. Also look for the Silver Coyote card to become the clean and easy 4-wheeling club of the future! Harry Lewellyn is *the* Silver Coyote.

CULTURAL
GOALS

Cultural goals are vital to the Program. By now, it must be clear the Silver Coyote promotes and practices respect for Mother Nature. We want to increase public acceptance for safe and responsible vehicular use in the backcountry, and have fun meeting our goals!